Anthony Casurella, Ph. D. (1981) in New
Testament, Durham University, England
is Professor on New Testament at Western Evangelical Seminary, Portland OR.
He has published on the Fourth Gospel,
in 1983 he published *The Johannine Para-*
clete in the Church Fathers (Beiträge zur
Geschichte der biblischen Exegese 25).

BIBLIOGRAPHY OF LITERATURE
ON FIRST PETER

NEW TESTAMENT TOOLS
AND STUDIES

EDITED BY

BRUCE M. METZGER, Ph.D., D.D., L.H.D., D. Theol., D. Litt.

Professor of New Testament Language and Literature, Emeritus
Princeton Theological Seminary
and
Corresponding Fellow of the British Academy

AND

BART D. EHRMAN, Ph.D.

Associate Professor, Department of Religious Studies
University of North Carolina at Chapel Hill

VOLUME XXIII

BIBLIOGRAPHY OF
LITERATURE
ON FIRST PETER

BY

ANTHONY CASURELLA

E.J. BRILL

LEIDEN · NEW YORK · KÖLN

1996

The paper in this book meets the guidelines for permanence and durability of the Committee on Production Guidelines for Book Longevity of the Council on Library Resources.

Library of Congress Cataloging-in-Publication Data

Casurella, Anthony.
    Bibliography of literature on First Peter / by Anthony Casurella.
       p.   cm. — (New Testament tools and studies, ISSN 0077-8842 ; v. 23)
    Includes indexes.
    ISBN 9004104887 (alk. paper)
    1. Bible. N.T. Peter, 1st—Criticism, interpretation, etc.-
-Bibliography.   I. Title. II. Series.
Z7772.P1C37   1996
[BS2795.2]
016.227'92—dc20

                                         95–53248
                                            CIP

Die Deutsche Bibliothek – CIP-Einheitsaufnahme

The CIP data has been applied for.

ISSN 0077-8842
ISBN 90 04 10488 7

PRINTED IN THE NETHERLANDS

FOR SHARON

TABLE OF CONTENTS

PREFACE

Aim

On one occasion my high school English teacher spoke to us about publishing. No one, she contended, ever publishes a book for purely altruistic reasons; authors are always out for personal ends. There may be some truth in what she said, though her horizons were undoubtedly limited to a certain kind of book in a certain limited realm. She had had little or no exposure to scholarly work in Biblical Studies.

Nevertheless, if her assertion is also even somewhat applicable to New Testament Studies, and if the motivation behind the present collection has been partly self-serving, it was only partly so. It is true that I wanted to acquaint myself with literature bearing on 1 Peter, but I have also desired to make this information accessible to the scholarly community.

My *modus operandi* was straightforward, though not simple. First I attempted to assemble the titles of everything ever published on 1 Peter in print. The only unpublished titles included are doctoral (but not master's) theses and dissertations. Secondly, I have tried to verify every detail through an examination of the printed works themselves in libraries in the U.S.A. and Great Britain, and through computer searches of on-line catalogues of libraries in western Europe and the Americas.

Titles Included

In general, but with notable exceptions, only titles of works specifically on 1 Peter are included in the bibliography. To accomplish this, however, was not as easy as might at first sight appear: for many works it is clear that they are exclusively about this New Testament book; but there are others that also contain additional material. Concerning these, the decision to include them or to exclude them from a bibliography on 1 Peter becomes problematic. It seemed advisable, therefore, that titles covering the Descent into Hades (if they were not exclusively dogmatic) or Peter as a New Testament figure should be incorporated here, since they impinge on 1 Peter to some greater or lesser extent. New Testament theologies and introductions, a vast field in their own right, are excluded, even though they often contain sections on 1 Peter. But dictionary and encyclopedia articles, though

they are at times hard to classify, are included. So also is any work
with a titled section or chapter devoted to part or all of 1 Peter.

Within these boundaries, I have tried to collect everything published through 1993. Subsequent titles were included as they came to
my attention. This is not to claim that the collection of titles published prior to 1994 is perfectly complete. Only a very bold bibliogra-
pher would assert anything like that, since the nature of the resources
does not allow for certainty. Nevertheless, completeness was intended, and the probability that everything of importance is here in-
creases as one moves further back in time from the present. January
1994 is the *terminus ante quem*.

The *terminus post quem* is of course the date of the publication of
1 Peter itself. But again, only work specifically dealing with 1 Peter
is listed. Furthermore, vis-à-vis even early titles, the bibliography is
limited to material that has actually been published. Unfortunately,
this automatically eliminates some things, such as some as yet unpublished medieval commentaries.

As regards the field from which titles have been garnered, I have
limited myself to the so-called Western world and the languages of or
derived from Europe. Most assuredly there are non-Western languages in which there has been writing on 1 Peter. Works in African
and Asian languages, however, have been excluded for both personal
and general reasons. Speaking personally, I know neither the languages nor the scripts in which these works are presented. More
generally, the world has not yet developed comprehensive tools for
collecting such titles nor comprehensive libraries for examining the
works themselves. Furthermore, publishing limitations curb the number and types of scripts that could be used even if they were collected
together.

In presenting this bibliography, decisions also had to be made concerning editions and reprints. For nineteenth and twentieth century
works other than encyclopedias, as many editions are listed as I have
been able to collect and verify. In form, multiple editions are shown
as in the entry for the commentary by Brox.

> BROX, N. *Der erste Petrusbrief.* EKKNT 21. Zürich,
> Einsiedeln, Köln, and Braunschweig: Benziger and
> Neukirchen-Vluyn: Neukirchener Verlag, 1979, ²1986,
> ³1989.

In the case of earlier authors, selected principal editions are shown, as
in the case of Bengel.

> BENGEL, J. A. "In epistolam Petri priorem," *Gnomon Novi
> Testamenti in quo ex nativa verborum vi simplicitas,
> profunditas, concinnitas, salubritas sensuum coeles-
> tium indicatur opera Jo. Alberti Bengelii.* Tübingen:

Schramm, 1742, [2]1759, [3]1773 (ed. E. Bengel), [5]1835-36 (ed. J. Steudel), and many editions and translations.

Reprints are listed only when an out-of-print work of a previous era is reissued, usually by a different firm, e.g., Klock and Klock of Minneapolis.

Reviews are collected together under the entry of the original book. Titles of review articles are not given.

If the number of titles falling into a given category is in excess of about twenty, that category has a separate section devoted to it. Categories of fewer than twenty titles are collected together in the section entitled "Miscellaneous." When an occasional title might have been assigned to two or more categories, I have with few exceptions chosen the grouping that seems most appropriate and excluded the other(s). Although users of this book may not always agree with my judgments, often made rapidly and with no leisure for subsequent reflection, they can always find anything by a given author by consulting the index.

Form and Format

A number of observations about the form of entries should be of help to the user of this book. Details are given here in the approximate order of the corresponding part of each entry.

Names of Authors

The names of authors appear in the script and lettering of the original languages. In all cases, forenames are given only as initials for the sake of consistency.

Titles

Titles of foreign language works appear as nearly as possible according to the conventions of capitalization of the original languages. French titles, for example, have only the first word and proper nouns capitalized, but in German titles the first word and all nouns are capitalized. But there are differences even then between editor and editor in the capitalization of, say, *Épître* in Épître de Pierre or *Saint* in Saint Pierre. In each case, I have tried to enter titles as the authors themselves have done, or, where this is not immediately apparent from the typography of the title itself, as they would do based on considerations internal to the text.

In some journals, titles on the first pages of articles are in upper case lettering. As may be imagined, this creates occasional difficulties in knowing whether to capitalize certain words. Therefore, but with some flexibility, in such cases the form of the title given here follows that given in the table of contents of the journal, if mixed lettering occurs there, or otherwise in the text of the article.

Details of the original have been followed wherever possible in every particular. Thus, for example, it differs from author to author whether the *First* in First Peter, when it is represented by a numeral, is *I, I., 1,* or *1.* or whether *St.* is or is not followed by a period. In an attempt to be faithful to the originals, these differences are reflected in the bibliography.

Alphabetization has been done according to the logic of my word processor and may or may not conform in detail to standards acceptable from place to place. Among other things, for example, the reader should observe that numerals take precedence over letters for alphabetical purposes, that articles are included, that *Mac* and *Mc* at the beginning of names are differentiated, and that umlauted letters are alphabetized as *a, o,* or *u* rather than as *ae, oe* or *ue.*

Other Details

In general other bibliographic details are dealt with according to American conventions, though place names are given the spellings of the publisher of the relevant works.

Abbreviations of journals and significant series and books are as those given in:

> *SBL: Society of Biblical Literature Membership Directory and Handbook.* Decatur, Ga.: The Society of Biblical Literature, 1994, 231-240.

They are also shown in the table of Abbreviations. All other series and journal titles are written out in full.

Parentheses (. . .) and brackets [. . .], where they occur, are present here because they also occur in the original, as in:

> ARICHEA, D. C., Jr. "God or Christ? A Study of Implicit Information [1 Peter 1:1-20]," *BT* 28 (1977) 412-418.

Braces {. . .}, however, always enclose additions which I have myself made for the sake of clarity, as in:

> ELLIOTT, J. H. "Salutation and Exhortation to Christian Behavior on the Basis of God's Blessings ({1 Peter} 1:1-2:10)," *RevExp* 79 (1982) 415-425.

The names of editors of well-known series (of commentaries, et al.) where editors change from time to time are omitted. But the names of editors of occasional works are included whenever they are known.

Publishers are given in shortened form, e.g. Fortress, Eerdmans, Mohr-Siebeck, except where more is required for the sake of clarity. Names of publishers are omitted only when I have been unsuccessful in finding them. Their absence for any given entry is usually a sign that the work in question is one of those for which I have not been able to examine hard copy or find on-line information. Only where names of publishing places or institutions are missing in the printed book is the designation *n.p.* given.

In addition to articles in journals, page numbers are given for articles in collections of essays of various sorts and in books of which the relevant material is only a part of the whole. For example,

> AGNEW, F. H. "1 Peter 1:2—An Alternative Translation," *CBQ* 45 (1983) 68-73.

> DELLING, G. "Der Bezug der christlichen Existenz auf das Heilshandeln Gottes nach dem ersten Petrusbrief," *Neues Testament und christliche Existenz. Festschrift für Herbert Braun zum 70. Geburtstag am 4. Mai 1973.* Ed. H. D. Betz and L. Schottroff. Tübingen: Mohr-Siebeck, 1973, 95-113.

> ACHTEMEIER, P. J. "1 Peter," Harper's Bible Commentary. Ed. J. L. Mays. San Francisco: Harper & Row, 1988, 1279-1285.

Additional details appropriate only to specific categories of titles are laid out in the introductions to relevant sections.

Finally, avoidance of omissions and errata in a work of this detail is nearly impossible to attain. Thousands of minute decisions and even deductions have to be made at every stage of production. I should be very grateful to receive any addenda or corrigenda that come to the user's attention.

ACKNOWLEDGEMENTS

If I had known how difficult and labor intensive the production of this book would be, I might have thought twice about undertaking it. Many individuals, however, have given help in what has become a "labor of love." First among those deserving thanks are the student assistants who have worked sedulously to ensure that this work came to the light of day. They are B. Brian Hanneken (1993-95), Yiik Sing (James) Wong (1992-93), and Greg C. Mozel (1990-92). Each in his own way has contributed more to this work and to me than any researcher has a right to expect. They have done invaluable service, and I consider them to be colleagues and friends. The mistakes and shortcomings of this work are mine, not theirs; that there are not more is owing to their careful and painstaking work.

Gratitude is due also to George E. McDonough, an exceptional librarian and esteemed colleague, and to other personnel at the library of Western Evangelical Seminary. They were always quick to help whenever I had occasion to call on them. The interlibrary loan staff, Patti Russell and Roger Kling, are worthy of special mention because of the extent and intensity of their efforts to help. I am grateful also for the courtesies shown me by the library personnel at:

> The University of Chicago Library, 13-20 August 1993
> Tyndale House Library, Cambridge, England, 25-30 July 1994
> Cambridge University Library, England, 25-30 July 1994
> Multnomah School of the Bible, Portland, Oregon, 30 August-2 September 1994
> Mount Angel Abbey Library, St. Benedict, Oregon, September-November 1994
> Western (Conservative Baptist) Seminary Library, Portland, Oregon, 27 September-7 October 1994
> Reed College Library, Portland, Oregon, 12 October 1994

Finally, I would like to mention the constant support and encouragement of my wife Sharon, to whom this book is dedicated, and of our children, Stephan, Joy, Jonathan, and Alison.

ABBREVIATIONS

Abbreviations used in this book are from the list printed in *SBL: Society of Biblical Literature Membership Directory and Handbook*. Decatur, Ga.: The Society of Biblical Literature, 1994, 231-240. The relevant ones are reproduced below for the convenience of the user.

AB	Anchor Bible
AJBI	Annual of the Japanese Biblical Institute
AnBib	Analecta biblica
Anton	*Antonianum*
ARW	*Archiv für Religionswissenschaft*
ASNU	Acta seminarii neotestamentici upsaliensis
ASSR	*Archives des sciences sociales des religions*
ATANT	Abhandlungen zur Theologie des Alten und Neuen Testaments
ATR	*Anglican Theological Review*
AusBR	*Australian Biblical Review*
AUSS	*Andrews University Seminary Studies*
BBET	Beiträge zur biblischen Exegese und Theologie
BeO	*Bibbia e oriente*
BETL	Bibliotheca ephemeridum theologicarum lovaniensium
BFCT	Beiträge zur Förderung christlicher Theologie
Bib	*Biblica*
BK	*Bibel und Kirche*
BLit	*Bibel und Liturgie*
BSac	*Bibliotheca Sacra*
BT	*The Bible Translator*
BTB	*Biblical Theology Bulletin*
BZ	*Biblische Zeitschrift*
BZNW	Beihefte zur *ZNW*
CB	*Cultura bíblica*
CBC	Cambridge Bible Commentary
CBQ	*Catholic Biblical Quarterly*
CChr	Corpus Christianorum
CGTC	Cambridge Greek Testament Commentaries
CH	*Church History*
CJT	*Canadian Journal of Theology*
ConNT	*Coniectanea neotestamentica*
CQ	*Church Quarterly*
CQR	*Church Quarterly Review*
CR	*Critical Review of Books in Religion*
CSCO	Corpus scriptorum christianorum orientalium
CTM	*Concordia Theological Monthly*
CurTM	*Currents in Theology and Mission*
DBSup	*Dictionnaire de la Bible, Supplément*
DTT	*Dansk teologisk tidsskrift*
Ebib	Etudes bibliques
EKKNT	Evangelisch-katholischer Kommentar zum Neuen Testament
EstBib	*Estudios bíblicos*

ETL	*Ephemerides theologicae lovanienses*
ETR	*Etudes théologiques et religieuses*
ETS	Erfurter theologische Studien
EvQ	*Evangelical Quarterly*
EvT	*Evangelische Theologie*
ExpTim	*Expository Times*
FB	Forschung zur Bibel
FRLANT	Forschungen zur Religion und Literatur des Alten und Neuen Testaments
GOTR	*Greek Orthodox Theological Review*
Greg	*Gregorianum*
HeyJ	*Heythrop Journal*
HNT	Handbuch zum Neuen Testament
IB	*Interpreter's Bible*
IBS	*Irish Biblical Studies*
IDB	*Interpreter's Dictionary of the Bible*
IDBSup	Supplementary volume to *IDB*
Int	*Interpretation*
ISBE	*International Standard Bible Encyclopedia*, rev.
JAAR	*Journal of the American Academy of Religion*
JBC	*The Jerome Biblical Commentary*
JBL	*Journal of Biblical Literature*
JBR	*Journal of Bible and Religion*
JEH	*Journal of Ecclesiastical History*
JES	*Journal of Ecumenical Studies*
JETS	*Journal of the Evangelical Theological Society*
JR	*Journal of Religion*
JRelS	*Journal of Religious Studies*
JRT	*Journal of Religious Thought*
JSNT	*Journal for the Study of the New Testament*
JSNTSup	Journal for the Study of the New Testament, Supplements
JSS	*Journal of Semitic Studies*
JTS	*Journal of Theological Studies*
LD	Lectio divina
LUÅ	Lunds universitets årsskrift
LW	*Lutheran World*
MeyerK	Kritisch-exegetischer Kommentar über das Neue Testament
MNTC	Moffatt New Testament Commentary
MScRel	*Mélanges de science religieuse*
MTZ	*Münchener theologische Zeitschrift*
NCB	New Century Bible
NCCHS	*New Catholic Commentary on Holy Scripture*
NedTTs	*Nederlands theologisch tijdschrift*
Neot	*Neotestamentica*
NICNT	New International Commentary on the New Testament
NJBC	*The New Jerome Biblical Commentary*

NorTT	*Norsk Teologisk Tidsskrift*
NovT	*Novum Testamentum*
NovTSup	Novum Testamentum, Supplements
NRT	*La nouvelle revue théologique*
NTAbh	Neutestamentliche Abhandlungen
NTD	Das Neue Testament Deutsch
NTF	Neutestamentliche Forschungen
NTS	*New Testament Studies*
PG	*Patrologia graeca* (Migne)
PL	*Patrologia latina* (Migne)
PO	Patrologia orientalis
PSTJ	*Perkins (School of Theology) Journal*
PW	*Real-encyclopädie der classischen Altertumswissenschaft* (Pauly-Wissowa)
QD	Quaestiones disputatae
RAC	*Reallexicon für Antike und Christentum*
RB	*Revue biblique*
RCB	*Revista de cultura biblica*
RE	*Realencyklopädie für protestantische Theologie und Kirche*
RelS	*Religious Studies*
RelSRev	*Religious Studies Review*
ResQ	*Restoration Quarterly*
RevExp	*Review and Expositor*
RevistB	*Revista bíblica*
RevScRel	*Revue des sciences religieuses*
RevThom	*Revue thomiste*
RGG	*Religion in Geschichte und Gegenwart*
RHE	*Revue d'histoire ecclésiastique*
RHPR	*Revue d'histoire et de philosophie religieuses*
RivB	*Rivista biblica*
RNT	Regensburger Neues Testament
RSPT	*Revue des sciences philosophiques et théologiques*
RSR	*Reserches de science religieuse*
RTL	*Revue théologique de Louvain*
RTP	*Revue de théologie et de philosophie*
SBLDS	SBL Dissertation Series
SBLMS	SBL Monograph Series
SBLSP	SBL Seminar Papers
SBM	Stuttgarter biblische Monographien
SBS	Stuttgarter Bibelstudien
ScEccl	*Sciences ecclésiastiques*
ScEs	*Science et esprit*
SE	*Studia Evangelica*
SEÅ	*Svensk exegetisk årsbok*
SJT	*Scottish Journal of Theology*
SNT	Studien zum Neuen Testament
SNTSMS	Society for New Testament Studies Monograph Series
ST	*Studia theologica*
STK	*Svensk teologisk kvartalskrift*
StudBib	Studia Biblica

SUNT	Studien zur Umwelt des Neuen Testaments
TD	*Theology Digest*
TGl	*Theologie und Glaube*
TLZ	*Theologische Literaturzeitung*
TQ	*Theologische Quartalschrift*
TRu	*Theologische Rundschau*
TS	*Theological Studies*
TSK	*Theologische Studien und Kritiken*
TT	*Teologisk Tidsskrift*
TToday	*Theology Today*
TTZ	*Trierer theologische Zeitschrift*
TynBul	*Tyndale Bulletin*
TZ	*Theologische Zeitschrift*
UNT	Untersuchungen zum Neuen Testament
USQR	*Union Seminary Quarterly Review*
VC	*Vigilae christianae*
VD	*Verbum domini*
WBC	Word Biblical Commentary
WTJ	*Westminster Theological Journal*
WUNT	Wissenschaftliche Untersuchungen zum Neuen Testament
WW	*Word and World*
ZKG	*Zeitschrift für Kirchengeschichte*
ZKT	*Zeitschrift für katholische Theologie*
ZMR	*Zeitschrift für Missionskunde und Religionswissenschaft*
ZNW	*Zeitschrift für die neutestamentliche Wissenschaft*
ZST	*Zeitschrift für systematische Theologie*
ZWT	*Zeitschrift für wissenschaftliche Theologie*

SECTION 1

COMMENTARIES

In this section works are assembled that comment on the entirety of 1
Peter, whether they are part of a larger work or are themselves book
length. Since knowledge of certain details peculiar to this material
will assist the reader in using the data, it should be noted that: (a)
Page numbers of sections on 1 Peter are supplied, insofar as possible,
for individual works (single or multivolume) that also comment on the
entire New Testament or Bible or for collections such as *PL* and *PG*.
Otherwise (e.g., where only one or a few New Testament books are
covered in the work cited) page numbers are not given. (b) Volume
numbers are given with the pages (in the form 5:335-457) only when
the book cited is part of a multivolume work, not a member of a series. For books in series, volume numbers appear immediately after
the series title. (c) Total volumes are not usually given and are never
shown for series, for multivolume-multiauthor commentaries, nor for
dictionaries and encyclopedias. (d) Here, as elsewhere, all major editions (not printings!) of contemporary works are shown when that information has been available. When complete information has been
unavailable, efforts have been made to list at least the earliest and lat-
est editions. (e) Only principal editions of commentaries from earlier
centuries (e.g., that by Bengel) are noted. (f) No attempt has been
made to distinguish serious (academic) commentaries from more
popular Bible study guides, but all have been included. It might be
possible to decide between works standing toward one end of the
spectrum or the other, but there is a middle ground where any taxon-
omy can be questioned.

1   ABDON, D. A. *The Hopeful Disciple: 1 Peter.* Living Dis-
     cipleship Series. Indianapolis: Parish Leadership Seminars,
     1986.

2   ACHTEMEIER, P. J. "1 Peter," *Harper's Bible Commentary.*
     Ed. J. L. Mays. San Francisco: Harper & Row, 1988, 1279-
     1285.

3   ADAMS, J. E. *Trust and Obey: A Practical Commentary on
     First Peter.* Philipsburg, N.J.: Presbyterian and Reformed,
     1978 and Grand Rapids: Baker, 1979.
     Review: Scharlemann, E., *Concordia Journal* 5 (1979) 194-195.

4   ALEXANDRE, N. *Commentarius litteralis et moralis in omnes*

epistolas Sancti Pauli Apostoli, et in septem epistolas catholicas. Rouen, 1710; Parisiis: T. Bettinelli, 1768.

5   ALFORD, H. "ΠΕΤΡΟΥ A," *The Greek Testament.* London: Rivingtons, 1849-1860; Boston: Lee and Shepard and New York: Lee, Shepard, and Dillingham, 4:[112-140] and 331-388; reprints, e.g., Chicago: Moody, 1958 and Grand Rapids: Baker, 1980. (An often edited and reprinted work with a complicated publication history. Revisions and editions were made on a volume-by-volume basis.)

6   ALULFUS. "Expositio super I Epistolam B. Petri Apostoli," *De expositione Novi Testamenti. PL* 79:1385-1388.

7   AMBROGGI, P. de. *Le Epistole cattoliche di Giacomo, Pietro, Giovanni e Giuda.* La Sacra Bibbia 14,1. Torino and Roma: Marietti, 1947, ²1949, reprint 1967.

8   AMMONIUS OF ALEXANDRIA. *Fragmentum in Primam S. Petri Epistolam. PG* 85:1607-1610.

9   AMYRAUT, M. *Paraphrase sur les épîtres catholiques de S. Jacqves, S. Pierre, S. Jean, & S. Jvde.* Saumur: Lesnier, 1646.

10   ANTONIDES, T. *Schriftmässige Erklärung über den ersten allgemeinen Brieff des Heil. Apostels Simonis Petri.* Ed. and trans. A. Plesken. Bremen: Saurmann, 1700.

11   ARETIUS, B. *Commentarii in Domini nostri Jesv Christi Novvm Testamentvm.* Bernae Helvetiorum: Ioannem le Prevx, 1607, 487-507; *In novum testamentum domini Jesu Christi commentarii doctissimi.* Editio postrema, omnium emendatissima, & utilissimis ad marginem notis illustrata. Genevae: Petru & Iacobus Chouet, 1618.

12   ARICHEA, D. C., and E. A. NIDA. *A Translator's Handbook on the First Letter from Peter.* Helps for Translators. New York, London, and Stuttgart: United Bible Societies, 1980.

13   AUGUSTI, J. C. W. *Die katholischen Briefe, neu übersetzt und erklärt und mit Excursen und einleitenden Abhandlungen herausgegeben.* Lemgo: Meyer, 1801-1808.

14   BALL, C. S. "First Peter," *The Wesleyan Bible Commentary.* Grand Rapids: Eerdmans, 1966, 6:239-278.

15   BARBIERI, L. A. *First and Second Peter.* Chicago: Moody, 1975, ²1977.

16   BARCLAY, W. *The Letters of James and Peter.* Daily Study Bible. Edinburgh: St. Andrew, 1958, ²1960; Philadelphia: Fortress, ²1960; Philadelphia: Westminster, 1961, ²1976.
      Review: Bunte, R. W. Vande {sic}, *Reformed Review* 15 (1961) 47.

17   BARNES, A. *Notes, Explanatory and Practical, on the General Epistles of James, Peter, John and Jude.* New York: Harper, 1855; reprint Grand Rapids: Baker, 1949.

18   BAUER, J. B. *Der erste Petrusbrief.* Die Welt der Bibel, Kleinkommentar 14. Düsseldorf: Patmos, 1971.

19   BAUER, W. *Die katholischen Briefe des Neuen Testaments.* Tübingen: Mohr-Siebeck, 1910.

20   BEARE, F. W. *The First Epistle of Peter: Introduction, Translation, and Commentary.* Ph.D. dissertation, University of Chicago, 1946.

21   ———. *The First Epistle of Peter: The Greek Text with Introduction and Notes.* Oxford: Blackwell, 1947, ²1958, ³1970.
      Review: Piper, O. A., *JR* 29 (1949) 62-63.

22   BECK, J. T. *Erklärung der Briefe Petri.* Ed. J. Lindenmeyer. Güttersloh: Bertelsmann, 1896.

23   BEDE, the Venerable. "Commentary on 1 Peter," *The Commentary on the Seven Catholic Epistles of Bede the Venerable.* Trans. D. Hurst. Cistercian Studies Series 82. Kalamazoo, Mich.: Cistercian, 1985, 69-122.

24   ———. "In primam epistolam Petri," *Super epistolas catholicas expositio, PL* 93:41-68.

25   BÉNÉTREAU, S. *La Première Épître de Pierre.* Commentaire évangélique de la Bible. Vaux-sur-Seine: Edifac, 1984.
      Review: Miller, L., *RHPR* 66 (1986) 236-237.

26   BENGEL, J. A. "Annotations on the First Epistle of Peter," *Gnomon of the New Testament . . . Now First Translated into English, with original notes Explanatory and Illustrative.* Trans. C. T. Lewis and M. R. Vincent. Edinburgh: T. & T. Clark, 1857-58; *John Albert Bengel's Gnomon of the New*

Testament. Pointing Out from the Natural Force of the Words, the Simplicity, Depth, Harmony and Saving Power of its Divine Thoughts. Trans. C. T. Lewis and M. R. Vincent from the German edition of 1855, ed. J. C. Steudel, which reproduces the edition of 1835; both retained the text of the standard (third) edition of 1773, ed. E. Bengel. Philadelphia: Perkinpine & Higgins and New York: Sheldon, 1860-62, 2:725-759 (the original printing was "entered according to Act of Congress, in the year 1860, by Perkinpine & Higgins, in the Clerk's Office of the District Court for the Eastern District of Pennsylvania" but apparently printed for the first time in 1862); reprinted as "Word Studies in First Peter," *New Testament Word Studies* (based on the 1864 edition by Perkinpine & Higgins). Grand Rapids: Kregel, 1971.

27   ——. "In epistolam Petri priorem," *Gnomon Novi Testamenti in quo ex nativa verborum vi simplicitas, profunditas, concinnitas, salubritas sensuum coelestium indicatur opera Jo. Alberti Bengelii.* Tübingen: Schramm, 1742, ²1759, ³1773 (ed. E. Bengel), ⁴1835-36 (ed. J. Steudel), and many editions and translations.

28   BENNETCH, J. H. "Exegetical Studies in 1 Peter," *Biblische Studien* 99 (1942) 180-192, 344-353, 440-452; 100 (1943) 263-272, 397-406, 524-531; 101 (1944) 83-94, 193-198, 304-318, 446. {See the studies begun by E. F. Harrison, of which these are a continuation.}

29   BENNETT, W. H. *The General Epistles: James, Peter, John, and Jude.* Century Bible 17. Edinburgh: Jack and New York: Frowde, 1901.

30   BENSON, G. *A Paraphrase and Notes on the Seven (Commonly Called) Catholic Epistles, viz. St. James, I St. Peter, II St. Peter, St. Jude, I, II, and III of St. John.* London: Waugh, 1749 and London: Waugh and Fenner, 1756.

31   ——. *Paraphrastische Erklärung und Anmerkungen über einige Bücher des Neuen Testaments.* Trans. J. P. Bamberger. Leipzig, 1761, 3:150-356.

32   BESSER, W. F. *Die Briefe St. Petri in Bibelstunden für die Gemeinde ausgelegt.* Bibelstunden 8. Halle, 1854.

33   BEST, E. *I Peter.* NCB. London: Oliphants and Grand Rapids: Eerdmans, 1971.

Reviews: Marshall, I. H., *EvQ* 43 (1971) 177-179; Thompson, J. W., *ResQ* 27 (1984) 232-233.

34   BIBLIANDER, T. *Richtige Harmonie der heiligen Schrifft Alten und Neuen Testamentes in 4 Theilen.* Görlitz, 1705.

35   BIGG, C. *A Critical and Exegetical Commentary on the Epistles of St. Peter and St. Jude.* The International Critical Commentary. Edinburgh: T. & T. Clark, 1901, ²1902.

36   BISPING, A. *Erklärung der sieben katholischen Briefe.* Exegetisches Handbuch zum Neuen Testament 8.   Münster: Aschendorf, 1871.

37   BLAIKLOCK, E. M. *First Peter: A Translation and Devotional Commentary.* Waco: Word, 1977.

38   BLAIR, J. *Study Guide for 1 Peter: Message of Encouragement.* Nashville: Convention, 1982.

39   BLAIR, J. A. *Living Peacefully: A Devotional Study of the First Epistle of Peter.* New York: Loizeaux, 1959.

40   BLENKIN, G. W. *The First Epistle General of Peter.* CGTC. Cambridge: University Press, 1914.

41   BLUM, E. A. "1 Peter," *The Expositor's Bible Commentary.* Ed. F. E. Gabelein.   Grand Rapids: Zondervan, 1976-88, 12:207-254.

42   BLUNT, J. H.   *The Annotated Bible, Being a Household Commentary upon the Holy Scriptures, Comprehending the Results of Modern Discovery and Criticism.* London and New York: Rivingtons, 1878-82.

43   BOATTI, A. *Le Lettere Cattoliche tradotte dal testo greco e annotate.* Sale Tortonexe: Ermite, 1932.

44   BOLKSTEIN, M. H.   *Die brieven van Petrus en Judas.* Nijkerk: Callenbach, 1963, ²1972.

45   BOWMAN, J. W. "The First Letter of Peter," *The Layman's Bible Commentary.*   Richmond: John Knox and London: SCM, 1959-63, 24:116-155.

46   BRATCHER, R. G. *A Translator's Guide to the Letters from James, Peter, and Jude.* Helps for Translators. London, New York, and Stuttgart: United Bible Societies, 1984.

47   BRESTIN, S., and D. BRESTIN. *First & Second Peter, Jude: Called for a Purpose.* Fisherman Bible Study Guides. Wheaton: Shaw, Harold, 1987.

48   BRISCOE, D. S. *1 Peter: Holy Living in a Hostile World.* Understanding the Book. Wheaton: Shaw, 1993.

49   BROWN, J. *Expository Discourses on the First Epistle of the Apostle Peter.* Edinburgh: Oliphant, 1848, ^{2}1849, ^{3}1886; reprint Marshallton, Del.: National Foundation for Christian Education, n.d.; New York: Carter, 1851, ^{2}1855; reprint as *First Peter*, Edinburgh and Carlisle, Penn.: Banner of Truth, 1975.

50   BROX, N. *Der erste Petrusbrief.* EKKNT 21. Zürich, Einsiedeln, Köln, and Braunschweig: Benziger and Neukirchen-Vluyn: Neukirchener Verlag, 1979, ^{2}1986, ^{3}1989.
      Review: Stöger, A., *BLit* 52 (1979) 261-265.

51   BRUN, L. *Forste Peters-Brev.* Oslo: Aschehoug, 1949.

52   BUGGE, F. W. *Apostlerne Peters og Judas's breve. Indledede, oversatte og forklarede.* Christiania: Steen, 1885, ^{2}1886.

53   BULLINGER, H. "In D. Petri Apostoli Epistolam vtranque," *Heinrychi Bullingeri Commentarius.* Zürich, 1534.

54   BURGER, K. *Der erste Brief Petri.* Strack-Zöcklers kurzgefaßter Kommentar über das Neue Testament 4. Nördlingen, 1888.

55   CAFFIN, B. C. *The First Epistle General of Peter.* The Pulpit Commentary. Ed. H. D. M. Spence and J. S. Excell. London: Kegan Paul, Trench, 1889; reprint Grand Rapids: Eerdmans, 1950 and Peabody, Mass.: Hendrickson, 1980, 22:i-xiv, 1-241.

56   CALLOUD, J., and F. GENUYT. *La première épitre de Pierre. Analyse sémiotique.* LD 109. Paris: Cerf, 1982.
      Reviews: Chevallier, M. A., *RHPR* 63 (1983) 350-351; Escande, J., *ETR* 58 (1983) 258-261; Genest, O., *ScEs* 35 (1983) 246-248; Lodge, J. G., *CBQ* 45 (1983) 681-682.

57 CALMES, T. *Les épîtres catholiques, L'Apocalypse.* Paris: Bloud, 1905, ³1907.

58 CALMET, A. *Commentaire littéral sur tous les livres de l'Ancien et du Nouveau Testament.* Paris, 1707-16 and 1726, 8:794-831.

59 CALOV, A. *Biblia Novi Testamenti illustrata.* Francofurti: Wustii, 1676; Dresdae et Lipsiae: Zimmermanni, ²1719, 2:1463-1531.

60 CALVIN, J. Commentaries. Badius, Geneva, 1561, 1562.

61 ———. "Epistola Petri Apostoli prior," *Ioannis Calvini opera quae supersunt omnia* {"Brunswick edition"}. Ed. G. Bauer, E. Cunitz, and E. Reuss. Corpus Reformatorum. Brunsvigae: Schwetschke, 1863-1900, 60:208-291; reprint New York and London: Johnson and Frankfurt: Minerva, 1964.

62 ———. I Peter, 1st ed. dedicated to Edward V. of England. Geneva, 1551.

63 CAMERLYNCK, A. *Commentarius in epistolas catholicas.* Brügge: Baetaert, 1876, ⁵1909.

64 CARROLL, B. H. *The Pastoral Epistles of Paul and I and II Peter, Jude, and I, II and III John.* Ed. J. B. Cranfill. An Interpretation of the English Bible. Nashville: The Sunday School Board of the Southern Baptist Convention, 1915 and Nashville: Broadman, ²1947.

65 CASSIODORUS, [F.] M. A. "Epistola Petri Apostoli ad gentes," *Complexiones canonicarum epistularum septem.* PL 70:1361-1368.

66 CATON, N. T. *A Commentary and an Exposition of the Epistles of James, Peter, John and Jude.* 1879.

67 CEDAR, P. A. *The Communicator's Commentary: James, First and Second Peter, Jude.* The Communicator's Commentary 11. Waco: Word, 1984, 105-200.
    Reviews: Baker, W. R., *JETS* 28 (1985) 97-99; Blok, A., *Reformed Review* 39 (1985) 57-58; Deppe, D., *Calvin Theological Journal* 20 (1985) 132-134; Kiehl, E. H., *Concordia Journal* 11 (1985) 195; Lea, T. D., *Southwestern Journal of Theology* 27 (1985) 72-73; Omanson, R. L., *RevExp* 82 (1985) 277-278.

68   CHARUE, A. *Les épîtres catholiques*. La Sainte Bible 12. Paris: Gabalda, 1938, ³1951.

69   CLARK, G. H. *I & II Peter*. (Two Books in One. Previously published separately as: *Peter Speaks Today: A Devotional Commentary on First Peter* and *II Peter: A Short Commentary*.) Phillipsburg, N.J.: Presbyterian and Reformed, 1980.

70   ——. *Peter Speaks Today: A Devotional Commentary on First Peter*. Philadelphia: Presbyterian and Reformed, 1967.

71   CLARKE, A. "The First General Epistle of Peter," *The Holy Bible Containing the Old and New Testaments. The Text Carefully Printed from the Most Correct Copies of the Present Authorized Translation Including the Marginal Readings and Parallel Texts. With a Commentary and Critical Notes; Designed as a Help to a Better Understanding of the Sacred Writings*. London: Butterworth, 1825; new edition, with the author's final corrections, London: Tegg, 1838, New Testament 2:1875-1908; New York: Sargent, 1811; second American edition, New York: Hitt and Paul, 1817; third American edition, New York: Hitt and Paul, 1817-25; royal octavo stereotype edition, New York: Waugh and Mason, 1832.

72   ——. *The New Testament of our Lord and Saviour Jesus Christ: The Text Taken from the Most Correct Copies of the Present Authorized Version, with the Marginal Readings—a Collection of Parallel Texts—and Copious Summaries to Each Chapter, With a Commentary and Critical Notes*. London: Butterworth, 1817; New York: Eastburn, Kirk, 1814 {vol. 1 only published}; New York: Smith, 1823; New York: Paul, 1825; New York: Smith, 1826; New York: Emory and Waugh (for the Methodist Episcopal Church), 1831; Philadelphia: Founder, 1823; White Plains: Smith, 1829.

73   CLEMENT OF ALEXANDRIA. "In Epistola Petri Prima catholica," *Adumbrationes Clementis Alexandrini in epistolas canonicas*. GCS 3:203-206.

74   CLOWNEY, E. P. *The Message of 1 Peter: The Way of the Cross*. The Bible Speaks Today. Leicester and Downers Grove: InterVarsity, 1988.
      Reviews: Grams, R., *East Africa Journal of Evangelical Theology* 8 (1989) 42-46; Guthrie, D., *Churchman* 103 (1989) 262; Milne, D. J. W., *Reformed Theological Review* 51 (1992) 31; Perkins, L., *JETS* 35

(1992) 543-544; Weima, J. A. D., *Calvin Theological Journal* 25 (1990) 267-269.

75   COCHRANE, E. E. *The Epistles of Peter: A Study Manual.* Shield Bible Study Series. Grand Rapids: Baker, 1965.

76   COFFMAN, B. *Commentary on James, 1 & 2 Peter, 1, 2 & 3 John, Jude.* Austin, Tex.: Firm Foundation, 1979.

77   COGLERUS, J. *In Epistolas Petri Commentarius.* Wittenberg, 1564.

78   COLEMAN, L., and R. PEACE. *1 Peter: A Pastor Directed Study Course for Small Groups.* Pastor/Teacher Commentary. Mastering the Basics: Personal Excellence through Bible Study. Littleton, Col.: Serendipity, 1988.

79   ———. *1 Peter.* Study Guide. Mastering the Basics: Personal Excellence through Bible Study. Littleton, Col.: Serendipity, 1988.

80   COOK, F. C. "The First Epistle General of Peter," *The Holy Bible According to the Authorized Version (A.D. 1611) with an Explanatory and Critical Commentary and a Revision of the Translation, by Bishops and Other Clergy of the Anglican Church. New Testament.* "The Speaker's Commentary." Ed. F. C. Cook. London: J. Murray, 1871-76 and New York: Scribner, Armstrong, 1871-81, 4:155-220.

81   CRAMER, G. H. *First and Second Peter.* Everyman's Bible Commentary. Chicago: Moody, 1967.

82   CRAMER, J. A. *Catenae graecorum patrum in Novum Testamentum.* Oxonii: E Typographeo Academico, 1844, 8:41-83.

83   CRANFIELD, C. E. B. *I and II Peter and Jude.* Torch Bible Commentaries. London: SCM, 1960 and New York: Harper and Row, 1961.
      Reviews: Heller, J., *Communio Viatorum* 4 (1961) 325; Mitton, C. L. *ExpTim* 72 (1961) 232-233; Smalley, S. S., *Churchman* 75 (1961) 54-55.

84   ———. "I Peter," *Peake's Commentary on the Bible.* Ed. M. Black and H. H. Rowley. London: Nelson, 1962, 1026-1030.

85   ——. "I Peter," *The Twentieth Century Bible Commentary*.
      New York: Harper, 1932, [2]1955, 506-510.

86   ——. *The First Epistle of Peter*. London: SCM, 1950.
      Reviews: Hunter, A. M., *ExpTim* 61 (1950) 236; Manson, W., *SJT* 5
      (1952) 334-336; Metzger, B. M., *Religion in Life* 19 (1950) 634-635.

87   CRELLIUS FRANCUS, J. "Commentarius in I. epistolae Petri
      duo priora capita," *Johannis Crellii Franci Opera omnia,
      exegetica, didactica, et polemica*. Freiburg, 1656, 2:269-284;
      *Johannis Crellii Opera omnia, exegetica, didactica, et po-
      lemica*. Bibliotheca Fratrum Polonorum qui Unitarii appel-
      lantur. Eleutheropoli: Philalethii, 1656.

88   CYRIL OF ALEXANDRIA. "In epistolam I B. Petri," *Fragmenta
      in epistolas catholicas*. *PG* 74:1011-1016.

89   DALTON, W. J. "I Peter," *NCCHS*. London, Melbourne, Jo-
      hannesburg, Don Mill (Ontario), and Camden (N.J.): Nelson,
      1953, [2]1969 (London), 1246-1251.

90   ——. "The First Epistle of Peter," *NJBC*. Ed. R. E. Brown,
      J. A. Fitzmyer, and R. E. Murphy. Englewood Cliffs, N.J.:
      Prentice Hall, 1990, 903-908.

91   DANKER, F. W. *Invitation to the New Testament Epistles IV:
      A Commentary on Hebrews, James, 1 and 2 Peter, 1, 2, and
      3 John and Jude*. Garden City, N.Y.: Image Books, 1980.

92   DAVIDS, P. H. *The First Epistle of Peter*. NICNT. Grand
      Rapids: Eerdmans, 1990.
      Reviews: Arichea, D. C., *BT* 42 (1991) 348-350; Bauckham, R., *NovT*
      35 (1993) 305-306; Blomberg, C. L., *Themelios* 17 (1992) 31;
      Bockmuehl, M., *Crux* 28 (1992) 47-48; Fleddermann, H., *CBQ* 54
      (1992) 557-559; Johnson, D. H., *Didaskalia* 2 (1991) 25-27; Jones, J.
      E., *RevExp* 88 (1991) 271; Kent, H. A., *Grace Theological Journal* 11
      (1990) 238-240; Kiehl, E. H., *Concordia Journal* 18 (1992) 105;
      Michaels, J. R., *CR* (1992) 192-193.

93   DE HAAN, R. W., and H. V. LUGT. *Good News for Bad
      Times: A Study of 1 Peter*. With a *Leader's Guide* prepared
      by T. Powell. Wheaton: Victor, 1975.

94   DEMAREST, J. T. *A Translation and Exposition of the First
      Epistle of the Apostle Peter*. New York: Moffet, 1851.

95   DE WETTE, W. M. L. *Kurze Erklärung der Briefe des
      Petrus, Judas und Jacobus*. Kurzgefaßtes exegetisches

Handbuch zum Neuen Testament 3,1. Leipzig: Weidmann, 1847 and Leipzig: Hirzel, ^{2}1853, ^{3}1885.

96 DÍAS, R. M. "1, 2 Sant Pere," *Epistoles Catòliques*. La Bíblia de Montserrat 22. Montserrat, 1958, 67-140.

97 DIDYMUS OF ALEXANDRIA. "In Epistolam S. Petri Primam enarratio," *In epistolas catholicas enarratio*. *PG* 39:1755-1772; *Didymi Alexandrini in Epstolas canonicas brevis ennaratio*. NTAbh 4,1. Ed. F. Zoepfl. Münster: Aschendorff, 1914.

98 DIONYSIUS BAR SALÎBI. *In Apocalypsim, Actus et Epistulas catholicas*, CSCO 53:134-137 (text), 60:103-105 (translation by I. Sedlacek).

99 DOWD, S. "1 Peter," *The Women's Bible Commentary*. Ed. C. A. Newsome and S. H. Ringe. London: SPCK and Louisville: Westminster/John Knox, 1992, 370-372.

100 DRACH {no forename given}. "Première épître catholique de l'apôtre Saint Pierre," *La Sainte Bible*. Paris: Lethielleux, 1890-1911, 25:76-110.

101 DUMMELOW, J. R., ed. "1 Peter," *A Commentary on the Holy Bible by Various Writers*. London: Macmillan, 1909 and New York: Macmillan, 1925, 1038-1048. {Authors of articles are cited in an opening table in this work, but it is apparently nowhere indicated which individual articles they wrote.}

102 EATON, R. "The First Epistle of St. Peter," *The Catholic Epistles of St. Peter, St. James, St. Jude, and St. John: Text and Commentary*. London: Burns Oates & Washbourne, 1937, 1-47.

103 EDWARDS, C. W. *Christian Being and Doing: A Study-Commentary on James and I Peter*. New York: Joint Comission on Education and Cultivation, Board of Missions, The Methodist Church, 1966.

104 EISENSCHMID, G. B. *Die Briefe des Apostels Petrus übersetzt, erläutert und mit erbaulichen Betrachtungen begleitet*. Ronnenberg, 1824.

105 ELLIOTT, J. H. "I-II Peter/Jude," *James, I-II Peter/Jude*. Augsburg Commentary on the New Testament. Minneapolis: Augsburg, 1982.

106 ELLISON, H. L. *1 and 2 Peter, 1, 2 and 3 John, Jude, Revelation.* Scripture Union Bible Study Books. Grand Rapids: Eerdmans, 1969.

107 EMMET, L. M. "1 Peter," *The Teachers' Commentary.* New York and London: Harper, 1932, 378-379 and [5]1948.

108 ERASMUS, D. *Annotationes in Novvm Testamentvm.* 1516, [2]1519; Basileam: Rauracorvm, [3]1522, [4]1527, [5]1535.

109 ———. *Paraphrases in Novvm Testamentvm.* 1516-23, [2]1524, [3]1532, [4]1534; *Opera Omnia* Leiden, 1706, 7:1081-1100; reprint Hildesheim: 1962.

110 ERDMAN, C. R. *The General Epistles: An Exposition.* Philadelphia: Westminster, 1918.

111 ESTIUS, G. *In omnes beati Pavli et septem catholicas apostolorvm epistolas commentarii.* Douai, 1614-16; *Absolvtissima in omnes Beati Pavli septem catholicas Apostolorvm epistolas commentaria.* Coloniae Agrippinae: Henningii, 1631; Parisiis: Leonarrd, 1658, 2:1149-1201.

112 EUTHALIUS (pseudo). "Prioris catholicae Petri episolae," *Elenchus capitum septem Epistolarum Catholicarum.* PG 85:679-682.

113 EUTHYMIUS ZIGABENUS. *Commentarius in XIV Epistolas S. Pauli et VII Catholicas.* Ed. N. Kalogeras. Athens, 1887, 2:519-566.

114 EVANS, W. *Peter, The Epistle of "The Living Hope".* Hollywood, Cal.: Gospel Light, 1941.

115 EWALD, H. "Petrus' Sendschreiben," *Sieben Sendschreiben des Neuen Bundes übersetzt und erklärt.* Göttingen: Dieterich, 1870, 1-73.

116 EXELL, J. S. *First Peter.* The Biblical Illustrator or Anecdotes, Similes, Emblems, Illustrations; Expository, Scientific, Geographical, Historical, and Homiletic, Gathered from a Wide Range of Home and Foreign Literature, on the Verses of the Bible. New York, Chicago, Toronto, London and Edinburgh: Revell, n.d., v-viii and 1-454; reprint Grand Rapids: Baker, 1954.

117   FABRIS, R.   *Lettera di Giacomo e Prima Lettera di Pietro.*
      Lettura Pastorale della Bibbia 8. Bologna, 1980.

118   FAUSSET, A. R.   "The First Epistle General of Peter," *A
      Commentary, Critical, Experimental, and Practical, on the
      Old and New Testaments.*   Glasgow: Collins, 1868-77,
      6:597-618; *A Commentary, Critical and Explanatory, on the
      Old and New Testamments.*   Hartford: Scranton and
      Hillsdale, Mich.:   Names, 1878, 2:494-514; reprint Grand
      Rapids: Eerdmans, ²1935, 494-514 and Regency Reference
      Library, Grand Rapids: Zondervan, 1961, 1460-1484.

119   FELTEN, J.   *Die zwei Briefe des hl. Petrus und der Judasbrief.*
      Regensburg: Manz, 1929.

120   FERMIN DE LA COT.   *Epistolas catolicas.*   Barcelona:
      Labrana, 1921.

121   FIELD, F.   "I Peter," *Notes on the Translation of the New
      Testament: Being the Otium Norvicense (pars tertia).*
      (Reprint with additions by the late author).   Cambridge: Uni-
      versity Press, 1899, 239.

122   FITZMYER, J. A.   "The First Epistle of Peter," *JBC*.   Ed. R. E.
      Brown, J. A. Fitzmyer, and R. E. Murphy.   Englewood Cliffs,
      N.J.:   Prentice-Hall, 1968, 2:362-368.

123   FRANCO, R.   *Cartas de San Pedro.*   La Sacrada Escritura,
      Neuvo Testamento.   Madrid, 1962, 3:219-334.

124   FRANKEMÖLLE, H.   *1. Petrusbrief. 2. Petrusbrief. Judas-
      brief.*   Die neue Echter Bibel.   Würzburg: Echter, 1987.

125   FRONMÜLLER, G. F. C.   *Die Briefe Petri und der Brief Judä.*
      J. P. Lange's   Theologisch-homiletisches   Bibelwerk   14.
      Bielefeld: Velhagen und Klasing, 1859, ²1862, ³1871, ⁴1890.

126   ———. *The Epistles General of Peter.*   A Commentary on the
      Holy Scriptures, New Testament 9.   Trans. J. I. Mombert.
      New York: Charles Scribner's Sons, 1867; reprint as *Lange's
      Commentary on the Holy Scriptures* 9, Grand Rapids: Zon-
      dervan, n.d.

127   FRONMÜLLER, J.   *Die zwei Briefe des hl. Petrus und der Ju-
      dasbrief.*   Regensburg, 1929.

128   FULLER, J. M. *Student's Commentary on the Holy Bible.*
      London, 1879-87, vol. 5.

129   GAEBELEIN, A. C. "The First Epistle of Peter," *The Anno-
      tated Bible.* New York: Loizeaux, 1913-21; reprint Chicago:
      Moody and Loizeaux, 1970, 4:49-88.

130   GALBREATH, M. L. *James and Peter.* Aldersgate Biblical
      Series, Leader's Guide. Winona Lake: Light and Life, 1962.

131   GARDNER, P. *1 Peter - Revelation.* Bible Study Commen-
      tary. London: Scripture Union, 1988.

132   GERHARD, J. *Commentarius super Priorem . . . D. Petri
      Epistolam.* Ed. J. E. Gerhard. Jenae: Reiffenberger, 1641.

133   GETTYS, J. M. *Living the Gospel: A Study of 1 Peter.*
      Richmond: CLC (Covenant Life Curriculum), 1970.

134   GOEBEL, S. *Die Briefe des Petrus, griechisch, mit kurzer
      Erklärung.* Gotha, 1893.

135   GOLTZIUS, D. *Schriftmatige verklaringe en toepassinge Tot
      geestelijck gebruyck, van de eerste algemeyne Sendbrief des
      apostels Petri.* Amsterdam: Boeckholt, 1689-91.

136   GOMARUS, F. "In Priorem S. Petri Epistolam explicatio," *Op-
      era Theologica Omnia.* Amstelodami: Janssonii, 1664, 679-
      705.

137   GOPPELT, L. *A Commentary on I Peter.* Ed. F. Hahn. Trans.
      from *Der erste Petrusbrief* (Göttingen: Vandenhoeck & Ru-
      precht, 1978) by J. E. Alsup. Grand Rapids: Eerdmans,
      1993.

138   ———. *Der erste Petrusbrief.* Ed. F. Hahn. MeyerK 12,1.
      Göttingen: Vandenhoeck & Ruprecht, [8]1978. {The 8th ed. is
      the only edition of the MeyerK on 1 Peter by Goppelt. For
      previous editions cf. Huther, Kühl, and Knopf.}
      Reviews: Achtemeier, P. J., *JBL* 100 (1981) 136-138; Bouttier, M.,
      ETR 53 (1978) 577-578; Dalton, W. J., *Bib* 60 (1979) 450-453; De
      Jonge, M., *NedTTs* 33 (1979) 242-243; Elliott, J. H., *CBQ* 41 (1979)
      647-649; Krentz, E., *CurTM* 8 (1981) 246-247; Laws, S., *JTS* 30
      (1979) 539-543; Miller, L., *RHPR* 60 (1980) 252-254; Rissi, M., *TZ* 35
      (1979) 249-251; Ubelacker, W. G., *STK* 56 (1980) 34-35; Weiss, K.,
      TLZ 104 (1979) 821-823.

139   GOURBILLON, J. G., and F. M. DU BUIT. *La premièr épître de S. Pierre.* Evangile 50. Paris, 1963.

140   GRAY, J. C. "The First Epistle General of St. Peter," *The Biblical Museum: A Collection of Notes, Explanatory, Homiletic, and Illustrative, on the Holy Scriptures, Especially Designed for the Use of Ministers, Bible Students, and Sunday-School Teachers.* London: Stock and New York: Randolph: 1871-80, 15:129-160.

141   GRAY, J. C., and G. M. ADAMS. "The First Epistle General of St. Peter," *The Biblical Encyclopedia: A Collection of Notes Explanatory, Homiletic and Illustrative Forming a Complete Commentary on the Holy Scriptures Expecially Designed for the Use of Ministers, Bible Students and Sunday-School Teachers. The New Testament.* Cleveland: Barton, 1903, 5:541-568.

142   ———. "The First Epistle General of St. Peter," *Gray and Adams' Bible Commentary.* (Formerly "Biblical Encyclopedia" and "Biblical Museum".) Grand Rapids: Zondervan, n.d., 5:541-568.

143   GREGORIUS BARHEBRAEUS. *Gregorii Abulfaragii Bar Ebhraya in Actus apostolorum et Epistulas catholicas adnotationes Syriace e recognitione M. Klamroth.* Göttingae: Aedibus Dieterichianis, 1878, 27-29.

144   GREIJDANUS, S. *De Brieven van de Apostelen Petrus en Johannes, en de Brief van Judas.* Kommentaar op het Nieuwe Testament 13. Amsterdam: van Bottenburg, 1929.

145   GROTIUS, H. *Annotationvm in Novvm Testamentvm, pars tertia ac vltima.* Parisiis: Pepingvé, 1650, 1-37.

146   GRUDEM, W. A. *The First Epistle of Peter: An Introduction and Commentary.* The Tyndale New Testament Commentaries 17. Leicester: Inter-Varsity and Grand Rapids: Eerdmans, 1988.

Reviews: Brooks, J. A., *Southwestern Journal of Theology* 31 (1989) 60-61; Dockery, D. S., *Criswell Theological Review* 4 (1990) 396-397; Grams, R., *East Africa Journal of Evangelical Theology* 8,2 (1989) 42-46; Klein, W. W., *JETS* 34 (1991) 267-269; Luter, A. B., *Grace Theological Journal* 11 (1990) 106-107; McCartney, D. G., *WTJ* 51 (1989) 394-396; Milne, D. J. W., *Reformed Theological Review* 49 (1990) 77-78; Motyer, J. A., *Churchman* 103 (1989) 167-168; Thompson, J. W., *ResQ* 33 (1991) 115-116; Weima, J. A. D., *Calvin Theological Journal* 25 (1990) 102-105.

147 GRYGLEWICZ, F. *Listy katolickie. Pierwszy list św. Piotra. Drugi list św Piotra. Wstęp-przekład—komentarz—ekskurski opracował.* Katolicki Uniw. Lubelski. Pismo święte Nowego Testamentu 11. Poznań: Pallotinum, 1959.

148 GUNKEL, H. "Der erste Brief des Petrus," *Die Schriften des Neuen Testaments.* Göttingen: Vandenhoeck & Ruprecht, 1906 (vol. 2); [3]1917 (vol. 3).

149 HARRISON, E. F. "Exegetical Studies in 1 Peter," *Biblische Studien* 97 (1940) 200-210, 325-334, 448-455; 98 (1941) 69-77, 183-193, 307-319, 459-468. {See the continuation of these studies by J. H. Bennetch.}

150 HARRISON, P. V. *James, 1,2 Peter, and Jude.* Nashville: Randall, 1992.

151 HART, J. H. A. "The First Epistle General of Peter," *The Expositor's Greek Testament.* Ed. W. R. Nicoll. London: Hodder & Stoughton and New York: Dodd, Mead, 1897-1910, 5:1-80; reprint Grand Rapids: Ecrdmans, 1979.

152 HAUCK, F. *Die Briefe des Jacobus, Petrus, Judas und Johannes.* NTD 10. Göttingen: Vandenhoeck & Ruprecht, 1936, [7]1954, [8]1957. {For the 9th and 10th editions see Schneider and for the 11th edition see Schrage.}

153 HEMMINGIUS, N. *Commentaria in omnes epistolas Apostolorvm, Pavli, Petri, Ivdae, Iohannis, Iacobi, et in eam qvae ad Hebraeos inscribitvr, scripta, recognita, emendata, et alicvbi avcta.* Francofurti, 1579, 667-708.

154 HENSLER, C. G. *Der erste Brief des Apostels Petrus übersetzt und mit einem Kommentar versehen.* Sulzbach: Seidel, 1813.

155 HESSELS, J. *In Priorem B. Pavli Apostoli ad Timothevm Epistolam commentarivs. Alter item eivsdem avthoris commentarivs in Priorem B. Petri Apostoli canonicam Epistolam.* Lovanii: Bogardvm (svb Bibliis Aureis), 1568.

156 HESYCHIUS. *Fragmentum in epistolam I S. Petri.* PG 93:1389-1390.

157 HIEBERT, D. E. *First Peter: An Expositional Commentary.* Chicago: Moody, 1984, [2]1992. {2[nd] ed. entitled *1 Peter.*}

158   HILARY (Irish pseudo). "Epistola Beati Petri Apostoli Prima,"
      Tractatvs Hilarii in Septem Epistolas Canonicas. CChr
      (Series Latina) 108B:77-98.

159   HILARY OF ARLES (pseudo). "Epistola Beati Petri Apostoli
      Prima," *Expositio in epistoles catholicas. PL Supplementum*
      3:83-106.

160   HILLYER, N. *1 and 2 Peter, Jude.* New International Biblical
      Commentary. Peabody, Mass.: Hendrickson, 1992.
      Review: Reese, R.-A., *JSNT* 51 (1993) 127.

161   HOFMANN, J. C. K. von. "Der erste Brief Petri," *Die heili-*
      gen Schrift Neuen Testaments zusammenhängend untersucht
      7,1. Nördlingen: Beck, 1869-86.

162   HOLMER, U., and W. DE BOOR. *Die Briefe des Petrus und*
      der Brief des Judas. Wuppertaler Studienbibel. Wuppertal:
      Brockhaus, 1976.

163   HOLTZMANN, O. *Die Petrusbriefe.* Das Neue Testament
      nach dem Stuttgarter griechischen Text übersetzt und erklärt.
      Giessen: Töpelmann, 1926.

164   HOLZMEISTER, U. *Commentarius in epistulas SS. Petri et Iu-*
      dae apostolorum. Cursus Scripturae Sacrae. Parisiis: Le-
      thielleux, 1937.

165   HORNEIUS, C. *In Epistolam catholicam Sancti Apostoli Petri*
      priorem. Expositio litteralis. Ed. J. Horneius. Brunsvigae:
      Dvnckeri, 1654.

166   HORT, F. J. A. *The First Epistle of Peter, I. 1-II. 17: The*
      Greek Text, with Introductory Lecture, Commentary, and
      Additional Notes. London and New York: Macmillan, 1898;
      reprint in *Exegetical and Expository Studies.* Minneapolis:
      Klock and Klock, 1980.

167   HOTTINGER, J. I. *Epistolae D. Iacobi atque Petri I cum ver-*
      sione germanica et commentario latino. Leipzig: Libraria
      Dyckiana, 1815.

168   ——. *Epistolae Jacobi atque Petri cum versione germanica et commentario latino*. Leipzig, 1815.

169   HUNDHAUSEN, L. J. *Das erste Pontificalschreiben des Apostelfürsten Petrus. Wissenschaftliche und praktische Auslegung des ersten Briefes des heil. Petrus im Geiste der Kirche und im Hinblick auf den Geist der Zeit.* Die beiden Pontificalschreiben des Apostelfürsten Petrus. Eine Festschrift zur Errinerung an das funfundzwanzigjahrige Papst-Jubilaum des heiligen Vaters Pius IX. Mainz: Kircheim, 1873.

170   HUNTER, A. M., and E. G. HOMRIGHAUSEN. "The First Epistle of Peter," *IB*. Introduction and exegesis by A. M. Hunter, exposition by E. G. Homrighausen. New York and Nashville: Abingdon, 1957, 12:77-159.

171   HUTHER, J. E. *Die Briefe Petri und Judae*. MeyerK 12. Göttingen: Vandenhoeck und Ruprecht, 1852, [2]1859, [3]1867, [4]1877. {These are the only editions of MeyerK 12 by Huther. For others cf. Kühl, Knopf, and Goppelt.}

172   ——. "The First Epistle of the Apostle Peter," *Critical and Exegetical Handbook to the General Epistles of Peter and Jude*. Critical and Exegetical Commentary on the New Testament (Meyer). Trans. D. B. Croom (1 & 2 Peter) and P. J. Cloag (Jude). Edinburgh: T. & T. Clark, 1881, 1-249; *Critical and Exegetical Handbook to the General Epistles of James, Peter, John, and Jude*. Trans. P. J. Cloag, D. B. Croom, and C. H. Irwin from the third German edition ([3]1867). New York: Funk and Wagnalls, 1884, 165-341; reprint of the 1884 Funk and Wagnalls edition Winona Lake, Ind.: Alpha, 1979.

173   IRONSIDE, H. A. *Expository notes on James and Peter*. New York: Loizeaux, 1947.

174   ISHO'DAD OF MERV.   *The Commentaries of Isho'dad of Merv, Bishop of Hadatha (c. 850 A.D.) in Syriac and Eng-*

lish. Horae Semiticae 5-7, 10-11. Ed. and trans. M. D. Gibson. Cambridge: University Press, 1911-16, 4:38-39, 51-53.

175   JACHMANN, K. R. *Commentar über die katholischen Briefe mit genauer Berücksichtigung der neuste Auslegungen.* Leipzig: Barth, 1838.

176   JAMES, E. C. *The Epistles of Peter: Practical Advice for the Last Days.* Chicago: Moody, 1964.

177   JENSEN, I. L. *1 & 2 Peter: A Self-Study Guide.* Bible Self-Study Guides. Chicago: Moody, 1971.

178   JEROME. "B. Petri Apostoli Epistola Prima," *Divina Bibliotheca. PL* 29:835-840.

179   JOHN CHRYSOSTOM. "In Primam S. Petri Epistolam," *Fragmenta in epistolas catholicas. PG* 64:1053-1058.

180   JOHNSTONE, R. *The First Epistle of Peter.* Edinburgh: T. & T. Clark, 1888; reprint Minneapolis: James Family, 1978.
       Review: Anonymous, *Methodist Review* 70 (1888) 633-634.

181   JONES, C. *First Peter.* Ministry School Publications, 1990.

182   JOWETT, J. H. *The Redeemed Family of God: Studies in the Epistles of St. Peter.* The Devotional and Practical Commentary. London: Hodder and Stoughton, 1904, ²1906, ³1910, ⁴1921; *The Epistles of St. Peter.* The Practical Commentary on the New Testament. New York: Armstrong, 1906; reprint as *The Epistles of St. Peter: A Practical and Devotional Commentary*, Grand Rapids: Kregel, 1970.

183   KEENER, C. S. "1 Peter," *The IVP Bible Background Commentary: New Testament.* Downers Grove: InterVarsity, 1993, 705-722.

184   KEIL, C. F. *Kommentar über die Briefe des Petrus und Judas.* Leipzig: Dorfeling & Franke, 1883.

185   KELLY, J. N. D. *A Commentary on the Epistles of Peter and of Jude.* Black's New Testament Commentaries. London:

A. & C. Black, 1969; Harper's New Testament Commentaries. New York: Harper and Row, 1969.

Reviews: Beare, F. W., *Theology* 72 (1969) 556-558; Beasley-Murray, P., *SJT* 24 (1971) 233-234; Bowne, D. R., *JBL* 89 (1970) 507-508; Caird, G. B., *ExpTim* 81 (1970) 151-152; Earle, R., *Christianity Today* 14 (5 June, 1970) 33; Krentz, E., *CTM* 42 (1971) 335-336; Leahy, T. W., *TS* 33 (1972) 585-586; Marshall, S. S., *JTS* 22 (1971) 211-213; Montague, G. T., *CBQ* 32 (1970) 456-457; Niel, W., *CQ* 2 (1970) 340-341; Pokorny, P., *TLZ* 95 (1970) 351-352; Schnackenburg, R., *BZ* 16 (1972) 267-268.

186 KELLY, W. *The First Epistle of Peter.* London: Weston, 1904, [2]1923.

187 KENDALL, D. W. "1 Peter," *Asbury Bible Commentary.* Ed. E. E. Carpenter and W. McCown. Grand Rapids: Zondervan, 1992, 1185-1197.

188 KENYON, D. J. *He That Will Love Life: A Daily-Reading Commentary on the First Epistle of Peter.* Harrisburg, Pa.: Christian Publications, 1968.

189 KETTER, P. *Hebräerbrief, Jacobusbrief, Petrusbriefe, Judasbrief.* Die Heilige Schrift für das Leben erklärt 16,1. Freiburg: Herder, 1950.

190 KEULERS, J. *De Katholieke Brieven en het Boek der Openbaring.* De boeken van het Nieuwe Testament 7. Roermond, 1946.

191 KISTEMAKER, S. J. *Exposition of the Epistles of Peter and of the Epistle of Jude.* New Testament Commentary. Grand Rapids: Baker, 1987.

192 KÜHL, E. *Die Briefe Petri und Judae.* MeyerK 12. Göttingen: Vandenhoeck & Ruprecht, [6]1897. {This and the following entry contain the only editions of MeyerK 12 by Kühl. For others cf. Huther, Knopf, and Goppelt.}

193 ——. *Kritisch exegetisches Handbuch über den 1. Brief des Petrus, den Brief des Judas und den 2. Brief des Petrus.* MeyerK 12. Göttingen: Vandenhoeck und Ruprecht, [5]1887. {This and the previous entry contain the only editions of MeyerK 12 by Kühl. For others cf. Huther, Knopf, and Goppelt}

194 KNOPF, R. *Die Briefe Petri und Judä.* MeyerK 12. Göttingen: Vandenhoeck & Ruprecht, [7]1912. {This is the only edi-

tion of MeyerK 12 by Knopf. For others cf. Huther, Kühl, and Goppelt.}

195   KRODEL, G. "The First Letter of Peter," *Hebrews. James. 1 and 2 Peter. Jude. Revelation.* Proclamation Commentaries. Philadelphia: Fortress, 1977; Minneapolis: Augsburg Fortress, [2]1995.

196   LANGE, J. *Urim ac Thummim (Licht und Recht) seu exegesis epistolarum Petri ac Joannis.* Hallae: Orphanotrophe, 1712, [2]1734.

197   LAPIDE, C. C. à. *Commentaria in epistolarvm canonicarvm.* Anterpiae: Martinvm Nuntivm, 1627, [2]1628, and frequently. {For a full account of the complicated publication history of Lapide's many commentaries, see Sommervogel, C., *Bibliotèque de la Compagnie de Jésus* (Bruxelles: Schepens and Paris: Picard, 1890-1932 [Suppl. 1960]), 4:1511-1525.}

198   LAURENTIUS, G. M. *Kurtze Erklärung des Ersten (u. andern) Briefs St. Petri. In Tabellen verfasset . . . Sammt angehängter kurtzen Paraphrasi.* Halle: Wäysenhauses, 1716.

199   LAURENTIUS, J. *S. Apostoli Petri Epistola catholica prior, perpetuo commentario explicata.* Campis: Sumptibus H. Laurentii, 1640.

200   LEANEY, A. R. C. *The Letters of Peter and Jude: A Commentary on the First Letter of Peter, a Letter of Jude and the Second Letter of Peter.* CBC. Cambridge: University Press, 1967.

201   LEA, T. [D.] "1 Peter—Outline and Exposition," *Southwestern Journal of Theology* 25,1 (Fall, 1982) 17-45.

202   LEIGHTON, R. *A Practical Commentary upon the First Epistle of St. Peter.* York: J. White, 1693 (vol. 1) and London: Sam. Keble, 1694 (vol. 2). Ed. W. West. London: Henry G. Bohn, 1853 and Longmans, 1870; reprint Grand Rapids: Kregel, 1972.

203   LENSKI, R. C. H. *The Interpretation of the Epistles of St. Peter, St. John and St. Jude.* Columbus, Ohio: Lutheran Book Concern, 1938, [2]1960 and Minneapolis: Augsburg, 1966.

204   LEUWIS, D. de. *In omnes Catholicas epistolas, necnon acta Apostelorum, & Apocalypsim, ac nonnullos hymnos ecclesiasticos, commentarii doctissimi.* Parisiis: Pocetum le Preux, 1542.

205   LILJE, H. *Die Petrusbriefe und der Judasbrief.* Bibelhilfe für die Gemeinde, Neutestmentliche Reihe 14. Kassel: Onken, 1954.

206   LILLIE, J. *Lectures on the First and Second Epistles of Peter.* New York: Charles Scribner's Sons, 1869; reprint Minneapolis: Klock and Klock, 1978, 1-344.

207   LINCOLN, W. *Lectures on the First and Second Epistles of Peter.* Kilmarnock, Scotland: John Richie, n.d.

208   LOVEJOY, T. R. *Standing Firm: A 22-week Group Bible Study in the Book of I Peter.* Panorama City, Cal.: Grace Community Church, 1985.

209   LUCULENTIUS. "Lectio epistolae I beati Petri apostoli," *In aliquot Novi Testamenti partes commentarii.* PL 72:857-860.

210   LUMBY, J. R. "The Epistles of St. Peter," *An Exposition of the Bible.* Hartford, Conn.: Scranton, 1903, 6:671-727.

211   ——. "The Epistles of St. Peter," *The Expositor's Bible.* London: Hodder and New York: Armstrong, 1893, 6:v-xiv and 671-754.

212   LUTHER, M. *Enarrationes Martini Lutheri in Epistolas D. Petri duas et Judae unam in quibus quidquid omnino ad Christianismum pertinet consumatissime digestum leges.* Trans. M. Butzer. Straßburg, 1524.

213   ——. *The Epistles of St. Peter and St. Jude.* Translation of *Enarrationes in epistolas Divi Petri duas et Iudae unam,* which combines the 1523 sermons with the 1539 commentary. Ed. and trans. J. N. Lenker. Minneapolis: Lutherans in All Lands, 1904; *Commentary on the Epistles of Peter and Jude.* Originally published as *The Epistles of St. Peter and St. Jude.* Ed. and trans. J. N. Lenker. Minneapolis: Lutherans in All Lands, 1904; reprint ed. P. W. Bennehoff, Grand Rapids: Kregel, 1982, updated 1990.

214   ——. *Utlaggning af Petri forsta bref.* Evang. Fosterlands-Stiftelesens Forlags-Expedition, 1905.

215 MACDONALD, W. *I Peter: Faith Tested, Future Triumphant: A Commentary.* Conerstone Commentaries. Wheaton: Shaw, 1972.

216 ———. "The First Epistle of Peter," *Believer's Bible Commentary, New Testament: An Exposition of Sacred Scripture.* Wichita, Kan.: A & O, 1989 and Nashville: Nelson, [2]1990, 1063-1100.

217 MACDUFF, J. R. *The Footsteps of St. Peter: Being the Life and Times of the Apostle.* New York: Carter, 1877; reprint Minneapolis: Klock and Klock, 1982, 562-580. {Cf. Mac-Duff in the section in this bibliography on Peter.}

218 MACKNIGHT, J. "I Peter," *A New Literal Translation, from the Original Greek of All the Apostolical Epistles.* Edinburgh: P. Elmsly, [2]1795; London: Longman, Hurst, [2]1806; Boston: W. Wells and T. B. Wait, 1810; London: T. Tegg, 1829; New edn. London: T. Tegg, 1832; New edn. Philadelphia: Thomas Wardle, 1841; New York: M. W. Dodd, 1850, 5:603-626; reprint Grand Rapids: Baker, 1969. "The First Epistle of the Apostle Peter," *A New Literal Translation from the Original Greek of All the Apostolical Epistles. With a Commentary, and Notes, Philological, Critical, and Practical. To Which is Added, a History of the Life of the Apostle Paul.* A New edition. London: Hurst, Reef, Orme, & Brown, Ogle, Duncan, & Co., and G. & W. B. Whittaker; Edinburgh: A. Constable & Co., J. Fairbairn, and J. Anderson Jun[r]; and Glasgow: M. Ogle, 1821, 5:413-507; 1821 edition reprinted as *Macknight on the Epistles*, Grand Rapids: Baker, 1984.

219 MACLAREN, A. "I. Peter," *The Epistles General of I. and II. Peter and I. John.* Expositions of Holy Scripture. New York: Armstrong and London: Hodder and Stoughton, 1910, 1-169; reprint Grand Rapids: 16(b):1-169

220 MACLEOD, A. N. *The First Epistle of Peter: A Commentary.* Hong Kong: Christian Witness, 1951.

221 MARGOT, J. C. *Les épîtres de Pierre.* Commentaire. Geneva: Labor et Fides, 1960.

222 MARSHALL, I. H. *1 Peter.* The IVP New Testament Commentary Series. Leicester and Downers Grove: InterVarsity, 1991.

Reviews: Ellis, E. E., *Southwestern Journal of Theology* 34 (1992) 61; Michaels, J. R., *CR* (1992) 233-235; Rosscup, J. E., *The Master's Seminary Journal* 2 (1991) 213-215; Wolfe, B. P., *Criswell Theological Review* 6 (1992) 140-141.

223　MARTH, D., and L. BUTH. *1 Peter and 1 John.* St. Louis: Concordia, 1991.

224　MARTINUS LEGIONENSIS. *Expositio in epistolam I B. Petri apostoli.* PL 209:217-252.

225　MASON, A. J. "The First Epistle General of Peter," *A New Testament Commentary for English Readers by Various Writers.* Ed. C. J. Ellicott. London, Paris, and New York: Cassell, 1884, 3:383-436; reprinted in *Ellicott's Commentary on the Whole Bible.* Grand Rapids: Zondervan, 1959, 4 (8):385-436.

226　MASTERMAN, J. H. B. *The First Epistle of St. Peter (Greek Text).* London and New York: Macmillan, 1900.

227　MATTHAEI, C. F. von. *SS. Apostolorum septem epistolae catholicae.* Rigae: Hartknochii, 1782.

228　MAUNEY, J. *1 Peter: A Four-Session Small-Group Bible Study on 1 Peter.* Minneapolis: Augsburg Fortress, 1988.

229　MAYCOCK, E. A. *A Letter of Wise Counsel: Studies in the First Epistle of Peter.* World Christian Books. London: Lutterworth and New York: Association, 1957.
　Review: MacKenzie, K., *SJT* 11 (1958) 206-207.

230　MAYERHOFF, E. T. *Historische-critische Einleitung in die petrinischen Schriften nebst einer Abhandlung über den Verfasser der Apostelgeschichte.* Hamburg: Perthes, 1835.

231　MCNAB, A. "I Peter," *The New Bible Commentary.* Grand Rapids: Eerdmans and London: Inter-Varsity, 1953, ²1954, 1129-1143. {Cf. Wheaton, D. H.}

232　MICHAELIS, J. D. *Anmerkungen für Ungelehrte, zu seiner Uebersetzung des Neuen Testaments.* Göttingen: Vandenhoeck und Ruprecht, 1790-1792, 4:242-257.

233　MICHAELS, J. R. *1 Peter.* WBC 49. Waco, Tex.: Word, 1988.

Reviews: Botha, P. J. J., *Theologia Evangelica* 22 (1989) 47-48; Brownson, J. V., *Reformed Review* 44 (1990) 82-84; Cranfield, C. E. B., *JTS* 40 (1989) 586-588; Deppe, D., *Calvin Theological Journal* 25 (1990) 272-274; Dockery, D. S., *RevExp* 87 (1990) 644; Elliott, J. H., *CR* (1990) 224-227; Ellis, E. E., *Southwestern Journal of Theology* 32 (1989) 48-49; Ericson, N. R., *Themelios* 17 (1992) 30-31; Kent, M., *AUSS* 27 (1989) 148-149; Krentz, E. M., *CurTM* 17 (1990) 233; McCartney, D. G., *WTJ* 51 (1989) 394-396; McKnight, S., *CBQ* 52 (1990) 353-355; Rodd, C. S., *ExpTim* 101 (1990) 184-190; Shogren, G. S., *JETS* 34 (1991) 533-534; Soards, M. L., *Perspectives in Religious Studies* 17 (1990) 71-73; Thompson, J. W., *ResQ* 33 (1991) 115-116.

234 ———. "First Peter," *Mercer Commentary on the Bible.* Macon, Ga.: Mercer University Press, 1995, 1295-1304.

235 MICHL, J. "1-2 Petrusbriefe," *Der Brief an die Hebräer und die Katholischen Briefe.* RNT 8. Regensburg: Pustet, 1953, 193-257.

236 ———. *Die katholischen Briefe.* RNT 8/2. Regensburg: Pustet, 1953, ²1968.

237 ———. "Primera carta de San Pedro," *Carta a los Hebreos y cartas católicas.* Comentario de Ratisbona al Nuevo Testamento 8. Barcelona: Herder, 1977, 437-521.

238 MILLER, J. *Notes on James, I and II Peter, I, II and III John, Jude, Revelation.* Bradford, England: Needed Truth Pub. Office, n.d.

239 MITCHELL, A. F. *Hebrews and the General Epistles.* The Westminster New Testament. London: Melrose and New York: Revell, 1911.

240 MOFFATT, J. *The General Epistles of James, Peter, and Judas.* MNTC. London: Hodder and Stoughton, 1928, ⁸1963 and Garden City, N.Y.: Doubleday, Doran, 1928.

241 MONNIER, J. *La Première Épître de l'Apôtre Pierre.* Macon: Protat Frères, 1900.

242 MOOREHEAD, W. G. *Catholic Epistles—James, I and II Peter, I, II, III John, and Jude.* Outline Studies in the New Testament. Pittsburgh: United Presyterian Board of Publication, 1910.

243 MORGAN, G. C. *An Exposition of the Whole Bible.* Westwood, N.J.: Revell, 1959, 522-524.

244 MORUS, S. F. N. *Praelectiones in Jacobi et Petri epistolas.* Ed. C. A. Donat. Lipsiae: Sumptibus Sommeri, 1794, 98-186.

245 MOTYER, S. "1 Peter," *Evangelical Commentary on the Bible.* Ed. W. A. Elwell. Grand Rapids: Baker, 1989, 1163-1170.

246 MOUNCE, R. H. *A Living Hope: A Commentary on 1 and 2 Peter.* Grand Rapids: Eerdmans, 1982.
Reviews: Omanson, R. L., *RevExp* 80 (1983) 138; Perkins, L., *JETS* 26 (1983) 237-238.

247 NAVARRA, UNIVERSIDAD DE, FACULTAD DE TEOLOGÍA. *Epistolas Catolicas.* Sagrada Biblia (Latin text with a commentary by members of the Faculty of Theology of the University of Navarre). Pamplona: Ediciones Universidad de Navarra, 1976-89, 11:123-173.

248 ———. *The Catholic Epistles.* The Navarre Bible in the Revised Standard Version and the New Vulgate, with a commentary by members of the Faculty of Theology of the University of Navarre. Blackrock [Dublin]: Four Courts, 1985—, vol. 11.

249 NAVPRESS. *A NavPress Bible Study on the Book of 1 Peter.* Life Change Series. Colorado Springs: NavPress, 1986.

250 NEYREY, J. H. *First Timothy, Second Timothy, Titus, James, First Peter, Second Peter, Jude.* Collegeville Bible Comentary 9. Collegeville, Minn.: Liturgical, 1993.

251 NICHOLSON, R. S. "I Peter," *Beacon Bible Commentary.* Kansas City: Beacon Hill, 1967, 10:253-309.

252 NIEBOER, J. *Practical Exposition of 1 Peter Verse by Verse.* Erie, Pa.: Our Daily Walk, 1948 (©1951).

253 NISBET, A. *A Brief Exposition of the First and Second Epistles General of Peter.* Southampton: Camelot, 1658; reprinted as *An Exposition of First and Second Peter.* The Geneva Series of Commentaries. Edinburgh and Carlisle, Penn.: Banner of Truth, 1982.

254 OBERST, B. *Letters from Peter.* Bible Study Textbook Series. Joplin, Mo.: College Press, 1962.

255   OECUMENIUS (pseudo). "Petri Apostoli prior epistola catho-
       lica," *Commentarii in Novum Testamentum*. *PG* 119:509-
       578.

256   OLHAUSEN, H. *Biblical Commentary on the New Testament:
       Adapted especially for Preachers and Students*. Trans. D.
       Fosdick, T. Brown, J. Gill, R. Garvey, and W. Lindsay. Ed-
       inburgh: T. & T. Clark, 1847-50; *Biblical Commentary on
       the New Testament*. Trans. and rev. A. C. Kendrick from the
       fourth German edition. New York: Sheldon, Blakeman,
       1857-58.

257   PAINE, S. W. "The First Epistle of Peter," *The Wycliffe Bible
       Commentary*. Ed. C. F. Pfeiffer and E. Harrison. Chicago:
       Moody, 1962, 1441-1452.

258   PARËUS, D. *Commentarii in epistolas canonicas Jacobi,
       Petri & Jvdae*. Ed. P. Parëus. Genevae, 1641.

259   PATERIUS. "In Epistolam S. Petri Primam," *Liber de exposi-
       tione Veteris ac Novi Testimenti*. *PL* 79:1097-1100.

260   PATTERSON, P. *A Pilgrim Priesthood: An Exposition of the
       Epistle of First Peter*. Nashville and Camden, N. Y.: Nelson,
       1982.
       Review: Stephenson, C. B., *JETS* 27 (1984) 354-355.

261   PEACE, R. *1 Peter. James: Living through Difficult Times*.
       Serendipity Group Bible Study Series. Littleton, Colo.: Ser-
       endipity, 1989.

262   PERKINS, P. *First and Second Peter, James, and Jude*. In-
       terpretation. Louisville: Knox, 1995.

263   PESCH, R. *Die Echtheit eures Glaubens. Biblische Orien-
       tierungen: I. Petrusbrief*. Freiburg, Basel, and Wien:
       Herder, 1980.

264   PHILLIPS, J. B. *Peter's Portrait of Jesus: A Commentary on
       the Gospel of Mark and the Letters of Peter*. London,
       Cleveland, and New York: Collins + World, 1976.

265   PLUMPTRE, E. H. *The General Epistles of St. Peter & St.
       Jude*. Cambridge Bible for Schools and Colleges. Cam-
       bridge: University Press, 1879.

266   POLKINGHORNE, G. J. "I Peter," *A Bible Commentary for Today Based on the Revised Standard Version*. Ed. G. C. D. Howley, F. F. Bruce, and H. L. Ellison. London and Glasgow: Pickering & Inglis and Grand Rapids: Zondervan, 1979, 1630-1644.

267   ——. "I Peter," *The International Bible Commentary with the New International Version*. Rev. ed. of *A Bible Commentary for Today*. Basingstoke: Marshall Pickering and Grand Rapids: Zondervan, 1986, 1550-1563.

268   ——. "The First Letter of Peter," *A New Testament Commentary*. Ed. G. C. D. Howley. Grand Rapids: Zondervan, 1969, 584-598.

269   POOLE, M. "The First Epistle General of Peter," *Annotation on the Holy Bible*. London: Richardson, 1683-85; reprinted as *A Commentary on the Holy Bible*, London: Banner of Truth, 1962-63, 3:898-917.

270   POTT, D. J. *Epistolae catholicae graece perpetua annotatione illustratae*. Göttingen, 1786.

271   PURKISER, W. T. *Hebrews. James. Peter*. Beacon Bible Expositions 11. Kansas City: Beacon Hill, 1974.

272   PURY, R. de. *Ein Petrusbrief in der Gefägniszelle. Auslegung des ersten Petrusbriefes*. Trans. V. D. M. H. Roth. Zollikon-Zürich. Evangelischer Verlag, 1944.

273   ——. *Pierres vivantes: Commentaire de la première Épître de Pierre*. Neuchâtel: Delachaux & Niestlé, 1944.

274   RAYMER, R. M. "I Peter," *The Bible Knowledge Commentary: New Testament*. Ed. J. F. Walvoord and R. B. Zuck. Wheaton: Victor, 1983, 837-858.

275   REICKE, B. *The Epistles of James, Peter, and Jude*. AB 37. Garden City, N.Y.: Doubleday, 1964, [2]1964.
       Reviews: Edwards, C. W., *JBR* 33 (1965) 352-354; Funk, R. W., *Int* 19 (1965) 468-472; Gilmour, S. M., R. J. Havighurst, and S. E. Karff, *Foundations* 9 (1966) 75-81; Kuehner, F. C., *WTJ* 28 (1965) 81-84; Maly, E. H., *CBQ* 27 (1965) 173-175; McAllaster, A. R., *Theology and Life* 9 (1966) 177-179; Minear, P. S., *JBL* 84 (1965) 181-184; Morris, L., *Christianity Today* 9 (May 21, 1965) 32-33; Pearson, B., *Dialog* 5 (1966) 73-74; Rhys, H., *Saint Luke's Journal of Theology* 11 (1967) 83-88; Terrien, S., *USQR* 20 (1965) 289-293; Walther, J. A., *Perspective* (Pittsburgh) 6 (June 1965) 35-37.

276   RENDTORFF, H. *Getrostes Wandern. Eine Einfürhung in den ersten Brief des Petrus.* Die urchristliche Botschaft 20. Berlin: Furche, 1929, [3-4]1931, [5]1936 and Hamburg: Furche, [7]1951.

277   RENOUX, C. *La chaîne sur les épîtres de Pierre.* La chaîne Arménienne sur les épîtres catholiques. PO 44,2, 66-173.

278   REUSS, J. *Die katholischen Briefe.* Die Heilige Schrift in deutscher Übersetzung, EB. Würzburg: Herder, 1959.

279   RICHARDS, L. O. "1 Peter," *The Bible Reader's Companion.* Wheaton: Victor, 1991, 876-883.

280   ———. "1 Peter," *The Teacher's Commentary.* Wheaton: Scripture Press, 1987, 1026-1036.

281   ———. "The Call to Submission (1 Peter 1:1-4:6)," *Small Group Member's Commentary.* Wheaton: Victor, 1992, 528-533.

282   ———. "The Call to Suffer (1 Peter 4:7-5:14)," *Small Group Member's Commentary.* Wheaton: Victor, 1992, 534-538.

283   ROBERTSON, A. T. "The First Epistle General of Peter," *Word Pictures in the New Testament.* New York and London: Harper, 1933, 6:69-136; reprint Nashville: Broadman, n.d.

284   ROLSTON, H. *The Apostle Peter Speaks to Us Today.* Atlanta: John Knox, 1977.

285   ROSS, J. M. E. *The First Epistle of Peter: A Devotional Commentary.* The "R. T. S." Devotional Commentary. London, Manchester, Madrid, Lisbon, and Budapest: Religious Tract Society, 1918.

286   ROTH, R. P. "I Peter," *The Biblical Expositor: The Living Theme of the Great Book.* Philadelphia: Holman, 1960, 3:417-427.

287   SALGUERO, J. "Prima Lettera de San Pedro," *Biblia Comentada.* Biblioteca de Autores Cristianos. Madrid, 1965, 7:88-146.

288   SCHELKLE, K. H.   *Die Petrusbriefe. Der Judasbrief.*
       HTKNT 13,2. Freiburg, Basel, and Wien: Herder, 1961,
       ²1964, ³1970, ⁵1980, ⁶1988.
       Reviews: Dalton, W. J., *Bib* 43 (1962) 230-232; Michl, J., *BZ* 9 (1965)
       143-145.

289   ——. *Cartas de Pedro. Carta de Judas. Texto y commen-
       tario.* (Translation of *Die Petrusbriefe. Der Judasbrief*
       ³1970.) Actualidad Biblica 39. Madrid: Fax, 1974.

290   SCHIWY, G. "An Petrus I," *Weg ins Neue Testament.* Würz-
       burg: Echter-Verlag, 1965-70, 4:189-219.

291   ——. *Die katholischen Briefe.* Der Christ in der Welt 6, Das
       Buch der Bücher 12. Aschaffenburg: Pattloch, 1973.

292   SCHLATTER, A.   *Die Briefe an die Thessalonicher. Die
       Briefe des Petrus und Judas.* Schlatters Erläuterungen zum
       Neuen Testament vol. 12. Stuttgart: Vereinsbuchhandlung,
       1910.

293   ——. *Erläuterungen zum Neuen Testament.* Stuttgart: Cal-
       wer, 1921, ⁴1928, 3:5-80.

294   SCHNEIDER, J.   *Die Briefe des Jacobus, Petrus, Judas und
       Johannes. Die katholischen Briefe.* NTD 10. Göttingen:
       Vandenhoek & Ruprecht, ⁹1961, ¹⁰1967. {The 9ᵗʰ ed. is the
       first edition of NTD 10 by this author. For previous editions
       see Hauck. For the 11ᵗʰ edition see Schrage.}
       Reviews: Forestell, J. T., *CBQ* 24 (1962) 333-334; Linss, W. C., *JBL*
       81 (1962) 322-323.

295   SCHOTT, T.   *Der erste Brief Petri erklärt.* Erlangen: A. De-
       ichert, 1861.

296   SCHRAGE, W.   "Der erste Petrus Brief" in Balz, H. R. and
       Schrage, W. *Die „Katholischen" Briefe. Die Briefe des Ja-
       cobus, Petrus, Johannes und Judas.* NTD 10. Göttingen:
       Vandenhoeck & Ruprecht, ¹¹1973 and 1985, 59-117. {The
       11ᵗʰ ed. is the first edition of NTD 10 by these authors. For
       previous editions see Hauck and Schneider}
       Reviews: Dunkly, J. D., *JBL* 93 (1974) 478-479; Vawter, B., *CBQ* 36
       (1974) 388-389.

297   ——. "La prima lettera di Pietro" in Balz, H. and Schrage,
       W. *Le lettere cattoliche. Le lettere di Giacomo, Pietro, Gio-*

vanni e Giuda. Nuovo Testamento 10. Trans. G. Forza. Brescia: Paideia, 1978, 111-213.

298 SCHROEDER, D. *First Peter: Faith Refined by Fire*. Faith and Life Bible Studies. Newton, Kan.: Faith and Life, 1985.

299 SCHWANK, B. *Der erste Brief des Apostels Petrus*. Geistliche Schriftlesung 20. Düsseldorf: Patmos, 1963.

300 ———. *La première lettre de l'Apôtre Pierre expliquè*. Trans. C. Nys. Paris: Desclée, 1967.

301 ———. "The First Epistle of Peter," *The Two Epistles of Saint Peter*. Trans. W. Kruppa. The New Testament for Spiritual Reading. London: Burns & Oates and New York: Herder, 1969, {22}:ix-xvii, 1-113.

302 SCHWEIZER, E. *Der erste Petrusbrief*. Prophetzei: Schweizerisches Bibelwerk für die Gemeinde, Zürcher Bibelkommentare. Zürich: Zwingli, 1942, [2]1949. {See following entry.}

303 ———. *Der erste Petrusbrief*. Zürcher Bibelkommentare, vormals Prophezei. Zürich: Theologischer Verlag, [3]1972.

304 SCOTUS ANONYMUS. "Petri <Epistola> Prima," *Commentarius in Epistolas Catholicas Scotti Anonymi*. CChr (Series Latina) 108B:28-35.

305 SELWYN, E. G. *The First Epistle of St. Peter: The Greek Text with Introduction, Notes and Essays*. London: Macmillan, 1946, [2]1947; reprint Grand Rapids: Baker, 1981.
Reviews: Achtemeier, P. J., *Theology and Life* (Lancaster) 1 (F 1958) 71-72; Beare, F. W, *JBL* 65 (1946) 329-333; Manson, T. W., *JTS* 47 (1946) 218-227.

306 SEMLER, J. S. *Paraphrasis in Epistolam I. Petri, cum latinae translationis varietate et multis notis*. Opera varia 7. Hallae: Impensis Bibliopolii Hemmerdiani, 1783.

307 SENIOR, D. *1 and 2 Peter*. New Testament Message 20. Wilmington, Del.: Michael Glazier, 1980.
Reviews: Neyrey, J. H., *CBQ* 43 (1981) 656; Omanson, R. L., *RevExp* 78 (1981) 117-120.

308 SERARIUS, N. *Prolegomena Bibliaca et Commentaria in omnes Epistolas Canonica*. Paris, 1612.

309 SETZER, S. M. *We are a Chosen People of God.* ELCA Lutheran Youth Organization 1989-90 Bible Studies. Ed. T. S. Hanson and H. Einess. Minneapolis: Augsburg Fortress, 1989.

310 SHOTANUS, M. *Conciones in I. Epistolam Petri.* Franeker, 1644.

311 SODEN, H. von. *Hebräerbrief, Briefe des Petrus, Jakobus, Judas.* Hand-Commentar zum Neuen Testament 3,2. Freiburg, Leipzig, and Tübingen: Mohr, 1890, ³1899.

312 SÖDERGREN, C. J. *The First Epistle of Peter.* Rock Island, Ill.: Augustana, 1925.

313 SPEYR, A. von. *Die katholischen Briefe.* 2 vols. Einsiedeln: Johannes, 1961.

314 SPICQ, C. *Les épîtres de Saint Pierre.* Source Bibliques. Paris: Gabalda, 1966.

315 STAFFELBACH, G. *Die Briefe der Apostel Jacobus, Judas, Petrus und Johannes: Eine Einführung.* Luzern: Räber, 1941.

316 STEIGER, W. *Der erste Brief Petri, mit Berücksichtigung des ganzen biblishen Lehrbegriffes ausgelegt.* Berlin: Oehmigke, 1832.

317 STIBBS, A. M., and A. F. WALLS. *The First Epistle General of Peter.* The Tyndale New Testament Commentaries 17. London: Tyndale (now Leicester: Inter-Varsity) and Grand Rapids: Eerdmans, 1959.
   Reviews: Anonymous, *ExpTim* 71 (1960) 111; Kruithof, B., *Reformed Review* 13 (Mr 1960) 39; Throckmorton, B. H., Jr., *Int* 14 (1960) 222; Tongue, D. H., *Churchman* 73 (1959) 153.

318 STOECKHARDT, G. *Lectures on the First Epistle of St. Peter.* Trans. by E. W. Koehlinger from *Kommentar über den ersten Brief Petri* by G. Stöckhardt. Ft. Wayne, Ind.: Concordia Theological Seminary Press, 1984(?).

319 STÖCKHARDT, G. *Kommentar über den ersten Brief Petri.* St. Louis: Concordia, 1912.

320 ΣΤΩΓΙΑΝΟς, Β. Π. ΠΡΩΤΗ ΕΠΙΣΤΟΛΗ ΠΕΤΡΟΥ. ΕΡΜΕΝΕΙΑ ΚΑΙΝΗΣ ΔΙΑΘΗΚΗΣ 15. Thessalonike, 1980.

321 STRACK, H. L., and P. BILLERBECK. *Kommentar zum Neuen Testament aus Talmud und Midrasch*. München: Beck, 1924-61, 3:762-768.

322 STRESON, C. *Meditationes in I et II Epistolas Petri*. Amsterdam, 1717.

323 STRONSTAD, R. *Models for Christian Living: The First Epistle of Peter*. Vancouver: CLM Educational Society, 1983.

324 SUMMERS, R. "1 Peter," *The Broadman Bible Commentary*. Nashville: Broadman, 1972, 12:141-171.

325 SUMNER, J. B. *A Practical Exposition of the General Epistles of James, Peter, John, and Jude in the Form of Lectures, Intended to Assist the Practice of Domestic Instruction and Devotion*. London: Hatchard, 1840.

326 SWINDOLL, C. R. *Hope in Hurtful Times: A Study of 1 Peter: Bible Study Guide*. Fullerton, Cal.: Insight for Living, 1990.

327 THEOPHYLACT (pseudo). *Expositio in Epistolam Primam S. Petri*. PG 125:1189-1252.

328 THOMAS (pseudo). *In septam epistolas canonicas*. Paris, 1873-82, 31:368-398. {Attributed to Nicolas de Gorran by P. J. Perrier; cf. C. Spicq, *Esquisse d'une histoire de l'exégèse latine au moyen âge* (Paris, 1944), 299 n. 6.}

329 THOMPSON, C. H. "The First Letter of Peter," *The Interpreter's One-Volume Commentary on the Bible*. Nashville and New York: Abingdon, 1971, 921-930.

330 TOSATTO, G. "La prima lettera di San Pietro," *Il messaggio della salvezza*, 5:909-948.

331 TRAPP, J. "The First Epistle General of St Peter," *A Commentary or Exposition upon All the Books of the New Testament*. London: R. W., 1647, ²1656; *A Commentary on the New Testament*. London: Dickinson, 1865; reprint Grand Rapids: Zondervan, 1958, 705-717.

332 ΤΡΕΜΠΕΛΑ, Π. Ν. Ἡ πρὸς Ἑβραίους καὶ αἱ ἑπτὰ καθολικαί. Ὑπόμνημα εἰς τὰς ἐπίστολας τῆς καινῆς

διαθήκης III. ᾿Αθῆναι· ᾿Αδελφότης θεολόγων ἡ "Ζωή,"
1956.

333   TUCK, R. "The First Epistle General of Peter," *A Homiletical Commentary on the General Epistles of I. and II. Peter, I. II. and III. John, Jude, and The Revelation of St. John the Divine*. The Preacher's Complete Homiletical Commentary on the New Testament. New York, London, and Toronto: Funk & Wagnalls, 1896, 1-167.

334   USTERI, J. M. *Wissenschaftlicher und praktischer Commentar über den ersten Petrusbrief*. Zürich: Höhr, 1887.

335   VACCARI, A. *Le Lettere cattoliche*. La Sacra Bibbia 9. Rome: Marietti, 1958.

336   VAGANAY, L. *L'Évangile de Pierre*. Ebib. Paris: Gabalda, ²1930.

337   VALENTINE, F. *Hebrews, James, 1 & 2 Peter*. Layman's Bible Book Commentary 23. Nashville: Broadman, 1981.

338   VAN ALPHEN, H. S. *De eerste algemeene sendbrief van den apostel Petrus, ontleedender wyse verklaard, en tot syn oogmerk toegepast*. Utrecht: van Paddenburg, 1734.

339   VAN DER HEEREN, A. *De Katholieke Brieven vertaald en uitgelegd*. Beelen NT. Brugge: Beyaert, 1932.

340   VAN KASTEREN, J. P. *De eerste Brief van den apostel Petrus*. Utrecht and Hertogenbosch: Van Rossum, 1911.

341   VAN NES, M. *De brief aan de Hebreen, de brief van Jakobus, de eerste brief van Petrus*. Tekst en Uitleg. Groningen: Wolters, 1931.

342   VAUGHAN, C. "1 Peter," *The Teacher's Bible Commentary*. Ed. H. F. Paschall and H. H. Hobbs. Nashville: Broadman, 1972, 785-791.

343   VAUGHAN, C., and T. D. LEA. *1-2 Peter, Jude*. Bible Study Commentary. Grand Rapids: Zondervan, 1988.
       Review: Luter, A. B., Jr, *Grace Theological Journal* 10 (1989) 248-249.

344 VREDE, W. "Der erste Petrusbrief," *Die katholischen Briefe*. Die heilige Schrift des Neuen Testaments, Bonner Neues Testament 9. Bonn: Hanstein, 1915, ⁴1932, 8:112-144.

345 WALAFRIDUS STRABO. "Epistola I B. Petri," *Glossa Ordinaria*. *PL* 114:679-688.

346 WALTEMYER, W. C. *The First Epistle of Peter*. New Testament Commentary. Philadelphia: United Lutheran Church of America, ²1944.

347 WAND, J. W. C. *The General Epistles of St. Peter and St. Jude*. Westminster Commentaries. London: Methuen, 1934.

348 WEISIGER, C. N. III *The Epistles of Peter*. Proclaiming the New Testament. Grand Rapids: Baker, 1961, ²1979 and London: Oliphants, 1962.

349 WEISS, B. *Das Neue Testament nach D. Martin Luthers bisherigen Übersetzung mit fortlangender Erläuterung versehen*. Leipzig: Hinrichs, 1902, ²1907.

350 WESLEY, J. *Explanatory Notes on the New Testament*. London: Boyer, 1755; Philadelphia: Crukshank, 1791; often reprinted, e.g. Grand Rapids: Francis Asbury Press, 1987, 577-580.

351 WESTWOOD, T. *The Epistles of Peter*. Glendale, Calif.: The Bible Treasury Hour, 1953.

352 WETTSTEIN, J. J. *Novum Testamentum Graecum editionis receptae cum lectionibus variantibus codicum mss., editionum aliarum, versionum, et patrum nec non commentario pleniore ex scriptoribus veteribus Hebraeis, Graecis et Latinis historiam et vim verborum illustrante*. Amstelaedami: Officina Dommeriana, 1751-52, 2:681-697; reprint Graz, 1962.

353 WHEATON, D. H. "1 Peter," *The New Bible Commentary Revised*. London: Inter-Varsity, ⁽³⁾1970 and Grand Rapids: Eerdmans, ⁽³⁾1970, 1236-1249; Downers Grove: InterVarsity, ⁴1994, 1369-1385. {Cf. McNab, A.}

354 WHEDON, D. D. *Commentary on the New Testament*. Vol. 1-2, New York: Carlton & Porter; vol. 3, New York: Carlton & Lanahan and Cincinatti: Hitchcock & Walden; vol. 4, New York: Nelson & Phillips and Cincinnati: Hitchcock & Wal-

den; vol. 5, New York: Phillips & Hunt and Cincinatti: Hitchcock & Walden, 1860-80, 5:188-222.

355 WIERSBE, W. W. *Be Hopeful.* Wheaton: Victor, 1982 and Amersham-on-the-Hill: Scripture Press, 1988.

356 ———. *The Bible Exposition Commentary.* Wheaton: Victor, 1989, 2:387-434.

357 WIESINGER, A. *Der erste Brief des Apostels Petrus.* Olhausens Commentar über sämtliche Schriften des Neuen Testaments 6,2. Königsberg: 1856.

358 WILLIAMS, G. *The Student's Commentary on the Holy Scriptures: Analytical, Synoptical, and Synthetical.* London: Oliphants, 1926, ^{4}1949, ^{5}1953, ^{6}1960 and Grand Rapids: Kregel, ^{4}1949, ^{5}1953, ^{6}1960, 998-1005.

359 WILLIAMS, N. M. *Commentary on the Epistles of Peter.* An American Commentary on the New Testament. Philadelphia: American Baptist Publication Society, 1888.

360 WILLMERING, H. "The First Epistle of St Peter," *A Catholic Commentary on Holy Scripture.* Ed. B. Orchard. London, Edinburgh, Paris, Melbourne, Toronto, and New York: Nelson, 1953, 1177-1180.

361 WINCKELMANN, J. *Commentarii in utramque Epistolam Petri.* Wittenberg, 1608.

362 WINDISCH, H. *Die katholischen Briefe.* HNT 15. Tübingen: Mohr-Siebeck, 1911, ^{2}1930, ^{3}1951 (3^d ed. revised and augmented by H. Preisker).

363 WOHLENBERG, G. *Der erste und zweite Petrusbrief und der Judasbrief.* Kommentar zum Neuen Testament 15. Leipzig: Scholl, $^{1\&2}$1915 and Leipzig: Deichert, ^{3}1923.

364 WOLF, J. C. *Cvrae philologicae et criticae in SS. apostolorvm Jacobi, Petri, Jvdae et Joannis epistolas, hvjvsqve Apocalypsin.* Hamburgi: Kisneri, 1735, 681-697.

365 WOODS, G. N. *A Commentary on the New Testament Epistles of Peter, John, and Jude.* Nashville: Gospel Advocate, 1974.

366 WORDSWORTH, C. *The New Testament of our Lord and Saviour Jesus Christ, Introduction and Notes*. London: Rivingtons, 1856-60, ²1861, ³1864, vol. 4.

367 WUEST, K. S. *First Peter in the Greek New Testament for the English Reader*. Word Studies in the Greek New Testament for the English Reader. Grand Rapids: Eerdmans, 1942, ²1944.

368 YEAGER, R. O. "ΠΕΤΡΟΥ Α," *The Renaissance New Testament*. Bowling Green, Ky.: Renaissance, 1976-78 (vols. 1-4) and Gretna, La.: Pelican, 1980-85 (vols. 5-18), 17:53-189.

369 ZERR, E. M. *Bible Commentary*. University City, Mo.: Missouri Mission Messanger, 1947-55.

DICTIONARY AND ENCYCLOPEDIA ARTICLES ON 1 PETER

Frequently edited and major dictionaries and encyclopedias have been checked for relevant articles only when accessible. Little attempt has been made to examine *every* edition of *every* encyclopedia.

370   ACHTEMEIER, P. J. "I Peter," *The Books of the Bible*. New York: Charles Scribner's Sons, 1989, 2:345-351.

371   ALEXANDER, P., and D. ALEXANDER, eds. "1 Peter," *The Lion Handbook to the Bible*. Berkhampstead, England: Lion, 1973, 636-638.

372   ALEXANDER, P., ed. "1 Peter," *The Lion Encyclopedia of the Bible*. Tring, Batavia: Lion and Sydney: Albatross, 1978 [2]1986, 106-107.

373   ALEXANDER, P. H. "Petrine Literature," *Dictionary of Pentecostal and Charismatic Movements*. Ed. S. M. Burgess and G. B. McGee. Grand Rapids: Zondervan, 1988, 712-714.

374   ANGUS, J., and S. G. GREEN. "First Epistle General of Peter," *The Cyclopedic Handbook to the Bible: An Introduction to the Study of Sacred Scripture* by Joseph Angus (1853). New edition, revised and in part rewritten by Samuel G. Green. New York: Revell, n.d., 741-745.

375   ANGUS, J. "First Epistle General of Peter," *The Cyclopedic Handbook to the Bible: An Introduction to the Study of Sacred Scripture*, 1853.

376   ANONYMOUS. "Peter, Epistles General of," *Chambers's Encyclopaedia*. London: Chambers, 1860, [2]1868, [3]1878, [4]1879, 7:446.

377   ANONYMOUS. "Peter, Epistles of," *Nelson's Illustrated Bible Dictionary*. Nashville: Nelson, 1986, 823-824.

378   ANONYMOUS. "Peter, Epistles of St.," *The Catholic Encyclopedia*. Ed. R. C. Broderick. Nashville, Camden, and New York: Nelson, 1976, [2]1987, 473-474.

379   ANONYMOUS. "Peter, Epistles of St.," *The Oxford Dictionary of the Christian Church*. Ed. F. L. Cross, 2nd edn. also ed. E. A. Livingstone. Oxford: University Press, 1957, ^{2}1974, 1051 (1st edn.), 1069 (2nd edn.).

380   ANONYMOUS. "Peter, Epistles of," *The Concise Oxford Dictionary of the Christian Church*. Ed. E. A. Livingstone. Oxford: University Press, 1977, 394.

381   ANONYMOUS. "Peter, Epistles of," *The Encyclopedia Americana*. New York: Scientific American, 1903-06, 11:n.p.

382   ANONYMOUS. "Peter, {Epistles of}," *The Illustrated Columbia Encyclopedia*. New York and London: Columbia University Press, ^{3}1963, 16:4820.

383   ANONYMOUS. "Peter, Epistles of," *The New International Encyclopaedia*. New York: Dodd, Mead, 1902-06, 15:650-652 and 1916-22, 17:418-421.

384   ANONYMOUS. "Peter, {Epistles}," *The New Columbia Encyclopedia*. New York and London: Columbia University Press, 1975, 2119-2120.

385   ANONYMOUS. "Peter, First Epistle of," *Concise Dictionary of the Bible*. London: Lutterworth, 1966, 245.

386   ANONYMOUS. "Peter, First Epistle of," *Cyclopaedia of Biblical, Theological, and Ecclesiastical Literature*. Ed. J. M'Clintock and J. Strong. New York: Harper, 1867-87, 8:15-21; reprint Grand Rapids: Baker, 1981.

387   ANONYMOUS. "Peter, First Epistle of," *Illustrated Dictionary & Concordance of the Bible*. Ed. (Gen. Ed.) G. Wigoder. New York: Macmillan and London: Collier Macmillan, 1986, 779-780.

388   ANONYMOUS. "Peter, First Epistle of," *Our Sunday Visitor's Catholic Encyclopedia*. Ed. P. M. J. Stravinskas. Huntington, Ind.: Our Sunday Visitor, 1991, 750.

389   ANONYMOUS. "Peter, First Epistle of," *Peloubet's Bible Dictionary*. Based upon the foundation laid by William Smith. Ed. F. N. Peloubet and A. D. Adams. Philadelphia and Chicago: Winston, 1912, 1925; New York: Holt, Rinehart and Winston, 1913; reprint Grand Rapids: Zondervan, 1971, 504-505.

390　ANONYMOUS. "Peter, First Epistle of," *The Bible Reader's Encyclopaedia and Concordance*. Based on *The Bible Reader's Manual* by C. H. Wright. Rev. and ed. W. M. Clow. London, New York, Glasgow, Toronto, Sydney, Auckland: Collins' Clear Type, 1962, 283-284.

391　ANONYMOUS. "Peter, First Epistle of," *The Encyclopedia of the Bible*. Originally published as *Elseviers Ecyclopedie van de Bijbel*. Trans. D. R. Welsh; emendations by C. Jones. Englewood Cliffs, N. J.: Prentice-Hall, 1965, 193.

392　ANONYMOUS. "Peter, First Epistle of," *Today's Dictionary of the Bible*. Compiled by T. A. Bryant. Minneapolis: Bethany House, 1982, 488.

393　ANONYMOUS. "Peter, First Letter of," *NIV Compact Dictionary of the Bible*. Ed. J. D. Douglas and M. C. Tenney. Grand Rapids: Zondervan, 1989, 451.

394　ANONYMOUS. "Peter, Letters of," *Encyclopaedia Britannica Micropaedia*. Chicago, London, Toronto, Geneva, Sydney, Tokyo, Manila, Seoul, Johannesburg: Encyclopaedia Britannica, [15]1974, 7:905-906.

395　ANONYMOUS. "Peter, Letters of," *Encyclopaedia Britannica Micropaedia*. Chicago, London, Toronto, Geneva, Sydney, Tokyo, Manila, Seoul, Johannesburg, Auckland, Paris, Rome: Encyclopaedia Britannica, [15]1987, 9:333-334.

396　ANONYMOUS. "Peter, Letters of," *The New World Dictionary-Concordance to the New American Bible*. New York: World, n.d. {copyright 1970 by C. D. Stampley Enterprises Inc.), 528-529.

397　ANONYMOUS. "Peter, or *Epistles of St*. Peter," *Encyclopaedia Britannica*. Edinburgh: Bell and Macfarquhar, 1771, 3:474.

398　ANONYMOUS. "Peter, The Epistles (Letters) of," *The New Westminster Dictionary of the Bible*. Ed. H. S. Gehman. Philadelphia: Westminster, 1970, 738-740.

399　ANONYMOUS. "Petrusbriefe," *Lexikon zur Bibel*. Ed. F. Rienecker. Wuppertal: Brockhaus, 1960, [2]1960, [3]1961, [4]1962, 1059-1062 (for [4]1962 only).

400   ANONYMOUS. "The First Epistle of Peter," *The Expositor's Dictionary of Texts: Containing Outlines, Expositions, and Illustrations of Bible Texts with Full References to the Best Homiletic Literature*. Ed. W. R. Nicoll and J. T. Stoddart. London: Hodder and Stoughton and New York: Doran, 1910, 2:920-934.

401   AYRE, J. "Peter, Epistles of," *The Imperial Bible-Dictionary*. Ed. P. Fairbairn. London, Glasgow, and Edinburgh: Blackie and Son, 1867, 2:580-587; 1891 ed. by Blackie and Son reprinted as *Fairbairn's Standard Imperial Bible Dictionary*, Grand Rapids: Zondervan, 1957, 5:208-215.

402   BEST, E. "Peter, The Letters of (1 Peter)," *The Oxford Companion to the Bible*. New York and Oxford: Oxford University Press, 1993, 583-586.

403   BOISMARD, M.-É. "Pierre (premièr épître de)," *DBSup* 7. Paris: Letouzey & Ané, 1966, 1415-1455.

404   BROOKS, J. A. "Peter, Letters of," *Mercer Dictionary of the Bible*. Ed. W. E. Mills (Gen. Ed.). Macon, Ga.: Mercer University Press, 1990, 677-679.

405   CASE, S. J. "Peter, Epistles of," *Dictionary of the Apostolic Church*. Ed. J. Hastings. New York: Charles Scribner's Sons and Edinburgh: T. & T. Clark, 1918, 2:201-209.

406   CHASE, F. H. "Peter, First Epistle of," *A Dictionary of the Bible*. Ed. J. Hastings. New York: Charles Scribner's Sons and Edinburgh: T. & T. Clark, 1898-1904, 3:779-796.

407   CONE, O. "Peter, The Epistles of," *Encyclopaedia Biblica*. Ed. T. K. Cheyne and J. S. Black. London: Black, 1899-1903, 3:3677-3685.

408   COOK, F. C. "Peter, First Epistle of," *A Dictionary of the Bible*. By {sic} William Smith. Rev. F. N. and M. A. Peloubet. Grand Rapids: Zondervan, 1948, 1967, 504. ("Copyright 1884 by Porter and Coates.")

409   COTRELL, R. F. "Peter, Epistles of," *Seventh-Day Adventist Bible Dictionary*. Commentary Reference Series 8. Washington, D. C.: Review and Herald, 1960, 846-847.

410   DINKLER, E. "Petrus, Apostel," *RGG*. Tübingen: Mohr-Siebeck, ³1957-65, 5:247-249.

411   ELLIOTT, J. H. "Peter, First Epistle of," *Anchor Bible Dictionary*. New York: Doubleday, 1992, 5:267-278.

412   ESTES, D. F. "Peter, Epistles of," *Encyclopedia Americana*. New York and Chicago: Americana, 1951, 21:657-659.

413   EZELL, D. "Peter, Epistles of," *Academic American Encyclopedia*. Princeton: Aretê, 1981 and Danbury, Conn.: Grollier, 1986, 15:199.

414   FALCONER, R. A. "Peter, First Epistle of," *Dictionary of the Bible*. Ed. J. Hastings. New York: Charles Scribner's Sons, 1909, 714-717.

415   FASCHER, E. "Petrusbriefe," *RGG*. Tübingen: Mohr-Siebeck, ³1957-65, 5:257-260.

416   FAUSSET, A. R. "Peter, Epistles of," *Bible Cyclopaedia*. Hartford, Conn.: Scranton, 1907, 562-564; reprint as *Fausset's Bible Dictionary*, Grand Rapids: Zondervan, 1961.

417   FILLION, L. "Pierre (Première Épitre de Saint)," *Dictionnaire de la Bible*. Paris: Letouzey et Ané, 1895-1912, 7:380-398.

418   FÖSTER, W. "Peter, First Epistle of," *Dictionary of the Bible*. Ed. J. Hastings; revised ed. by F. C. Grant and H. H. Rowley. New York: Charles Scribner's Sons, 1963, 754-757.

419   GOODSPEED, E. J. "Peter, First and Second Letters of," *An Encyclopedia of Religion*. Ed. V. Ferm. New York: The Philosophical Library, 1945, 578.

420   GRANT, F. C., and F. J. SHEEN. "Peter, Epistles of," *The World Book Encyclopedia*. Chicago, Frankfurt, London, Paris, Rome, Sydney, Tokyo, and Toronto: World Book-Childcraft, 1978, 15:284.

421   HARDON, J. A. "Peter, Epistles of," *Modern Catholic Dictionary*. Garden City, N. Y.: Doubleday, 1980, 419.

422   HOBERG, {no forename given}. "Die canonischen Briefe Petri," *Wetzer und Welte's Kirchenlexikon*. Ed. J. Hergenröther and F. Kaulen. Freiburg, Wein, Straßburg, München, and St. Louis: Herder, ²1882-1903, 9:1868-1876.

423   JOHNSON, L. T. "Peter, Epistles of," *Encyclopedia Americana*. Danbury, Conn.: Grolier, 1989, 21:808.

424 KENNEDY, H. A. A. "Peter, First Epistle of," *A New Standard Bible Dictionary.* New York and London: Funk & Wagnalls, [2]1925, [3]1936, 699-700.

425 LAKE, K. "Peter, Epistles of," *Encyclopaedia Britannica.* Cambridge: University Press and New York: Encyclopaedia Britannica, [11]1911, 21:295-297; London and New York: Encyclopaedia Britannica, [13]1926, 21:295-297.

426 LANG, J. P. "Peter, The First Epistle of," *Dictionary of the Liturgy.* New York: Catholic Book, 1989, 507.

427 LAWS, S. "Peter, First," *A Dictionary of Biblical Interpretation.* Ed. R. J. Coggins and J. L. Houlden. London: SCM and Philadelphia: Trinity, 1990, 534-535.

428 LEAHY, T. W. "Peter, Epistles of St.," *New Catholic Encyclopedia.* New York, St Louis, San Francisco, Toronto, London, Sydney: McGraw-Hill, 1967, 11:231-233.

429 LÉON-DUFOUR, X. "Peter (Epistles of)," *Dictionary of the New Testament.* Trans. T. Prendergast. San Francisco: Harper & Row, 1980, 320.

430 MARTIN, R. P. "Peter, First Epistle of," *International Standard Bible Encyclopedia.* Grand Rapids: Eerdmans, [3]1979-88, 3:807-815.

431 MCKENZIE, J. L. "Peter, Epistles of," *Dictionary of the Bible.* Milwaukee: Bruce, 1965, 666-668.

432 MILLER, M. S., and J. L. MILLER. "Peter, the First Epistle of," *Harper's Bible Dictionary.* New York: Harper, 1952, 542-543; New York, Evanston, and London: Harper & Row, [7]1961, 542-543.

433 MOORHEAD, W. G. "Peter, The First Epistle of," *The International Standard Bible Encyclopedia.* Chicago: Howard-Severance, 1915, [2]1929, 4:2351-2355.

434 NEYREY, J. H. "Peter, The First Letter of," *Harper's Bible Dictionary.* Ed. P. J. Achtemeier (gen ed.). San Francisco: Harper & Row, 1985, 778-780.

435 PAYNE, J. B. "I Peter," *Encyclopedia of Biblical Prophecy.* New York, Evanston, San Francisco, and London: Harper & Row, 1973, 580-582.

44 DICTIONARY AND ENCYCLOPEDIA ARTICLES

436 PIPER, J. "Peter, First Letter of," *Baker Encyclopedia of the Bible*. Ed. W. A. Elwell. Grand Rapids: Baker, 1988, 2:1651-1657.

437 PLUMMER, A. "St. Peter," *The Bible Reader's Manual: Or, Aids to Biblical Study for Students of the Holy Scriptures*. Ed. C. H. H. Wright. London and Glasgow: William Collins and New York: International Bible Agency, 1892, 49.

438 RICHARDS, H. J. "1 Peter," *ABC of the Bible*. London: Chapman and Milwaukee: Bruce, 1967, 46.

439 SCHELKLE, K. H. "Pedro, Cartas de," *Sacramentum Mundi: Enciclopedia Teológica*. Barcelona: Herder, 1974, ²1977, 5:374-378. {Dates of publication are for volume 5 only, as each of the six volumes seem to have been issued and edited independently.}

440 ——. "The Letters of Peter. A. 1 Peter," *Sacramentum Mundi: An Encylopedia of Theology*. New York: Herder and London: Burns & Oates, 1969, 4:205-206.

441 ——. "The Letters of Peter. A. I Peter," *Encyclopedia of Theology: The Concise Sacramentum Mundi*. Ed. K. Rahner. New York: Seabury, 1975, 1059-1060.

442 STANLEY, D. N. "Peter, St., Epistles of," *The Catholic Encyclopedia for School and Home*. New York, San Francisco, Dallas, Toronto, London, and Sydney: McGraw-Hill, 1965, 8:354-356.

443 STEINMUELLER, J. E., and K. SULLIVAN. "Peter, First Epistle of," *Catholic Biblical Encyclopedia: New Testament*. New York: Wagner, 1950, 504.

444 STENDAHL, K., and E. T. SANDER. "The First Letter of Peter," *The New Encyclopaedia Britannica Macropaedia*. Chicago, London, Toronto, Geneva, Sydney, Tokyo, Manila, Seoul, Johannesburg: Encyclopaedia Britannica, ¹⁵1974, 2:969-970.

445 ——. "The First Letter of Peter," *The New Enclopaedia Britannica Macropaedia*. Chicago, Auckland, Geneva, London, Manila, Paris, Rome, Seoul, Sydney, Tokyo, and Toronto: Encyclopaedia Britannica, ¹⁵1987, 14:842-843.

446 TENNEY, M. C. "Peter, First Epistle of," *The Zondervan Pictorial Bible Dictionary*. Ed. M. C. Tenney. Grand Rapids: Zondervan, 1963, [2]1964, [3]1967, 642-643.

447 ———. "Peter, First Letter of" *The New International Dictionary of the Bible*. Grand Rapids: Zondervan and Basingstoke: Marshall Pickering, 1987, 773-774. {Originally published as *The Zondervan Pictorial Bible Dictionary*}.

448 UNGER, M. F. "Peter, First Epistle of," *Unger's Bible Dictionary*. Chicago: Moody, 1957, 850-851.

449 VAN DER HEEREN, A. "Peter, Epistles of Saint," *The Catholic Encyclopedia*. New York: Appleton, 1911 and Encyclopedia Press, 1913, 11:752-755.

450 VAN DODEWAARD, J. A. E. "Peter, Epistles of St." Trans. L. F. Hartman. *Encyclopedic Dictionary of the Bible*. Ed. L. F. Hartman. Translated and adapted from A. van den Born's *Bijbels Woordenboek*, [2]1954-57. New York, Toronto, and London: McGraw-Hill, 1963, 1818-1821.

451 VAN ELDEREN, B. "Peter, First Epistle," *Zondervan Pictorial Encyclopedia of the Bible*. Grand Rapids: Zondervan, 1975, 4:723-726.

452 ———. "Petrine Ethics," *Baker's Dictionary of Christian Ethics*. Ed. C. F. H. Henry. Grand Rapids: Baker, 1973, 506-508.

453 VAN UNNIK, W. C. "Peter, First Letter of," *IDB*. New York and Nashville: Abingdon, 1962, 3:758-766.

454 WALLS, A. F. "Peter, First Epistle of," *The Illustrated Bible Dictionary*. Ed. J. D. Douglas. Leicester: Inter-Varsity, Wheaton: Tyndale, and Sydney and Auckland: Hodder and Stoughton, 1980, 3:1202-1205.

455 ———. "Peter, First Epistle of," *The New Bible Dictionary*. Leicester: Inter-Varsity and Wheaton: Tyndale, 1962, [2]1982, 918-921.

456 WRIGHT, W. "Peter, Epistles of," *The Cyclopaedia of Biblical Literature*. Ed. J. Kitto. New York: American Book Exchange, 1880, 2:505-512.

457   ——. "Peter, The Epistles of," *The Popular and Critical Bible Encyclopaedia and Scriptural Dictionary*. Ed. S. Fallows. Chicago: Howard-Severance, 1901, 2:1321-1328.

SECTION 3

THE DESCENT TO HADES

This section is a bibliography of works on the theology of the descent of Christ to Hades. Among them are books and articles that are not in their entirety devoted to particular New Testament passages. But since there is in them usually some greater or lesser reference to 1 Peter and for the sake of completeness, the following list seeks to be inclusive. For related titles, see the relevant material in the section "Exposition and/or Application of Individual Passages."

458   ALTHAUS, P. "'Niedergefahren zur Hölle,'" *ZST* 19 (1942) 365-384.

459   BIEDER, W. "Der Descensus Jesu Christi und die Mission der Christen," *Kirchenblatt für die reform Schweiz* 119 (1963) 306-309.

460   ——. *Die Vorstellung von der Höllenfahrt Jesu Christi. Beitrag zur Entstehungsgeschichte der Vorstellung vom sog. Descensus ad inferos.* ATANT 19. Zürich: Zwingli, 1949.
       Reviews: Bonsirven, J., *Bib* 31 (1950) 518-520; Grant, R. M., *ATR* 33 (1951) 53-56.

461   BISER, E. "Abstiegen zur Hölle," *Münchener theologische Zeitschrift* 9 (1958), 205-212, 283-293.

462   BOUMAN, C. A. "He Descended into Hell," *Worship* 33 (1958-59) 194-203.

463   BOUSSET, W. "Zur Hadesfahrt Christi," *ZNW* 19 (1919-20) 50-66.

464   BRUSTEN, C. *La Descente du Christ aux enfers, d'après les apôtres et d'après l'église.* Paris: Fischbacher, 1897.

465   CHAINE, J. "Descente du Christ aux enfers," *DBSup* 2. Paris: Letouzey & Ané, 1934, 395-431.

466   CLEMEN, C. *"Niedergefahren zu den Toten." Ein Beitrag zur Würdigung des Apostolikums.* Giessen: Ricker, 1900.

467   DOEHLER, G. "Altes oder 'neues' Apostolikum?" *Lutheri-scher Rundblick* 21 (1973) 210-230.

468   ——. "The Descent into Hell," trans. and annotated by W. C. Daib. *The Springfielder* 39,1 (June 1975) 2-19.

469   GALOT, J. "Christ's Descent into Hell," *TD* 13 (1965) 89-94.

470   ——. "La descente du Christ au enfers," *NRT* 83 (1961) 471-491.

471   GRILLMEIER, A. "Der Gottessohn im Totenreich. Soteriologische und christologische Motivierung der Descensuslehre in der älteren christlichen Überlieferung," *ZKT* 71 (1949) 1-53, 184-203; *Mit Ihm und in Ihm. Christologische Forschungen und Perspektiven.* Freiburg, Basel, and Wien: Herder, 1975, 76-174.

472   GSCHWIND, K. *Die Niederfahrt Christi in die Unterwelt. Ein Beitrag zur Exegese des Neuen Testaments und zur Geschichte des Taufsymbols.* Neutestamentliche Abhandlungen 2,3,5. Münster: Aschendorff, 1911.

473   GÜDER, E. *Die Lehre von der Erscheinung Jesu Christi unter den Toten in ihrem Zusammenhänge mit der Lehre von den letzten Dinge.* Bern: Jent und Reinert, 1853.

474   HOLTZMANN, H. "Höllenfahrt im Neuen Testament," *ARW* 11 (1908) 285-297.

475   HUIDEKOPER, F. *The Belief of the First Three Centuries Concerning Christ's Mission to the Underworld.* New York: D. G. Francis, 1854, [7]1887, [8]1890.

476   JENSEN, P. *Laeren om Kristi Nedfahrt til de döde. En Fremstilling of Laerpunctets Historie tilligemed et Indloeg i dette.* Copenhagen, 1903.

477   JEREMIAS, J. "Zwischen Karfreitag und Ostern. Descensus und Ascensus in der Karfreigtagstheologie des Neuen Testaments," *ZNW* 42 (1949) 194-201; *Abba: Studien zur neutestamentlichen Theologie und Zeitgeschichte.* Göttingen: Vandenhoeck & Ruprecht, 1966, 323-331.

478   JOSEPHSON, H. "Niedergefahren zur Hölle," *Der Beweiss des Glaubens* 33 (1897) 400-418.

479 KÖNIG, J. L. *Die Lehre von Christi Höllenfahrt nach der heiligen Schrift, der ältesten Kirche, den christlichen Symbolen und nach ihrer vielumfassenden Bedeutung dargestellt.* Frankfurt: Zimmer, 1842.

480 KÖRBER, J. *Die katholische Lehre von der Höllenfahrt Jesu Christi.* Lanshut: Wölfe, 1860.

481 KOWALSKI, S. "De descensu Christi ad inferos in prima S. Petri epistola," *Collectanea Theologica* 21 (1949) 42-76.

482 ———. *La descente de Jésus-Christ aux enfers selon la doctrine de Saint Pierre.* Roznan, 1938.

483 KROLL, J. *Gott und Hölle. Der Mythos vom Descensuskampfe.* Studien der Bibliothek Warburg 20. Leipzig and Berlin: Teubner, 1932.

484 KÜRZINGER, J. "Descenso de Cristo a los infiernos," *Diccionario de Teología Bíblica.* Trans. D. R. Bueno from "Höllenfahrt Christi," *Bibeltheologisches Wörterbuch,* ed. J. B. Bauer (Graz, Wien, and Köln: Styria, ²1962). Barcelona: Herder, 1967, 259-264.

485 ———. "Descent into Hell," *Sacramentum Verbi: An Encyclopedia of Biblical Theology.* Trans. from „Höllenfahrt Christi," *Bibeltheologisches Wörterbuch,* ed. J. B. Bauer (Graz, Wien, and Köln: Styria, ³1967). New York: Herder, 1:202-206.

486 ———. "Höllenfahrt Christi," *Bibeltheologisches Wörterbuch.* Ed. J. B. Bauer. Graz, Wien, and Köln: Styria, 1959, ²1962, ³1967, 2:670-675 {pp. are those of ²1962}.

487 LAUTERBURG, M. "Höllenfahrt Christi," *RE.* Ed. J. J. Herzog. Leipzig, 1854-68, ³1896-1913, 7:199-206.

488 LOOFS, F. "Descent to Hades (Christ's)," *Encyclopedia of Religion and Ethics.* Ed. J. Hastings. New York: Charles Scribner's Sons, 1908-27, 4:654-663.

489 MAAS, W. *Gott und die Hölle. Studien zum Descensus Christi.* Einsiedeln: Johannes, 1979.

490 MACCULLOUGH, J. A. *The Harrowing of Hell: A Comparative Study of Early Christian Doctrine.* Edinburgh: T. & T. Clark, 1930.

491 MONNIER, J. *La descente aux enfers. Étude de pensée re-ligieuse d'art et de littérature.* Paris: Fischbacher, 1905.

492 NORDBLAD, C. *Föreställningen om Kristi hadesförd under-soekt till sitt ursprung. En religionshistorisk studie.* Upsala, 1912.

493 ODEBERG, H. "Nederstigen till dodsriket," *Bibliskt Manads-hafte* 18,12 (1944) 357-359.

494 PERROT, C. "La descente du Christ aux enfers dans le Nou-veau Testament," *Lumière et Vie* 87 (1969) 5-29.

495 PLUMPTRE, E. H. "The Spirits in Prison," and "The Descent Into Hell," *The Spirits in Prison and Other Studies on the Life After Death.* London: Isbister, 1885, [2]1886; New York: Whittaker, 1884, 3-28 and 75-121.

496 QUILLIET, H. "Descente de Jésus aux Enfers," *Dictionnaire de théologie catholique.* Paris: Letouzey et Ané, 1903-72, 4:565-619.

497 RÖDDING, G. "Descendit ad inferna," *Kerygma und Melos. Christhard Mahrenholz 70 Jahre.* Ed. W. Blankenburg, H. von Schade, and K. Schmidt-Clausen assisted by A. Völker. Kassel, Basel, Tours, London: Bärenreiter and Berlin and Hamburg: Lutherisches Verlaghaus, 1970, 94-102.

498 ROUSSEAU, O. "La descente aux enfers, fondement soté-riologique du baptême chrétien," *Mélanges Jules Lebreton. RSR* 40 (1951-52), 2:273-297.

499 SCHMIDT, B. *Die Vorstellungen von der Höllenfahrt Christi in der alten Kirche.* N.p., 1906.

500 SCHMIDT, C. "Der Descensus ad inferos in der alten Kirche," *Gespräche Jesu mit seinen Jüngern nach der Auferstehung. Ein katholisch-apostolisches Sendschreiben des 2. Jahrhun-derts.* Leipzig: Hinrichs, 1919, 453-576; reprint Hildesheim: Olms, 1967.

501 STRYNKOWSKI, J. J. *The Descent of Christ among the Dead.* Doctoral dissertation, Pontificia Universitas Gregoriana, 1972.

502 VOGELS, H.-J. *Christi Absteig ins Totenreich und das Läuterungsgericht an den Toten. Eine bibeltheologisch-*

dogmatische Untersuchung zum Glaubensartikel 'descendit ad inferos.' Freiburger Theologische Studien 102. Freiburg: Herder, 1976.

503 VORGRIMMLER, H. "Questions relatives à la descente du christ aux enfers," *Concilium* 11 (1966) 129-139.

504 ———. "The Significance of Christ's Descent into Hell," *Concilium* 11 (1966) 147-159.

505 WEXELS, W. A. *Aaben erklaering til mine Medkristne om min Anskülse og Bekjendfelse angaaende Christi Nederfahrt till Helvede og Muligheden af en Omvendelse efter Doden.* N.p.: Christiania, 1845.

506 YATES, J. "'He Descended into Hell': Creed, Article and Scripture, Part I," *Churchman* 102 (1988) 240-250.

EXPOSITION AND/OR APPLICATION OF INDIVIDUAL PASSAGES

The following works do not include what might be described as essentially sermonic or homiletical material. For such titles, see the Section headed "Sermons and Preaching."

Chapter 1

507   AGNEW, F. H. "1 Peter 1:2—An Alternative Translation," *CBQ* 45 (1983) 68-73.

508   ANONYMOUS. "Illustration of 1 Peter I:6," *Methodist Review* 3 (1820) 409-411.

509   ARICHEA, D. C., JR. "God or Christ? A Study of Implicit Information [1 Peter 1:1-20]," *BT* 28 (1977) 412-418.

510   BLENDINGER, C. "Kirche als Fremdlingschaft (1. Petrus 1,22-25)," *Communio Viatorum* 10 (1967) 123-134.

511   BRUMMACK, C. "Eis elpida zoosan - zur lebendigen Hoffnung (1 Petr 1,3)," *Kirche, Recht und Land: Festschrift Weihbischof Prof. Dr. Adolf Kindermann dargeboten z. 70 Lebensjahre.* Ed. K. Reiss and H. Schutz. Königstein: Südetendt. Priesterwerk and München: Ackerman-Gemeinde, 1969, 276-279.

512   CALLOUD, J. "Ce que parler veut dire (1 P 1,10-12)," *Études sur la première lettre du Pierre. Congrès de l'ACFEB, Paris 1979.* LD 102. Ed. C. Perrot. Paris: 1980, 175-206.

513   CIPRIANI, S. "Lo « Spirito di Cristo » come « spirito di profezia » in 1 Pt. 1,10-12," *Ecclesiae Sacramentum. Studi in onore di P. Alfredo Marranzini S. J.* Pontificia facoltà teologica dell'Italia meridionale 2. Ed. G. Lorizio and V. Scippa. Napoli: D'Auria, 1986, 157-167.

514   COUTTS, J. "Ephesians i.3-14 and I Peter i.3-12," *NTS* 3 (1956-57) 115-127.

515   DALMER, J. "Zu 1. Petr 1,18-19," BFCT 2,6 (1898-99) 75-

87.

516   DALTON, W. J. "La rigenerazione alla vita cristiana (1 Pt 1,3)," *Parola Spirito e vita* 5 (1982) 234-246.

517   ———. "So That Your Faith May Also Be Your Hope In God (1 Peter 1:21) {1 Peter 1:3-25}," *Reconciliation and Hope: New Testament Essays on Atonement and Eschatology Presented to L. L. Morris on his 60th Birthday.* Ed. R. Banks. Exeter: Paternoster and Grand Rapids: Eerdmans, 1974, 262-274.

518   DAUTZENBERG, G. "Σωτηρία ψυχῶν (1 Petr 1,9)," *BZ* 8 (1964) 262-276.

519   DEICHGRÄBER, R. "1. Petrus 1,3-5," *Gotteshymnus und Christushymnus in der frühen Christenheit. Untersuchungen zu Form, Sprache und Stil der frühchristlichen Hymnen.* SUNT 5. Göttingen: Vandenhoeck & Ruprecht, 1967, 77-78.
Reviews: Dreyfus, F., *RB* 77 (1970) 133-134; Elliott, J. H., *CBQ* 30 (1968) 440-441; Krentz, E., *CTM* 39 (1968) 500-501; Mack, B. L., *JBL* 87 (1968) 358-359; Osten-Sacken, P. von der, *LW* 15 (1968) 357; Schille, G., *TLZ* 94 (1969) 121-123; Schnackenburg, R., *BZ* 14 (1970) 294-296; Visser, A. J., *NedTTs* 24 (1969) 61-63.

520   DU TOIT, A. B. "The Significance of Discourse Analysis for New Testament Interpretation and Translation: Introductory Remarks with Special Reference to 1 Peter 1:3-13," *Neot* 8: *Linguistics and Bible Translating* (1974) 54-79.

521   EVANG, M. "'Εκ καρδίας ἀλλήλους ἀγαπήσατε ἐκτενῶς. Zum Verständnis der Aufferorderung und ihrer Begründungen in 1 Petr 1,22f," *ZNW* 80 (1989) 111-123.

522   FURNISH, V. P. "Elect Sojourners in Christ: An Approach to the Theology of I Peter {1 Peter 1:1-12}," *PSTJ* 28,3 (Spring 1975) 1-11.

523   GATZWEILER, K. "Prix et exigencies de la condition chrétienne (1 P 1,17-21)," *Assemblées du Seigneur* 24 (1970) 16-20.

524   GROSCHEIDE, F. W. "1 Petrus 1:1-12," *Gereformeerd Theologisch Tijdschrift* 60 (1960) 6-7.

525   ——. "Kol 3,1-4; 1 Petr 1,3-5; 1 Jo 3,1-2," *Gereformeerd Theologisch Tijdschrift* 54 (1954) 139-147.

526   HIEBERT, D. E. "Designation of the Readers in 1 Peter 1:1-2," *BSac* 137 (1980) 64-75.

527   ——. "Peter's Thanksgiving for our Salvation {1 Peter 1:3-12}," *Studia Missionalia* 29 (1980) 85-103.

528   HOLZMEISTER, U. "Exordium prioris epistulae S. Petri (1 Petr. 1, 1.2)," *VD* 2 (1922) 209-212.

529   HUNTER, A. M. "The Christian Idea of God (I Peter 1.3)," *Gospel and Apostle*. London: SCM, 1975, 170-173.

530   KAISER, W. C., JR. "The Single Intent of Scripture {Alleged Proof Texts for 'Double Meaning': Daniel 12:6-8; John 11:49-52; 14:25, 26; 15:26, 27; 16:12-15; 1 Peter 1:10-12; 2 Peter 1:19-21}," *Evangelical Roots: A Tribute to Wilbur Smith*. Ed. K. S. Kantzer. Nashville and New York: Nelson, 1978, 123-141.

531   KENDALL, D. W. "I Peter 1:3-9: On Christian Hope," *Int* 41 (1987) 66-71.

532   ——. *The Introductory Character of 1 Peter 1:3-12*. Ph.D. dissertation, Union Theological Seminary (Virginia), 1984.

533   ——. "The Literary and Theological Function of 1 Peter 1:3-12," *Perspectives on First Peter*. Ed. C. H. Talbert. National Association of Baptist Professers of Religion Special Studies Series 9. Macon, Ga: Mercer University Press, 1986, 103-120.

534   KILPATRICK, G. D. "1 Peter 1:11 τίνα ἢ ποῖον καίρον," *NovT* 28 (1986) 91-92.

535   KOKOT, M. "Znaczenie 'nasienia niezniszczalnego' w 1 P 1,23 [Signification du 'germe incorruptible' dans 1 P 1,23]," *Collectanea Theologica* 44 (1974) 35-44.

536   KÜHSCHELM, R. "Lebendige Hoffnung (1 Petr 1,3-12)," *BLit* 56 (1983) 202-206.

537   LAVERDIÈRE, E. A. "Covenant Theology in 1 Peter 1:1-2:10," *Bible Today* 42 (1969) 2909-16.

538   ——. "A Grammatical Ambiguity in 1 Pet 1:23," *CBQ* 36 (1974) 89-94.

539   LE DÉAUT, R. "Le Targum de *Gen.* 22, 8 et 1 *Pt.* 1, 20," *RSR* 49 (1961) 103-106.

540   MACARTHUR, J., JR. *Chosen for Eternity: A Study of Election* {1 Peter 1:1-2}. Chicago: Moody, 1989, 7-49.

541   ——. *Our Great Salvation {1 Peter 1:3-12}.* Panorama City, Cal.: Grace to You and Chicago: Moody, 1990.

542   MARGOT, J.-C. "1 Pierre 1.3-9," *Traduire sans trahir. La théorie de la traduction et son application aux textes bibliques.* Lausanne: L'Age D'Homme, 1979, 231-242.

543   MARTIN, T. W. "The Present Indicative in the Eschatological Statements of 1 Peter 1:6, 8," *JBL* 111 (1992) 307-312.

544   NESTLE, E. "1 Pet 1.2," *ExpTim* 10 (1898-99) 188-189.

545   PARSONS, S. *We Have Been Born Anew: The New Birth of the Christian in the First Epistle of Peter (I Peter 1:3, 23).* Doctoral dissertation, St. Thomas Aquinas Pontifical University, Roma, 1978.

546   RIGATO, M.-L. "Quali i profeti di cui nella 1 Pt 1,10?" *RivB* 38 (1990) 73-90.

547   SCHARLEMANN, M. H. "An Apostolic Descant: An Exegetical Study of 1 Peter 1:3-12," *Concordia Journal* 2 (1976) 9-17.

548   ——. "An Apostolic Salutation: An Exegetical Study of 1 Peter 1:1-2," *Concordia Journal* 1 (1975) 108-118.

549   ——. "Why the *Kuriou* in 1 Peter 1:25?" *CTM* 30 (1959) 352-356.

550   SCHENK, W. "I. Petr. I,3," *Der Segen im Neuen Testament. Eine begriffsanalytische Studie.* Theologische Arbeiten XXV. Berlin: Evangelische Verlagsanstalt, 1967, 101.

551   SCOTT, C. A. "The 'Sufferings of Christ': A Note on 1 Peter I. 11," *Expositor* 6,12 (1905) 234-240.

552   SHIMADA, K.   "A Critical Note on 1 Peter 1,12," AJBI 7
       (1981) 146-150.

553   VALLAURI, E.   "'Succincti lumbos mentis vestrae' (1 Piet.
       1,13). Nota per una traduzione," *BeO* 24 (1982) 19-22.

554   VAN UNNIK, W. C.   "De verlossing I Petrus i 18-19 en het
       probleem van den eersten Petrusbrief," *Mededelingen der
       Nederlandsche Akademie van Wetenschappen, Afdeeling
       Letterkunde* 5,1. Amsterdam: Noord-Hollandsche Uitgever-
       maatschappij, 1942, 1-106.

555   ——. "The Critique of Paganism in I Peter 1:18," *Neotesti-
       mentica et Semitica: Studies in Honor of Matthew Black*.
       Ed. E. E. Ellis and M. Wilcox. Edinburgh: T. & T. Clark,
       1969, 129-142.

556   ——. "The Redemption in I Peter I 18-19 and the Problem of
       the First Epistle of Peter," *Sparsa Collecta: The Collected
       Essays of W. C. van Unnik*. NovTSup 29-31. Leiden: Brill,
       1977-87, 2:3-82.

557   WARDEN, D.   "The Prophets of 1 Peter 1:10-12," *ResQ* 31
       (1989) 1-12.

558   WENGST, K. "1. Petr. 1,20; 3,18.22," *Christologische For-
       meln und Lieder des Urchristentums*. SNT 7. Revision of
       the author's 1967 Bonn thesis. Gütersloh: Gütersloher Ver-
       lagshaus, 1972, [2]1974, 161-165.
       Review: Schille, G., *TLZ* 98 (1973) 755-758.

Chapters 1-2

559   BOISMARD, M.-É. "La typologie baptismale dans la première
       épître de saint Pierre {1 Peter 1,13-2,10}," *La Vie spirituelle*
       94 (1956) 339-352.

560   DANKER, F. W.   "I Peter 1_{24}-2_{17}—A Consolatory Pericope,"
       ZNW 58 (1967) 93-102.

561   ELLIOTT, J. H.   "Salutation and Exhortation to Christian Be-
       havior on the Basis of God's Blessings ({1 Peter} 1:1-2:10),"
       RevExp 79 (1982) 415-425.

562   GRAY, J. M. "The Obligation of Love {1 Peter 1:22-23; 2:1-3}," *Fundamentalist Journal* 5,4 (April 1986) 48-49. {"Adapted by permission from *Moody Monthly*"}

563   HAMBLIN, R. L. "Expositor's Corner: First Peter {1 Peter 1:1-2:10}," *Theological Educator* 13,1 (Fall 1982) 83-88.

Chapters 1 and 3

564   WENGST, K. "1. Petr. 1,20; 3,18.22," *Christologische Formeln und Lieder des Urchristentums*. SNT 7. Revision of the author's 1967 Bonn thesis. Gütersloh: Gütersloher Verlagshaus, 1972, ²1974, 161-165.

Chapter 2

565   ADINOLFI, M. "Stato civile dei cristiani « forestieri e pellegrini » (1 Pt 2, 11)," *Anton* 42 (1967) 420-434; "Stato civile dei cristiani « forestieri e pellegrini » (1 Piet. 2,11)," *Questione bibliche di storia e storiografia*. Esegesi biblica 5. Brescia: Paideisa, 1969, 1901-208.

566   ANONYMOUS. "Questions. {Quel est le vrai sens de 'tradebat autem judicanti se *iniuste*' de la Ire Epître de S. Pierre II,23?}," *L'Ami du clergé* 49 (1932) 48.

567   BAMMEL, E. "The Commands in I Peter ii.17," *NTS* 11 (1964-65) 279-281.

568   BARTINA, S. "Pedro manifiesta su poder primacial (1 P 2,25)," *CB* 21 (1964) 333-336.

569   BEST, E. "I Peter II 4-10—A Reconsideration," *NovT* 11 (1969) 270-293.

570   ———. "A First Century Sect {1 Peter 2:17}," *IBS* 8 (1986) 115-121.

571   ———. "I Peter II 4-10—A Reconsideration," *NovT* 11 (1969) 270-293.

572   BIEDER, W. "Das Volk Gottes in Erwartung von licht und Lobpreis. Neutestamentlich-missionstheologische Erwägungen zur Ekklesiologie {1 Peter 2:9-12}," *TZ* 40 (1984) 137-148.

573   BISHOP, E. F. F. "The Word of a Living and Unchanging God: 1 Peter 2,23," *Muslim World* 43 (1953) 15-17.

574   BLINZLER, J. "IEPATEYMA. Zur Exegese von 1 Petr 2,5 u. 9," *Episopus. Studien über das Bischofsamt seiner Eminenz Michael Kardinal von Faulhaber, Erzbischof von München-Freising zum 80. Geburtstag.* Ed. Theologischer Fakultät der Universität München. Regensburg: Gregorius, 1949, 49-65.
        Review: Fiorenza, E. S., "Zur Interpretation von 1 Petr 2,5.9 ," *Priester für Gott: Studien zum Herrschafts- und Priestmotiv in der Apkalypse.* NTAbh 7. Münster: Aschendorff, 1972, 51-59.

575   CARREZ, M. "L'esclavage dans la première épître de Pierre {1 Peter 2:18-25}," *Études sur la première lettre de Pierre. Congrès de l'ACFEB, Paris 1979.* LD 102. Ed. C. Perrot. Paris: 1980, 207-217.

576   CERFAUX, L. "Regale sacerdotium {Exodos 19:6; 1 Peter 2:9}," *RSPT* 28 (1939) 5-39; *Recueil Lucien Cerfaux. Études d'exégèse et d'histoire religieuse de Monseigneur Cerfaux.* BETL 6-7. Gembloux: Duculot, 1954, 2:283-315.

577   CHRYSSAVGIS, J. "The Royal Priesthood ({1} Peter 2.9)," *GOTR* 32 (1987) 373-377.

578   COLECCHIA, L. F. "Rilievi su 1 Piet. 2,4-10," *RevistB* 25 (1977) 179-194.

579   CONGAR, Y. M.-J. "Saint Pierre {1 Peter 2:4-10}," *Le mystère du temple ou l'économie de la présence de Dieu à sa créature de la Genèse à l'Apocalypse.* LD 22. Paris: Cerf, 1958, ²1963, 207-222.
        Reviews: Anonymous, *Irénikon* 33 (1960) 401-402; Henkey, C. H. *CBQ* 21 (1959) 242-244; Phillips, G., *ETL* 36 (1960) 97-98.

580   ———. "San Pedro {1 Peter 2:4-10}," *El misterio del templo.* Colección ecclesia 6. Trans. A. R. Resina. Barcelona: Estela, 1964, ²1967, 200-214.

581   ———. "St Peter {1 Peter 2:4-10}," *The Mystery of the Temple Or the Manner of God's Presence to His Creatures from Genesis to the Apocalypse.* Trans. R. F. Trevett. London: Burns and Oates, 1962, 175-188.

582   COPPENS, J. "Le sacerdoce royal des fidèles: un commentaire de I Petr., ii. 4-10," *Au service de la parole de Dieu:*

Mélanges offerts à Monseigneur André-Marie Charue. Gembloux: Duculot, 1969, 61-75.

583 CORDERO, M. G. "El « sacerdocio real » en 1 P 2, 9," *CB* 16 (1959) 321-323.

584 DABIN, P. "Le sacerdoce royal et prophétique dans Saint Pierre {1 Peter 2:1-10}," *Le sacerdoce royal des fidèles dans les livres saints.* Gembloux: Duculot, 1941, 171-197.

585 DALE, R. W. "A Spiritual House (1 Peter ii.5)," *Expositor* (1896-A) 127-136.

586 DEICHGRÄBER, R. "1. Petrus 2,21 ff," *Gotteshymnus und Christushymnus in der frühen Christenheit. Untersuchungen zu Form, Sprache un Stil der frühchristlichen Hymnen.* SUNT 5. Göttingen: Vandenhoeck & Ruprecht, 1967, 140-143.

587 DEIST, F. E. "'Van die duisternis tot sy merkwaardige lig' (1 Petr. 2 : 9) in die lig van Elephantine," *Nederduitse gereformeerde teologiese tydskrif* 11 (1970) 44-48.

588 DE JONGE, M. "Vreemdelingen en bijwoners. Enige opmerkingen naar aanleiding van 1 Petr. 2:11 en verwante Teksten," *NedTTs* 11 (1956-57) 18-36.

589 D'HÉROUVILLE, P. "I Petr. 2, ₂, 3 et saint Bernard. In festo omn. Sanct., Sermo I,4," *RSR* 6 (1916) 131-133.

590 ELLIOTT, J. H. "Backward and Forward 'In His Steps': Following Jesus from Rome to Raymond and Beyond. The Tradition, Redaction, and Reception of 1 Peter 2:18-25," *Discipleship in the New Testament.* Ed. F. F. Segovia. Philadelphia: Fortress, 1985, 184-208.

591 ——. *The Elect and the Holy: An Exegetical Examination of I Peter 2:4-10 and the Phrase* βασίλειον ἱεράτευμα. NovTSup 12. Leiden: Brill, 1966.
Reviews: Brown, R. E., *CBQ* 29 (1967) 255-257; Cothenet, E., *Esprit et Vie* 11 (1969) 169-173; Danker, F. W., *CTM* 38 (1967) 329-332; Fiorenza, E. S., "Zur Interpretation von 1 Petr 2,5.9 ," *Priester für Gott: Studien zum Herrschafts- und Priestmotiv in der Apkalypse.* NTAbh 7. Münster: Aschendorff, 1972, 51-59; Grob, R., *TZ* 23 (1967) 445-446; Meyer, P. W., *JBL* 87 (1968) 483-484; Moule, C. F. D., *JTS* 18 (1967) 471-474; Schnackenburg, R., *BZ* 12 (1968) 152-153; Schweizer, E., *Int* 22 (1968) 103-105.

592   FEUILLET, A. "Les « sacrifices spiritueles » du sacerdoce royal des baptisés (1 P 2,5) et leur préparation dans l'Ancien Testament," *NRT* 96 (1974) 704-728.

593   FITCH, W. "The Glory of the Cross {1 Peter 2:21-25}," *Christianity Today* 3,12 (16 March 1959) 7-9.

594   FRANCIS, J. "'Like Newborn Babes'—The Image of the Child in 1 Peter 2:2-3," *StudBib* 1978. Ed. E. A. Livingstone. JSNTSup 3 (1980) 3:111-117.

595   GÄRTNER, B. "I Pet. ii. 3-6," *The Temple and the Community in Qumran and the New Testament: A Comparative Study in the Temple Symbolism of the Qumran Texts and the New Testament.* SNTSMS 1. Cambridge: University Press, 1965, 72-88.

596   GIESEN, H. "Kirche als Gottes erwähltes Volk. Zum Gemeindeverständnis von 1 Petr 2,4-10," *Theologie der Gegenwart* 29 (1986) 140-149.

597   GOLDSTEIN, H. "Das heilige Volk, das zuvor kein Volk war. Christengemeinde ohne Judenpolemik: 1 Petr 2,4-10," *Gottesverächter und Menschenfeinde? Juden zwischen Jesus und frühchristlicher Kirche.* Ed. H. Goldstein. Düsseldorf: Patmos, 1979, 279-302.

598   HALAS, S. "Sens dynamique de l'expression λαὸς εἰς περιποίησιν en 1 P 2.9," *Bib* 65 (1984) 254-258.

599   HIEBERT, D. E. "Selected Studies from 1 Peter. Part 1: Following Christ's Example: An Exposition of 1 Peter 2:21-25," *BSac* 139 (1982) 32-45.

600   HILLYER, N. "'Spiritual milk . . . Spiritual House' {1 Peter 2:2-4}," *TynBul* 20 (1969) 126.

601   HUNTER, A. M. "The Christian Gentleman (I Peter 2,12.18)," *Gospel and Apostle.* London: SCM, 1975, 174-176.

602   JONES-HALDEMAN, M. *The Function of Christ's Suffering in I Peter 2:21.* Th.D. dissertation, Andrews University, 1988.

603   KETTER, P. "Das allgemeine Priestertum der Gläubigen nach dem ersten Petrusbrief {1 Peter 2:1-10}," *TTZ* 56 (1947) 43-51.

604 LANGKAMMER, H. "Jes 53 und 1 Petr 2,21-25. Zur christologischen Interpretation der Leidenstheologie von Jes 53," *BLit* 60 (1987) 90-98.

605 LEA, T. D. "How Peter Learned the Old Testament {1 Peter 2:4-8}," *Southwestern Journal of Theology* 22,2 (Spring 1980) 96-102.

606 LÉGASSE, S. "La Soumission aux Autorités d'après I Pierre 2.13-17: Version Spécifique d'une Parénèse Traditionelle," *NTS* 34 (1988) 378-396.

607 MACARTHUR, J., JR. *The Believer's Privileges {1 Peter 2:4-10}*. Panorama City: Grace to You and Chicago: Moody, 1990.

608 MANNS, F. "« La maison où réside l'Esprit. » 1 P 2,5 et son arrière-plan juif," *Studium Biblicum Franciscanum Liber Annuus* 34 (1984) 207-224.

609 MARSHALL, J. S. "'A Spiritual House an Holy Priesthood' (1 Petr ii,5)," *ATR* 28 (1946) 227-228.

610 MEECHAM, H. G. "A Note on 1 Peter ii. 12," *ExpTim* 65 (1953-54) 93.

611 MIGUÉNS, M. "La « Passion » du Christ total (1 P 2, 20b-25)," *Assembleés du Seigneur* 25 (1969) 26-31.

612 MINEAR, P. S. "The House of Living Stones: A Study of 1 Peter 2:4-12," *Ecumenical Review* 34 (1982) 238-248.

613 MOL, L. "As Newborn Babes {1 Peter 2:2}," *Other Side* 21,6 (August/September 1985) 32-33.

614 MORGAN, G. C. *Peter and the Church {1 Peter 2:9}*. New York: Revell, 1938.

615 OGARA, F. "In hoc enim vocati estis: quia et christus passus est pro nobis . . . (1 Pet. 2,21-25) (1 Pet. 2,11-19)," *VD* 16 (1936) 97-106.

616 OSBORNE, T. P. "Guide Lines for Christian Suffering: A Source-Critical and Theological Study of 1 Peter 2,21-25," *Bib* 64 (1983) 381-408.

617   PATSCH, H. "Zum alttestamentlichen Hintergrund von Römer 4$_{25}$ und I. Petrus 2$_{24}$," *ZNW* 60 (1969) 278-279.

618   PÉREZ, G., and J. F. HERNÁNDEZ. "Epístolas dominicales. Epístola de la Dominica III de Pascua (I P 2, 11-19)," *CB* 13 (1956) 92-98.

619   PRIGENT, P. "I Pierre 2,4-10," *RHPR* 72 (1992) 53-60.

620   RAMOS, F. F. "El sacerdocio de los creyentes (1 Pet 2,4-10)," *Sacerdocio ministerial y laical. Teologia del sacerdocio 2.* Burgos, Spain: Aldecoa, 1970, 11-47.

621   ROBINSON, P. J. "Some Missiological Perspectives from I Peter 2:4-10," *Missionalia* 17 (1989) 176-187.

622   RYAN, T. J. *The Word of God in First Peter: A Critical Study of 1 Peter 2:1-3.* S.T.D. dissertation, Catholic University of America, 1973.

623   SANDEVOIR, P. "Un royaume de prêtres {1 Peter 2:9}?" *Études sur la première lettre de Pierre. Congrès de l'ACFEB, Paris 1979.* LD 102. Ed. C. Perrot. Paris: Cerf, 1980, 219-229.

624   SCHRAGE, W. "I. Petrus 2 {esp. 1 Peter 2:13-17}," *Die Christen und der Staat nach dem Neuen Testament.* Gütersloh: Mohn, 1971, 63-68.

625   SCHRÖGER, F. "'Lasst euch auferbauen zu einem geisterfüllten Haus' (1 Petr 2,4-5). Eine Überlegung zu dem Verhältnis von Ratio und Pneuma," *Theologie—Gemeinde—Seelsorge.* Ed. W. Friedberger and F. Schnider. München: Kosel, 1979, 138-145.

626   SCHWANK, B. "Wie Freie—aber als Sklaven Gottes (1 Petr 2,16). Das Verhältnis der Christen zur Staatsmacht nach dem ersten Petrusbrief," *Erbe und Auftrag* 36 (1960) 5-12.

627   SISTI, A. "Il cristiano nel mondo (1 Piet. 2,11-19)," *BeO* 8 (1966) 70-79.

628   SISTI, P. A. "Sulle orme di Gesù sofferente (1 Piet. 2,21-25)," *BeO* 10 (1968) 59-68.

629   SNODGRASS, K. R. "I Peter ii. 1-10: Its Formation and Literary Affinities," *NTS* 24 (1977-78) 97-106.

630   SNYDER, S. "1 Peter 2:17: A Reconsideration," *Filologia Neotestamentaria* 4 (1991) 211-215.

631   STANFORD, W. B. "St Peter's Silence on the Petrine Claims {1 Peter 2:3-8}," *Theology* 48 (1945) 15.

632   STEUERNAGEL, V. R. "An Exiled Community as a Missionary Community: A Study Based on 1 Peter 2:9, 10," *Evangelical Review of Theology* 10 (1986) 8-18.

633   STEVICK, D. B. "A Matter of Taste: 1 Peter 2:3," *Review for Religious* 47 (1988) 707-717.

634   TEICHERT, H. "1 Petr. 2,13—eine crux interpretum?" *TLZ* 74 (1949) 303-304.

635   THOMPSON, J. W. "'Be Submissive to Your Masters': A Study of I Peter 2:18-25," *ResQ* 9 (1966) 66-78.

636   VANHOYE, A. "{1 Peter 2:1-10}," *Old Testament Priests and the New Priest According to the New Testament.* Studies in Scripture. Trans. J. B. Orchard. Petersham, Mass.: St. Bede's, 1986, 243-267.

637   ———. "La foi qui construit l'eglise (1 P 2,4-9)," *Assemblées du Seigneur* 26 (1973) 12-17.

638   ———. "La maison spirituelle (1 P 2,1-10)," *Assemblées du Seigneur* 43 (1964) 16-29.

639   ———. "L'Église du Christ, organisme sacerdotal {1 Peter 2:1-10}," *Prêtres anciens, prêtre nouveau selon le Nouveau Testament.* Parole de Dieu. Paris: Seuil, 1980, 269-306.

640   WAINWRIGHT, G. "Praying for Kings: The Place of Human Rulers in the Divine Plan of Salvation {1 Timothy 2:1-8; Titus 3:1-2; 1 Peter 2:11-17; Revelation 13:1-10}," *Ex Auditu* 2 (1986) 117-127.

641   WINTER, B. W. "The Public Honouring of Christian Benefactors: Romans 13.3-4 and 1 Peter 2.14-15," *JSNT* 34 (1988) 87-103.

642   ZAŁĘSKI, J. "Posłuszeństwo władzy świeckiej według 1 [P]t 2, 13-17," *Collectanea Theologica* 54 (1984) 39-50; "L'obbedienza al potere civile in 1 Pt 2, 13-17," *Collectanea Theologica* 55 (Special issue 1985) 153-162.

Chapters 2-3

643 BALCH, D. L. "Early Christian Criticism of Patriarchal Authority: 1 Peter 2:11-3:12," *USQR* 39 (1984) 161-173.

644 DALE, R. W. "Christians and Social Institutions (1 Peter ii.11-iii.7)," *Expositor* (1896-A) 287-295.

645 MACARTHUR, J., JR. *Through Suffering to Triumph {1 Peter 2:21-25; 3:18-22}.* Panorama City, Cal.: Grace to You and Chicago: Moody, 1991.

646 SCHULZ, S. "Evangelium und Welt. Hauptprobleme einer Ethik des Neuen Testaments {1 Cor 7:29 *ff,* Gal 3:27 *f,* 1 Peter 2:13-3:7}," *Neues Testament und christliche Existenz. Festschrift für Herbert Braun zum 70. Geburtstag am 4. Mai 1973.* Ed. H. D. Betz and L. Schottroff. Tübingen: Mohr-Siebeck, 1973, 483-501.

647 SENIOR, D. "The Conduct of Christians in the World ({1 Peter} 2:11-3:12)," *RevExp* 79 (1982) 427-438.

Chapter 3

648 AALEN, S. "Oversettelsen av ordet ἐπερώτημα i dåpsstedet 1 Pet. 3, 21," *Tidsskrift for Teologi og Kirke* 43 (1972) 161-175.

649 ANONYMOUS. "Remarks on 1 Peter III,18,19,20," *Methodist Review* 10 (1827) 161-163.

650 ANONYMOUS. "Thoughts on 1 Peter III:19," *Methodist Review* 2 (1819) 375-379.

651 ARCHER, G. L. "1 Peter: Is There a Second Chance after Death {1 Peter 3:19}," *Encyclopedia of Bible Difficulties.* Grand Rapids: Zondervan, 1982, 423-424.

652 ARVEDSON, T. "Syneideseos agathes eperotema. En studie til I Petr. 3, 21," *SEÅ* 15 (1950) 55-61.

653 BALTENSWEILER, H. "Erster Petrusbrief (Kap. 3,1-7)," *Die Ehe im Neuen Testament. Exegetische Untersuchungen über Ehe, Ehelosigkeit und Ehescheidung.* ATANT 52. Zürich and Stuttgart: Zwingli, 1967, 243-249.

654 BANKS, W. L. "Who are the Spirits in Prison? {1 Peter 3:18-19}," *Eternity* 17,2 (February, 1966) 23, 26.

655 BARTH, G. "Taufe als Bitte um ein gutes Gewisen in 1 Peter 3,21," *Die Taufe in früchristlicher Zeit.* Biblische-theologische Studien 4. Neukirchen-Vluyn: Neukirchener Verlag, 1981, 111-116.

656 BARTH, M. *Die Taufe—ein Sakrament? Ein exegetischer Beitrag zum kirchlichen Gespräch über die kirchliche Taufe {1 Peter 3:18-21}.* Zollikon-Zürich: Evangelischer Verlag, 1951, 480-522.
Reviews: Filson, F. V., *Today* 10 (Ap 1953) 130-131; Héring, J., *RHPR* 33 (1953) 255-260.

657 BARTON, J. M. T. "What are we to understand by the 'spirits that were in prison' referred to in I Peter iii, 19?" *Scripture* 4 (1949-51) 181-182.

658 BEASLEY-MURRAY, G. R. "I Peter 3.20-21," *Baptism in the New Testament.* London, 1962; reprint Grand Rapids: Eerdmans 1973, 358-362.

659 BINDLEY, T. H. "1 Peter iii. 18f," *ExpTim* 41 (1929-30) 44.

660 BISHOP, E. F. F. *"Oligoi* in 1 Pet. 3:20," *CBQ* 13 (1951) 44-45.

661 BORNHÄUSER, K. "Jesu Predigt für die Geister (Nach 1. Petri 3, 19. 20)," *Allgemeine Evangelisch-Lutherische Kirchenzeitung* 54 (1921) 322-324.

662 BROOKS, O. S. "I Peter 3:21—The Clue to the Literary Structure of the Epistle," *NovT* 16 (1974) 290-305.

663 COOK, D. "I Peter iii. 20: An Unnecessary Problem," *JTS* 31 (1980) 72-78.

664 CURRY, D. "Christ Preaching to the Spirits in Prison {1 Peter 3:18-20}," *Methodist Review* 67 (1885) 69-82.

665 DALE, R. W. "Like minded (1 Peter iii.8-12)," *Expositor* (1896-A) 349-357.

666 DALTON, W. J. "1 Peter 3:19 Reconsidered," *The New Testament Age: Essays In Honor of Bo Reicke.* Ed. W. C. Weinrich. Macon: Mercer, 1984, 1:96-105.

667   ——. "Christ's Proclamation to the Spirits (1 Peter 3:19)," *Australasian Catholic Record* 41 (1964) 322-327.

668   ——. "Interpretation and Tradition: An Example from 1 Peter {1 Peter 3:19}," *Greg* 49 (1968) 11-37.

669   ——. "Le christ, espérance des chrétiens dans un monde hostile (1 P 3,15-18)," *Assemblées du Seigneur* 27 (1970) 18-23.

670   DAVIDSON, R. M. "Τύπος Structures in 1 Pet 3:18-22," *Typology in Scripture: A Study of Hermeneutical τύπος Structures*. D.Th. dissertation, Seventh-day Adventist Theological Seminary of Andrews University, 1981, 313-336.

671   ——. "Τύπος Structures in 1 Pet 3:18-22," *Typology in Scripture: A Study of Hermeneutical τύπος Structures*. Andrews University Seminary Doctoral Dissertation Series 2. Berien Springs: Andrews University Press, 1981, 313-336.

672   DE RU, G. "De Heilige Doop—gebed of gave? (1 Petrus 3,20b. 21)," *NedTTs* 20 (1966) 255-268.

673   DINKLER, E. "Die Taufaussagen des Neuen Testaments {1 Peter 3:18-22}," *Zu Karl Barths Lehre von der Taufe*. Ed. F. Viering. Gütersloh: Mohn, 1971, 60-153 (article), 181-121 (section).

674   DUBLIN, J. {J. A. Bernard, Archbishop of Dublin}. "The Descent into Hades and Christian Baptism (A Study of 1 Peter III, 19 ff)," *Expositor* ser. 8/64 (1916) 241-274.

675   FEINBERG, J. S. "1 Peter 3:18-20, Ancient Mythology, and the Intermediate State," *WTJ* 48 (1986) 303-336.

676   FERNANDEZ, J. "Epístola del Domingo quinto después de Pentecostés (1 Pe 3,8-15)," *Cultura Bíblica* 10 (1962) 290-304.

677   FRANCE, R. T. "Exegesis in Practice: Two Samples {Mt 8:5-13; 1 Pet 3:18-22}," *New Testament Interpretation: Essays on Principles and Methods*. Ed. I. H. Marshall. Exeter: Paternoster and Grand Rapids: Eerdmans, 1977, 252-281.

678   FRIDRICHSEN, A. "Scholia in Novum Testamentum. '3. Till 1 Petr. 3:7,'" *SEÅ* 12 (1947) 127-131.

679 GHIBERTI, G. "Le « Sante Donne » di una volta (1Pt 3,5)," *RivB* 36 (1988) 287-297.

680 GOLDINGAY, J. "Expounding the New Testament {Mt 8:5-13; 1 Pet 3:18-22}," *New Testament Interpretation: Essays on Principles and Methods*. Ed. I. H. Marshall. Exeter: Paternoster and Grand Rapids: Eerdmans, 1977, 351-365.

681 GOODSPEED, E. J. "Some Greek Notes: IV. Enoch in I Peter 3:19," *JBL* 73 (1954) 91-92.

682 GOURGUES, M. "La première épître de Pierre {1 Peter 3:18-22}," *A la droite de Dieu. Résurrection de Jésus et actualisation de Psaume 110:1 dans le Nouveau Testament*. Ebib. Paris: Gabalda, 1978, 75-87.

683 GRIFFITH THOMAS, W. H. "A Study of 1 Peter 3:19ff," *Expositor* 8,12 (1916) 237-241.

684 GROSS, C. D. "Are the Wives of 1 Peter 3.7 Christians?" *JSNT* 35 (1989) 89-96.

685 GRUDEM, W. [A.] "Christ Preaching through Noah: 1 Peter 3:19-20 in the Light of Dominant Themes in Jewish Literature," *Trinity Journal* 7,2 (Fall, 1986) 3-31.

686 HANSON, A. T. "Salvation Proclaimed: I. Peter 3:18-22," *ExpTim* 93 (1982) 100-105.

687 HEIKEL, I. A. "1. Petr. 3, 4" in "Konjekturen zu einigen Stellen des neutestamentlichen Textes," *TSK* 106 (1934-35) 314-317 (article), 316-317 (section).

688 HIEBERT, D. E. "Selected Studies from 1 Peter. Part 2: The Suffering and Triumphant Christ: An Exposition of 1 Peter 3:18-22," *BSac* 139 (1982) 146-158.

689 HOWARD, G. "The Tetragram and the New Testament [1 Pet 3:14-15]," *JBL* 96 (1977) 63-83.

690 HUNZINGER, C.-H. "Zur Structur der Christus-Hymnen in Phil 2 und 1. Petr 3 {1 Peter 3:18-22}," *Der Ruf Jesu und die Antwort der Gemeinde. Exegetische Untursuchungen. Joachim Jeremias zum 70. Geburtstag gewidmet von seinen Schülern*. Ed. E. Lohse, C. Burchard, and B. Schaller. Göttingen: Vandenhoeck & Ruprecht, 1970, 142-156.

691   HUTTON, J. A. "A Ruling from First Peter {1 Peter 3:1-2}," *Expositor* 8,23 (1922) 420-427.

692   KELLY, W. *The Preaching to the Spirits in Prison: I Peter III. 18-20.* London: Weston, 1900; reprint Denver: Wilson Foundation, 1970.

693   KILEY, M. "Like Sara: The Tale of Terror Behind 1 Peter 3:6," *JBL* 106 (1987) 689-692.

694   KÜCHLER, M. "Sara und 'Herr' Abraham. Die Unterordnung als Schmuck der Frau (1Petr 3,1-6)," *Schweigen, Schmuck und Schleier. Drei neutestamentliche Vorschriften zur Verdrängung der Frauen auf dem Hintergrund einer frauenfeindlichen Exegese des Alten Testaments im antiken Judentum.* NTOA 1. Freiburg, Schweiz: Universitätsverlag and Göttingen, Vandenhoeck & Ruprecht, 1986, 64-70.

695   KVANVIG, H. "Bruken av Noahtradisjonene i 1 Pet 3,20f," *Tidskrift for teologi og kirche* 56 (1985) 81-98.

696   LANDEIRA, J. *Descensus Christi ad inferos in 1 Pet. 3:18-20.* Doctoral dissertation, Pontifical University, Lateranensis, 1966.

697   LECOMTE, P. "Aimer la vie. 1 Pierre 3/10 (Psaume 34/13) {1 Peter 3:8-18}," *ETR* 56 (1981) 288-293.

698   LINDARS, B. "Enoch and Christology {1 Peter 3^{18-22}}," *ExpTim* 92 (1981) 295-299.

699   LUMBY, J. R. "1 Peter III.17," *Expositor* 4,1 (1890) 142-147.

700   LUNDBERG, P. "Le Déluge et la baptême dans I Pierre 3:19 ss.," *La typologie baptismale dans l'ancienne église.* ASNU 10. Leipzig : Lorentz and Upsala: Lundequistska, 1942, 98-116.

701   MANNS, F. "Sara, modèle de la femme obéissante. Étude de l'arrière-plan juif de 1 Pierre 3,5-6," *BeO* 26 (1984) 65-73.

702   MICHAELS, J. R. "Eschatology in I Peter iii. 17," *NTS* 13 (1966-67) 394-401.

703   NIXON, R. E. "The Meaning of 'Baptism' in 1 Peter 3,21," *SE* 4 (TU 102) Berlin: Akademie-Verlag, 1968, 437-441.

704 ODELAND, S. "Kristi praediken for 'aanderne i forvaring' (1 Petr. 3, 19)," *NorTT* 2 (1901) 116-144, 185-229.

705 OGARA, F. "'Quis est qui vobis noceat, si boni simulatores fueritis?' In epistolam (1 Pet. 3,8-15) Domenica V post Pentecoste," *VD* 17 (1937) 161-165.

706 PATTERSON, D. K. "Roles in Marriage: A Study in Submission: 1 Peter 3:1-7," *Theological Educator* 13,2 (Spring 1983) 70-79.

707 PIPER, J. "Hope as the Motivation of Love: I Peter 3:9-12," *NTS* 26 (1979-80) 212-231.

708 REICKE, B. "Die Gnosis der Männer nach I. Ptr 3[7]," *Neutestamentliche Studien für Rudolf Bultmann zu seinem siebzigsten Geburtstag am 20. August 1954.* BZNW 21. Ed. W. Eltester. Berlin: Töpelmann, 1954, [2]1957, 296-304.
Reviews: Barrett, C. K., *JTS* 86 (1955) 267-270; Boismard, M.-É., *RB* 63 (1956) 101-106; Campenhausen, H. von, *ZKG* 66 (1954-1955) 303-305; Grech, P., *Bib* 38 (1957) 214-216.

709 ———. *The Disobedient Spirits and Christian Baptism: A Study of 1 Peter iii. 19 and its Context.* ASNU 13. Ed. A. Fridrichsen. København: Munksgaard, 1946; reprint Ann Arbor, Mich.: University Microfilms, 1979.
Review: Dessain, C. S., *Downside Review* 66 (1948) 212-213.

710 RICHARDS, G. C. "I Pet. iii 21," *JTS* 32 (1931) 77.

711 RIGAUX, B. "1 Tm 3,16; 1 P 3,18-22; He 1,3-4," *Dieu l'a ressuscité. Exégèse et théologie biblique.* Studii biblici franciscani analecta 4. Gembloux: Duculot, 1973, 160-169.

712 RUBINKIEWICZ, R. "'Duchy zamknięte w wiezięniu.' Interpretacja 1 P 3,19 w świetla Hen 10,4.12 ['Die Geister im Gefängnis.' Interpretation von 1. *Petr.* 3,19 im Licht von *Hen.* 10,4.12]," *Roczniki Teologiczno-Kanoniczne* 28 (1981) 77-86.

713 SANDERS, J. T. *The New Testament Christological Hymns: Their Historical Religious Background {1 Peter iii.18-22}.* SNTSMS 15. Cambridge: University Press, 1971, 17-18, 95.
Reviews: Caird, G. B., *ExpTim* 83 (1972) 153; Fuller, R. H., *TS* 32 (1971) 533-535; Herter, T. J., *WTJ* 35 (1973) 342-344; Jones, P. R., *RevExp* 69 (1972) 376-377; de Jonge, M., *NedTTs* 26 (1972) 399-401; Mack, B. L., *JBL* 91 (1972) 431-433; Moule, C. F. D., *JTS* 23 (1972) 212-214; Murphy-O'Connor, J., *RB* 79 (1972) 309-310; O'Rourke, J. J., *BQ* 33 (1971) 605-606; Pearson, B. A., *VC* 28 (1974) 151-153; Per-

rin, N., *JR* 52 (1972) 459-461; Robinson, D. W. B., *Reformed Theological Review* 33 (1974) 59-60; Schille, G., *TLZ* 96 (1971) 915-917; Smith, D. M., *Duke Divinity School Review* 37 (Winter 1972) 53-54.

714   SCHARLEMANN, M. H. "'He Descended into Hell': An Interpretation of 1 Peter 3:18-20," *Concordia Theological Monthly* 27 (1956) 81-94; reprint *Concordia Journal* 15 (1989) 311-322.

715   SCHENK, W. "I. Petr. 3,9," *Der Segen im Neuen Testament. Eine begriffsanalytische Studie.* Theologische Arbeiten XXV. Berlin: Evangelische Verlagsanstalt, 1967, 62-64.

716   SCHLOSSER, J. "1 Pierre, 3,5b-6," *Bib* 64 (1983) 409-410.

717   SCHOLER, D. M. "Woman's Adornment: Some Historical and Hermeneutical Observations on the New Testament Passages {1 Timothy 2:9-10; 1 Peter 3:3-4}," *Daughters of Sarah* 6 (1980) 3-6.

718   SCHWANK, B. "Des éléments mythologiques dans une profession de foi (1 P 3,18-22)," *Assemblées du Seigneur* 14 (1973) 41-44.

719   ──── . "Lecture chrétienne de la Bible (1 P 3,8-15)," *Assemblées du Seigneur* 59 (1956) 16-32.

720   SCHWEIZER, A. *Hinabgefahren zur Hölle als Mythus ohne biblische Begrundung durch Auslegung der Stelle 1 Petr. 3,17-22 nachgewiesen.* Zürich: Schulthness, 1868.

721   SHIMADA, K. "The Christological Credal Formula in 1 Peter 3,18-22—Reconsidered," AJBI 5 (1979) 154-176.

722   SISTI, A. "Testimonianza di virtù cristiane (1 Piet. 3,8-15)," *BeO* 8 (1966) 117-126.

723   SLAUGHTER, J. R. *The Dynamics of Marriage in 1 Peter 3:1-7.* Th.D. dissertation, Dallas Theological Seminary, 1992.

724   SLY, D. I. "1 Peter 3:6b in the Light of Philo and Josephus," *JBL* 110 (1991) 126-129.

725   SMITH, M. L. "1 Peter iii.21: Ἐπερώτημα," *ExpTim* 24 (1912-13) 46-47.

726 SPITTA, F. *Cristi predigt an die Geister (1 Petr. 3:19ff): Ein Beitrag zur neutestamentliche Theologie.* Göttingen: Vandenhoek & Ruprecht, 1890.

727 SYLVA, D. "Translating and Interpreting 1 Peter 3.2," *BT* 34 (1983) 144-147.

728 SYNGE, F. C. "1 Peter 3$^{18-21}$," *ExpTim* 82 (1970-71) 311.

729 TRIPP, D. H. "Eperotema (I Peter 3^{21}): A Liturgist's Note," *ExpTim* 92 (1980-81) 267-270.

730 VANDER BROEK, L. "Women and the Church: Approaching Difficult Passages {1 Peter 3:1-7; 1 Timothy 2:8-15; 1 Corinthians 11:2-16}," *Reformed Review* 38 (1984-85) 225-231.

731 VÖGTLE, A. "Die TKe der Petrusbriefe {1 Peter 3:8; 2 Peter 1:5-7}," *Die Tugend- und Lasterkataloge im Neue Testament. Exegetisch, religions- und formgeschichtlich Untersucht* Neutestamentliche Abhandlungen 16, 4-5. Münster: Aschendorff, 1936, 188-191.

732 WALSH, J. B. *1 Peter 3:18-20: Christ's Descent into Hell.* Ft. Wayne, Ind.: Concordia Theological Seminary Press, 1984.

733 ZEILINGER, F. "Das 'zweite Petrusbekenntnis'. Zur Rezeption von 1 Kor 15,3ff in 1 Petr 3,18-22," *Anfänge der Theologie. ΧΑΡΙΣΤΕΙΟΝ Johannes B. Bauer zum Janner 1987.* Ed. N. Brox, A. Felber, and W. Gombocz. Graz, Wien, and Köln: Styria, 1987, 81-99.

734 ZEZSCHWITZ, C. A. G. von. *Petri Apostole de Christi ad inferas descensu sententia ex loco nobilissimo. 1 ep. 3,19 erata, exacta et epistolae argumentum.* Lipsiae: Ackermanni et Glaseri, 1857.

Chapters 3-4

735 BULLINGER, E. W. "The Spirits in Prison: 1 Pet. III. 17-IV. 6," *Selected Writings.* London: Lamp, 1960, 141-163.

736 CRAMER, J. "Exegetica et critica. Het glossematisch karakter van 1 Petr. 3:19-21 en 4:6," *Nieuwe Bijdragen op het gebied van godgeleerdheid en wijsbegeerte.* Amsterdam: Hirberger, 1891, 7:73-149.

737   CRANFIELD, C. E. B. "The Interpretation of I Peter iii. 19 and iv. 6," *ExpTim* 69 (1957-58) 369-372.

738   DALTON, W. J. *Christ's Proclamation to the Spirits: A Study of 1 Peter 3:18-4:6.* AnBib 23. Rome: Pontifical Biblical Institute, 1965, ²1989.
       Reviews: Elliott, J. H., *CTM* 39 (1968) 276-277; Elliott, J. H., *BTB* 23 (1993) 135; Giet, S., *RevScRel* 40 (1966) 411; Grassi, J. A., *TS* 27 (1966) 103-105; Holtz, T., *TLZ* 92 (1967) 359-360; Martin, R. P., *EvQ* 64 (1992) 283-284; Panella, D. A., *CBQ* 27 (1965) 422-423; Paproth, D., *AusBR* 39 (1991) 79-80; Perry, M. C., *JTS* 17 (1966) 456-458; Proctor, J., *ExpTim* 101 (1990) 215; Scharlemann, M. H., *JBL* 84 (1965) 470-472.

739   ——. "Proclamatio Christi spiritibus facta: inquisitio in textum ex Prima Epistola S. Petri 3:18-4:6," *VD* 42 (1964) 225-240.

740   ——. "The Interpretation of 1 Peter 3,19 and 4,6: Light from 2 Peter," *Bib* 60 (1979) 547-555.

741   DIDERICHSEN, B. "Αλλοτριοεπισκοποσ (1 Pet 4,15) og Επηρωτημα (1 Pet 3,21) belyst ved Plinius dys brev til Trajan (ep x, 96)," *Hilsen til Noack. Fra kolleger og medarbejdere til Bent Noack pa 60-arsdagen den 22. August 1975.* Ed. N. Hyldahl and E. Nielsen. København: Gad, 1975, 35-41.

742   FELTEN, J. "Zur Predigt Jesu an 'die Geister im Gefängnis' 1 Petr. 3,19f und 4,6," *Festschrift der Vereinigung katholischer Theologen „Aurelia."* Bonn, 1926.

743   FRINGS, J. "Zu 1 Petr 3, 19 und 4, 6," *BZ* 17 (1925-26) 75-88.

744   JOHNSON, S. E. "The Preaching to the Dead {1 Peter 3:18-22; 4:5-6}," *JBL* 79 (1960) 48-51.

745   KIRA, K. "1 Pe. 3:18-4:6 et la descente aux enfers du Christ," *JRelS* 34 (1960) 62-76.

746   KNAPP, P. "1 Petri 3, 17 ff und die Höllenfahrt Jesu Christi," *Jahrbücher für Deutsche Theologie* 23 (1878) 177-228.

747   KNOX, J. "Pliny and I Peter: A Note on I Pet 4:14-16 and 3:15," *JBL* 72 (1953) 187-189.

748 KOWALSKI, S. "Le problème de la descente du Christ aux enfers dans la 1 Épître de S. Pierre," *Collactanea theologica Societatis theologorum Poloniae edita* 21 (1949) 42-76.

749 OMANSON, R. "Suffering for Righteousness' Sake ({1 Peter} 3:13-4:11)," *RevExp* 79 (1982) 439-450.

750 PERROT, C. "La descente aux enfers et la prédication aux morts {1 Peter 3:19; 4:6}," *Études sur la première lettre de Pierre: Congrès de l'AFCEB, Paris 1979.* LD 102. Ed. C. Perrot. Paris: Cerf, 1980, 231-246.

751 PINTO DA SILVA, A. "A proposito del significatio di 1 Pt 3,18-4,6," *Salesianum* 46 (1984) 473-486.

752 PLOOIJ, D. "De Descensus in 1 Petrus 3:19 en 4:6," *TT* 47 (1913) 145-162.

753 SALVONI, F. "Cristo andò nello spirito a proclamare agli spiriti in carcere (1 Pietro 3,18-20 e 4,6)," *Ricerche Bibliche e Religiose* 6 (1971) 57-86.

754 SKRADE, C. E. *The Descent of the Servant: A Study of I Peter 3:13-4:6.* Ph.D. dissertation, Union Theological Seminary (Virginia), 1966.

755 SPOTO, D. M. *Christ's Preaching to the Dead: An Exegesis of I Peter 3,19 and 4,6.* Ph.D. dissertation, Fordham University, 1971.

756 STEUER, A. "1 Petr 3, 17-4, 6," *TGl* 30 (1938) 675-678.

757 USTERI, J. M. *Hinabgefahren zur Hölle. Eine Wiedererwägung der Schriftstellen: 1. Petr. 3,18-22 und Kap. 4, Vers 6.* Zürich: Höhr, 1886.

758 VITTI, A. "Descensus Christi ad inferos ex 1 Petri 3, 19-20; 4, 6," *VD* 7 (1927) 111-118.

759 VÖLTER, D. "Bemerkungen zu I. Pe 3 und 4," *ZNW* 9 (1908) 74-77.

Chapter 4

760 BARR, J. "באר‎—μόλις: Prov. xi.31, I Pet. iv.18," *JSS* 20 (1975) 149-164.

761   BAUER, J. B. "Aut maleficus aut alieni speculator (1 Petr 4,15)," *BZ* 22 (1978) 109-115.

762   BISCHOFF, A. "Ἀλλοτρι[ο]επίσκοπος {1 Peter 4:15}," *ZNW* 7 (1906) 271-274.

763   BLAZEN, I. T. "Suffering and Cessation from Sin According to 1 Peter 4:1," *AUSS* 21 (1983) 27-50.

764   DIERKENS, L. H. B. E. "Bladvulling: 'Nauwelijks zalig' (1 Pt 4:18)," *Nieuwe theologische Studien* 2 (1919) 188.

765   ERBES, K. "Noch etwas zum ἀλλοτριοεπίσκοπος 1 Petr 4₁₅," *ZNW* 20 (1921) 249.

766   ——. "Was bedeutet ἀλλοτριοεπίσκοπος 1 Pt 4, 15?" *ZNW* 19 (1919-20) 39-44.

767   GARCÍA DEL MORAL, A. "El sujeto secundario de los dones del Espiritu Santo a la luz de 1 Pedro, IV, 14," *Teología Espirtual* 5 (1961) 443-458.

768   ——. "¿Reposo o morada del Espíritu? {1 Peter 4:14}," *EstBib* 20 (1961) 191-206.

769   ——. "Sentido trinitario de la expressión 'Espíritu de Yavé' de Is. XI, 2 en I Pdr. IV, 14," *EstBib* 20 (1961) 169-206.

770   GARCÍA DEL MORAL, A., and O. P. GARRIDO. *Interpretacion apostolica de Is. XI,2 en I Pdr. IV,14*. Pont. Athen. Intern. Anglicum. Granada, 1962.

771   HIEBERT, D. E. "Selected Studies from 1 Peter. Part 3: Living in the Light of Christ's Return: An Exposition of 1 Peter 4:7-11," *BSac* 139 (1982) 243-254.

772   HOLZMEISTER, U. "'Dei . . . Spiritus super vos requiescat' (1 Petr. 4, 14)," *VD* 9 (1929) 129-131.

773   JOHNSON, D. E. "Fire in God's House: Imagery from Malachi 3 in Peter's Theology of Suffering (1 Pet 4:12-19)," *JETS* 29 (1986) 285-294.

774   KLINE, L. "Ethics for the End Time: An Exegesis of 1 Peter 4:7-11," *ResQ* 7 (1963), 113-123.

775   OGARA, F. "Caritas operit multitudinem peccatorum (1 Pet. 4,7b-11)," *VD* 16 (1936) 129-135.

776   SANDER, E. T. *ΠΥΡΩΣΙΣ and the First Epistle of Peter 4:12.* Ph.D. dissertation, Harvard University, 1967.

777   SCHUTTER, W. L. "1 Peter 4:17, Ezekiel 9:6, and Apocalyptic Hermeneutics," SBLSP 26 (1987) 276-284.

778   SCHWANK, B. "Le « Chrétien Normal » selon le Nouveau Testament (1 P 4,13-16)," *Assemblées du Seigneur* 14 (1973) 26-30.

779   SCHWEIZER, E. "1. Petrus 4,6," *TZ* 8 (1952) 152-154.

780   SISTI, A. "La vita cristiana nell'attesa della Parusia (1 Piet. 4,7-11)," *BeO* 7 (1965) 123-128.

781   SPICQ, C. "Prière, charité, justice . . . et fin des temps (1 P 4:7-11)," *Assemblées du Seigneur* 50 (1966) 15-29.

782   STROBEL, A. "Macht Leiden von Sünde frei? Zur Problematik von 1. Petr. 4,1f," *TZ* 19 (1963) 412-425.

783   WHITE, N. J. D. "Love that Covers Sins {1 Peter 4:8; James 5:20}," *Expositor* (1913-A) 541-547.

Chapters 4-5

784   Borchert, G. L. "The Conduct of Christians in the Face of the 'Fiery Ordeal,' ({1 Pet} 4:12-5:11)," *RevExp* 79 (1982) 451-462.

Chapter 5

785   APPLEGATE, J. K. "The Co-Elect Woman of I Peter {1 Peter 5:13}," *NTS* 38 (1992), 587-604.

786   BROWN, E. F. "1 Peter v 9," *JTS* (1907) 450-452.

787   GAMBA, G. G. "L'Evangelista Marco Segretario—« Interprete » della prima lettera di Pietro? {1 Peter 5:12-13}," *Salesianum* 44 (1982) 61-70.

788 GIAQUINTA, C. "« Vuestra hermandad que está en el mundo » (1 Pe 5,9). Apuntos biblicos para una eclesiogia," *Teologia* 17 (1980) 14ff.

789 GOLEBIEWSKI, E. "Dieu nous console dans l'épreuve (1 P 5,6-11)," *Assemblées du Seigneur* 57 (1965) 17-23.

790 HARRIS, J. R. "The Religious Meaning of 1 Peter V. 5," *Expositor* 8,18 (1919) 131-139.

791 HEUSSI, K. "Der erste Petrusbrief {1 Peter 5:14}," *War Petrus in Rom?* Gotha: Klotz, 1936, 34-39.

792 HIEBERT, D. E. "Selected Studies from 1 Peter. Part 4: Counsel for Christ's Undershephrds: An Exposition of 1 Peter 5:1-4," *BSac* 139 (1982) 330-341.

793 LÖVESTAM, E. "1 Peter 5:6-10," *Spiritual Wakefulness in the New Testament.* Trans. W. F. Salisbury. LUÅ 1,3. Lund: Gleerup, 1963, 60-64.
   Reviews: Boismard, M.-É., *RB* 71 (1964) 635-636; Klijn, A. F. J., *VC* 19 (1965) 190; Kohler, M. E., *TZ* 25 (1969) 135-137; Kugelman, R., *TS* 25 (1964) 85-87; Price, J. L., *JBL* 83 (1964) 90-91; Vanhoye, A., *Bib* 45 (1964) 119.

794 MICHL, J. "Die Presbyter des ersten Petrusbriefes {1 Peter 5:1-4}," *Ortskirche-Weltkirche. Festgabe für Julius Kardinal Döpfner.* Ed. H. Fleckenstein, G. Gruber, G. Schwaiger, and E. Tewes. Würzburg: Echter, 1973, 48-62.

795 NAUCK, W. "Probleme des früchristlichen Amtsverständnisses (I Ptr 5₂f)," *ZNW* 48 (1957) 200-220.

796 OGARA, F. "'Adversarius . . . diabolus tamquam leo rugiens'. In epistolam (1 Pet. 5,6-11) Domenica III post Pentecoste," *VD* 16 (1936) 166-173.

797 PÉREZ, G. and J. F. HERNÁNDEZ. "Epístolas dominicales. Epístola del Domingo III de Pentecostés (I P. 5, 6-11)," *CB* 13 (1956) 144-148.

798 PRETE, B. "L'espressione ἡ ἐν βαβυλῶνι συνεκλεκτή di 1 Pt. 5,13," *Vetera Christianorum* 21 (1984) 335-352.

799 RIGGENBACH, B. "Die Poimenik des Apostels Petrus (I Petri 5,1-5) nach ihrer geschichtlichen und praktischen Bedeutung," *Schweizerische theologische Zeitschrift* 7 (1889) 185-195.

800 SANFORD, M. *Are They Elders? {1 Peter 5:1-4}.* Carlsborg, Wash.: Circa, 1987.

801 SCHWANK, B. "Diabolus tamquam leo rugiens (1 Petr 5,8)," *Erbe und Auftrag* 38 (1962) 15-20.

802 SILVOLA, K. "'Kristuksen kärsimysten todistaja' 1 Pt 5:1," *Teologinen Aikakauskirja* 83 (1978) 416-423.

803 THIEDE, C. P. "Babylon, der andere Ort: Anmerkungen zu 1 Petr 5,13 und Apg 12,17," *Bib* 67 (1986) 532-538; *Das Petrusbild in der neueren Forschung.* Ed. C. P. Thiede. Monographien und Studienbücher. Wuppertal: Brockhaus, 1987, 221-229.

804 VISCHER, W. "Le temps de l'Eglise. 3ᵉ dimanche après la Trinité. 1 Pierre 5: 5b-11. Dieu s'opose aux orgueilleux mais aux humbles il donne grace," *ETR* 27,2 (1952) 19-20.

EXPOSITIONS OF THE ENTIRE BOOK

The works listed here are overall examinations of the form, nature, purpose, significance, structure, themes, or theology of 1 Peter, though a few may concentrate on individual passages. Excluded are commentaries and dictionary and encyclopedia articles, which are collected in other sections.

805   ACHTEMEIER, P. J. "Newborn Babes and Living Stones: Literal and Figurative in 1 Peter," *To Touch the Text: Biblical and Related Studies in Honor of Joseph Fitzmyer, S. J.* Ed. M. P. Horgan and P. J. Kobelski. New York: Crossroad, 1989, 207-236.

806   ADINOLFI, M. "Temi dell'esodo nella 1 Pt," *Studi Biblici Franciscani Liber Annus* 16 (1965-66) 299-317.

807   ———. "Temi dell'Esodo nella 1 Petr.," *San Pietro. Atti della XIX Settimana biblica.* Brescia: Paideia, 1967, 319-336.

808   AMBROGGI, P. de. "Il concetto di salute nei discorsi e nelle lettere di S. Pietro," *La Scuola Cattolica* 6 (1933) 289-303, 431-446.

809   ———. "Il sacerdozio dei fideli secondo la prima di Pietro," *La Scuola Cattolica* 75 (1947) 52-57.

810   ANDRIANOPOLI, L. *Il misterio di Gesù nelle lettere di San Pietro.* Torino: Società editrice internationale, 1935.

811   ANTONIAZZI, A. "A saida é . . .ficar. O conflito dos critâos com sociedade segundo a primeira epístola de Pedro," *Estudos Baianos* 15 (1987) 57ff.

812   ANTONIOTTI, L.-M. "Structure littéraire et sens de la première épître de Pierre," *RevThom* 85 (1985) 533-560.

813   ASHCRAFT, M. "Theological Themes in I Peter," *Theological Educator* 13,1 (Fall 1982) 55-62.

814   BALCH, D. L. "Hellenization/Aculturation in 1 Peter," *Perspectives on First Peter.* Ed. C. H. Talbert. National Asso-

ciation of Baptist Professors of Religion Special Study Series 9. Macon, Ga.: Mercer University Press, 1986, 79-101.

815 BALDWIN, H. A. *The Fisherman of Galilee.* New York, Chicago, London, and Edinburgh: Revell, 1923.

816 BARKER, F. M. *A Living Hope: Guidelines for God's People from I Peter.* Philadelphia: Great Commission, 1987.

817 BARR, A. "Submission Ethic in the First Epistle of Peter," *Hartford Quarterly* 2 (1961-62) 27-33.

818 BAUMEISTER, T. "Der 1. Petrusbrief," *Die Anfänge der Theologie des Martyriums.* Münsterische Beiträge zur Theologie 45. Münster: Aschendorff, 1980, 204-209.

819 BEARE, F. W. "The Teaching of First Peter," *ATR* 27 (1945) 284-296.

820 BIEDER, W. *Grund und Kraft der Mission nach dem I. Petrusbrief.* Theologische Studien 29. Zollikon-Zürich: Evangelischer Verlag, 1950.

821 BISHOP, E. F. F. "Palestine and Islam in the Letters of Saint Peter," *Apostles of Palestine: The Local Background to the New Testament Church.* London: Lutterworth Press, 1958, 203-224.

822 BOISMARD, M.-É. Quatre hymnes baptismales dans la première épître de Pierre {I Petr I, 3-5; 2, 22-25; 3, 18-22; 5, 5-9}. LD 30. Paris: Cerf, 1961.
    Reviews: Benoit, P., *RB* 70 (1963) 133-135; Maly, E. H., *TS* 23 (1962) 290-292; Michl, J., *BZ* 9 (1965) 145-147.

823 BOJORGE, H. "Fundamentación y normas de la conducta cristiana según la 1ª carta de Pedro," *RevistB* 37 (1975) 269-277.

824 BOLKESTEIN, M. H. "De Kerk in haar vreemdelingschap volgens de eerste brief van Petrus," *Nieuwe Theologische Studiën* 25 (1942) 181-194.

825 ———. "Het tijdbegrip in de eerste brief van Petrus," *Woord en Wereld: Opgedragen aan Prof. Dr. K. H. Miskotte naar aanleiding von zijn aftreden als kerkelijk hoogleraar te Leiden.* Ed. H. C. Touw. Amsterdam: De Arbeiderspers, 1961, 140-149.

826   BORCHERT, G. L. "The Conduct of Christians in the Face of the 'Fiery Ordeal' ({1 Peter} 4:12-5:11)," *RevExp* 79 (1982) 451-462.

827   BORNEMANN, W. "Der erste Petrusbrief—eine Taufrede des Silvanus?" *ZNW* 19 (1919-20) 143-165.

828   BOSETTI, E. *Il pastore. Cristo e la chiesa nella prima lettera di Pietro.* Supplementi alla Rivista Biblica 21. Bologna: Dehoniane, 1990.

829   ——. Ποιμὴν καὶ επίσκοπος {sic}*: The Image of the Shepherd in First Peter (2,18-25; 5,1-4).* Doctoral dissertation, Pontificia Universitas Gregoriana, 1989.

830   BOTHA, J. "Christians and Society in 1 Peter: Critical Solidarity," *Scriptura* 24 (1988) 27-37.

831   BOVON, F. "Foi chrétienne et religion populaire dans la première épître de Pierre," *ETR* 53 (1978) 25-41.

832   BRANDT, W. "Wandel als Zeugnis nach dem 1. Petrusbrief," *Verbum Dei manet in aeternum. Eine Festschrift für Prof. D. Otto Schmitz zu seinem siebzigsten Geburtstag am 16. Juni 1953.* Ed. W. Foerster. Witten: Luther-Verlag, 1953, 10-25.

833   BROWN, R. E. "The Petrine Heritage in I Peter: The Church as the people of God," *The Church the Apostles Left Behind.* New York and Ramsey, N.J.: Paulist and London: Chapman, 1984, 75-83.

834   BROX, N. "'Sara zum Beispiel . . .'; Israel im 1. Petrusbrief," *Kontinuität und Einheit. Für Franz Mussner.* Ed. P.-G. Müller and W. Stenger. Freiburg, Basel, and Wien: Herder, 1981, 484-493.

835   ——. "Situation und Sprache der Minderheit im ersten Petrusbrief," *Kairos* 19 (1977) 1-13.

836   ——. "Zur pseudepigraphischen Rahmung des ersten Petrusbriefes," *BZ* 19 (1975) 78-96.

837   BRUNI, G. "La communita christiana nella prima lettera di Pietro," *Servitum* 7 (1973) 278-286.

838   BRUNK, G. R. "The Missionary Stance of the Church in 1 Peter," *Mission Focus: Current Issues*. Ed. W. R. Shenk. Scottdale, Pa.: Herald, 1980, 70-81.

839   BRUNK, G. R. III. "The Missionary Stance of the Church in 1 Peter," *Mission-Focus* 6 (1978) 1-4.

840   BULTMANN, R. K. "Bekenntnis- und Liedfragmente im ersten Petrusbrief," *ConNT* 11 (1947) 1-14; *Exigetica. Aufsätze zur Erforschung des Neuen Testaments*. Ed. E. Dinkler. Tübingen: Mohr-Siebeck, 1967, 285-297.

841   BUSE, S. I. "Baptism in Other New Testament Writings," *Christian Baptism: A Fresh Attempt to Understand the Rite in Terms of Scripture, History, and Theology*. Ed. A. Gilmore. London: Lutterworth, 1959, 170-186.

842   CANNON, A. *1 Peter: Encounter in Christian Living: A Study in Christian Living for All Youth*. Nashville: Convention, 1986.

843   CARRIER, R. R. *The Petrine Doctrines of the Word of God*. Ph.D. dissertation, Bob Jones University, 1964.

844   CERVANTES GABARRON, J. *The Suffering of Christ in the First Epistle of Peter: The Literary and Theological Centre of the Epistle*. dissertation, Pontificia Universitas Gregoriana, 1989.

845   CHEVALLIER, M.-A. "1 Pierre 1/1 à 2/10. Structure littéraire et conséquences exégétiques," *RHPR* 51 (1971) 129-142.

846   ———. "Comment lire 1 Pierre aujourd'hui la première épître de Pierre. De l'actualisation interne à l'Écriture à l'actualisation contemporaine," *Études sur la première lettre de Pierre. Congrès de l'ACFEB, Paris 1979*. Ed. C. Perrot. Paris: Cerf, 1980, 129-152.

847   ———. "Condition et vocation des chrétiens en diaspora: remarques exégétiques sur la 1re Épître de Pierre," *RevScRel* 48 (1974) 387-400.

848   ———."Israël et l'Église selon la Première Épître de Pierre," *Paganisme, Judaïsme, Christianisme: Influences et affrontemonts dans le monde antique. Mélanges offerts à Marcel Simon*. Paris: de Boccard, 1978, 117-130.

849 CHIN, M. "A Heavenly Home for the Homeless: Aliens and Strangers in 1 Peter," *TynBul* 42 (1991) 96-112.

850 CIPRIANI, S. "« Evangelizzazione » e « missione » nella prima lettera di Pietro," *Richerche storico bibliche* 2 (1990) 125-138.

851 ———. "L'unitarietà dei disegno della storia della salvezza nella I Lettera di S. Pietro," *RevistB* 14 (1966) 385-406.

852 ———. "Sacerdozio « comune » e « ministeriale » nella 1ª lettera di Pietro," *Lateranum* 47 (1981) 31ff.

853 ———. "Unitarietà dei disegno della storia della salvezza nella 1ª Lettera di Pietro," *Jalones de la historia de la salvación en el Antiguo y Nuevo Testamento*. Madrid: Suarez, 2:201-217.

854 CLARK, R. *Messages for Today from Simon Peter for Today's Church: 10 Studies in the First Letter of Peter*. Fortitude Valley: PCE, 1990.

855 CLARK, S. D. "Persecution and the Christian Faith," *Theological Educator* 13,1 (Fall 1982) 72-82.

856 CLEMEN, C. "Die Einheitlichkeit des 1. Petrusbriefes," *TSK* 78 (1905) 619-628.

857 COMBRINK, H. J. B. "The Structure of 1 Peter," *Neot* 9: *Essays on the General Epistles of the New Testament* (1975, ²1980) 34-63.

858 COTHENET, É. "La portée salvifique de la résurrection du Christ d'après I Pierre," *La pâque du Christ, mystère de salut. Mélanges offerts au P. F.-X. Durrwell pour son 70ᵉ annniversaire*. LD 112. Ed. M. Benzerath, A. Schmid, and J. Guillet. Paris: Cerf, 1982, 249-262.

859 ———. "La première Épître de Pierre; l'Épître de Jacques," *Le Ministère et les ministères selon le Nouveau Testament. Dossier exégétique et réflexion théologique*. Ed. J. Delorme. Paris: Seuil, 1974, 138-154.

860 ———. "Le réalisme de l'espérance chrétienne selon I Pierre," *NTS* 27 (1980-81) 564-572.

861 ———. "Liturgie et vie chrétienne d'après 1 Pierre," *Conférences Saint-Serge* 25 (1979) 97-113.

862   CROSS, F. L. *1 Peter: A Paschal Liturgy*. London: Mow-
       bray, 1954, [2]1957.

863   DACQUINO, P. "Il sacerdozio del nuovo popolo di Dio e la
       prima lettera di Pietro," *San Pietro. Atti della XIX settimana
       biblica*. Brescia: Paideia, 1967, 291-317.

864   DALTON, W. J. "The Church in I Peter," *Jerusalem: Seat of
       Theology*. Ed. D. Burrell, P. Du Brul, and W. Dalton. Jerusa-
       lem: Ecumenical Institute for Theological Research, 1982,
       79-91.

865   DAVIDSON, A. K. *The Petrine Conception of the Christian
       Life*. Doctoral dissertation, Temple University, 1940.

866   DAVIDSON, J. A. "The Congregation: Priest and Servant {1
       Peter 1,9; 5,2}," *ExpTim* 85 (1973-74) 336-337.

867   DAVIES, P. E. "Primitive Christology in 1 Peter," *Festschrift
       to Honor F. Wilbur Gingrich*. Ed. E. H. Barth and R. E.
       Cocroft. Leiden: Brill, 1972, 115-122.

868   DEERING, R. F. *The Humiliation-Exaltation Motif in I Peter*.
       Th.D. dissertation, The Southern Baptist Theological Semi-
       nary, 1961.

869   DELLING, G. "Der Bezug der christlichen Existenz auf das
       Heilshandeln Gottes nach dem ersten Petrusbrief," *Neues
       Testament und christliche Existenz. Festschrift für Herbert
       Braun zum 70. Geburtstag am 4. Mai 1973*. Ed. H. D. Betz
       and L. Schottroff. Tübingen: Mohr-Siebeck, 1973, 95-113.

870   ———. "Taufe und Taufmotive im I. Petrusbrief, im Johannes-
       Evangelium und im I. Johannesbrief," *Die Taufe im Neuen
       Testament*. Berlin: Evangelische Verlaganstalt, 1963, 82-96.

871   DIJKMAN, J. H. L. "1 Peter: A Later Pastoral Stratum?" *NTS*
       33 (1987) 265-271.

872   ———. *The Socio-Religious Condition of the Recipients of I
       Peter: An Attempt to Solve the Problems of Date, Authorship
       and Addressees of the Letter*. Ph.D. dissertation, University
       of the Witwatersrand, 1984.

873   DIXON, M. C. *Discipleship in I Peter as a Model for Contex-
       tual Mission*. Ph.D. dissertation, The Southern Baptist
       Theological Seminary, 1989.

874   DURKEN, D. "First Peter," *Worship* 29 (1955) 382-384.

875   ELLIOTT, J. H. "1 Peter, Its Situation and Strategy: A Discussion with David Balch," *Perspectives on First Peter*. Ed. C. H. Talbert. National Association of Baptist Professors of Religion Special Studies Series 9. Macon, Ga.: Mercer University Press, 1986, 61-78.

876   ——. *A Home for the Homeless: A Sociological Exegesis of 1 Peter, Its Situation and Strategy*. Philadelphia: Fortress, 1981 and London: SCM, 1982; *A Home for the Homeless: A Social Scientific Criticism of I Peter, Its Situation and Strategy, With a New Introduction*. Minneapolis: Fortress, ²1990.
Reviews: Achtemeier, P. J., *JBL* 103 (1984) 130-133; Best, E., *SJT* 36 (1983) 554-555; Burnett, F., *CBQ* 55 (1993) 364-366; Chevallier, M. A., *ETR* 58 (1983) 117-18; Clark, N., *The Baptist Quarterly* 29 (1982) 330-331; Danker, F. W., *Int* 37 (1983) 84-88; Dubois, J. D., *ASSR* 31 (n.d.; 62 No. 2) 266-267; Edwards, O. C., *ATR* 65 (1983) 431-448; Furnish, V. P., *PSTJ* 36 (1983) 61-62; Guthrie, D., *EvQ* 55 (1983) 236-237; Harrington, D. J., *TS* 43 (1982) 358; Harris, O. G., *Lexington Theological Quarterly* 19 (1984) 110-111; Hemer, C. J., *JSNT* 24 (1985) 120-123; Holmberg, B., *STK* 62 (1986) 43-45; Karris, R. J., *Horizons* 9 (1982) 352; Klauck, H. J., *BZ* 26 (1982) 290-292; Kraemer, R. S., *The Second Century* 4 (1985) 185-187; Laws, S., *Theology* 86 (1983) 64-66; Marrow, S. B., *CBQ* 45 (1983) 483-484; Maynard-Reid, P. U., *AUSS* 23 (1985) 203-205; McKnight, E. V., *Dialog* 22 (1983) 152-154; Moxnes, H., *NorTT* 84 (1983) 195-196; Olsson, B., *SEÅ* 49 (1984) 89-108; Omanson, R. L., *BT* 33 (1982) 344-345; Osborne, G. R., *Theological Students Fellowship Bulletin* 7,5 (1984) 21; Penna, R., *Greg* 66 (1985) 342-343; Porter, S. E., *JSNT* 51 (1993) 126; Rhoads, D., *WW* 4 (1984) 97-98; Rodd, C. S., *ExpTim* 94 (1983) 161-162; Tidball, D. J., *EvQ* 55 (1983) 237-239; Walton, W. J., *Bib* 64 (1983) 442-444; Wire, A., *RelSRev* 10 (1984) 209-216; Wolff, C., *TLZ* 109 (1984) 443-445.

877   ——. "Death of a Slogan: From Royal Priests to Celebrating Community," *Una Sancta* 25,3 (Michaelmas 1968) 18-31.

878   ——. "Social-Scientific Criticism of a Biblical Text: 1 Peter as an Example," *What is Social-Scientific Criticism?* Guides to Biblical Scholarship, New Testament Series. Ed. D. O. Via. Minneapolis: Fortress, 1993.

879   ELLUL, D. "Un exemple de cheminement rhétorique: 1 Pierre," *RHPR* 70 (1990) 17-34.

880   ERICSON, N. R. "Interpreting the Petrine Literature," *The Literature and Meaning of Scripture*. Ed. M. A. Inch (Gen.

Ed.) and C. Hassell (Consulting Ed.). Grand Rapids: Baker, 1981, 243-266.

881 FARRAR, F. W. "The First Epistle of St. Peter," *The Early Days of Christianity*. London: Cassell, Petter, Galpin, 1882 and New York: Funk and Wagnalls, 1883, 83-97.

882 FELDMEIER, R. *Die Christen als Fremde. Die Metapher der Fremde in der antiken Welt, im Urchristentum und im 1. Petrusbrief.* Habilitationschrift, Universität Tübingen, 1991.

883 ———. *Die Christen als Fremde. Die Metapher der Fremde in der antiken Welt, im Urchristentum und im 1. Petrusbrief.* WUNT 64. Tübingen: Mohr-Siebeck, 1992.

884 FERRIN, H. W. *"Strengthen Thy Brethren": Pointers from Peter for Power in Christian Living: A Devotional Exposition of the First Epistle of Peter.* Grand Rapids: Zondervan, 1942.

885 FILSON, F. V. "Partakers with Christ: Suffering in First Peter," *Int* 9 (1955) 400-412.

886 FINKBINER, F. L. *Church and State from Paul to 1 Peter.* Th.D. dissertation, Southern California School of Theology, 1960.

887 FRANSEN, I. "Une homélie chrétienne (la premiére épître de Pierre)," *Bible et Vie Chrétienne* 31 (1960) 28-38.

888 FRATTALONE, R. "Antropologia naturale e soprannaturale nella prima lettera di San Pietro," *Studia Moralia* 5 (1967) 41-111.

889 ———. *Fondamenti dottrinali dell'agire morale christiano nella prima lettera di S. Pietro.* Doctoral dissertation, Academiae Alfonsianae, 1966.

890 FREDERICK, S. C. *The Theme of Obedience in the First Epistle of Peter.* Ph.D. dissertation, Duke University, 1975; Ann Arbor: University Microfilms, 1978.

891 GALBIATI, E. "L'escatologia delle lettere di S. Pietro," *San Pietro: Atti della XIX settimana biblica.* Brescia: Paideia, 1967, 413-423.

892   ———. "L'eschatologia delle lettere di S. Pietro," *Scritti minori* 1. Brescia: Paideia, 1979, 259-269.

893   GAUDEMET, J. "Ersten Petrusbrief" in „Familie I (Familienrecht)," *RAC* 7:286-358.

894   GENNRICH, P. "Der 1. Petrusbrief," *Die Lehre von der Wiedergeburt, die christliche Zentrallehre in dogmengeschichtlicher und religionsgeschichtlicher Beleuchtung.* Leipzig: Deichert, 1907, 42-46.

895   GEYSER, A. S. "Die Name van Petrus en I Petrus," *Hervormde teologiese studies* 15 (1959) 92-100.

896   GINGRICH, R. E. *Outline and Analysis of the First Epistle of Peter.* Th.D. dissertation, Grace Theological Seminary, 1937.

897   GOLDSTEIN, H. *Das Gemeindeverständnis des Ersten Petrusbriefs. Exegetische Untersuchungen zur Theologie der Gemeinde im 1 Pt.* Dissertation, Münster, 1973.

898   ———. "Die Kirche als Schar derer, die ihrem leidenden Hernn mit dem Ziel der Gottesgemeinshaft nachfolgen. Zum Gemeindeverständnis von 1 Petr 2:21-25 und 3:18-22," *Bibel und Leben* 15 (1974) 38-54.

899   ———. *Paulinische Gemeinde im Ersten Petrusbrief.* SBS 80. Stuttgart: KBW, 1975.
        Review: Des Places, D., *Bib* 57 (1976) 589-590.

900   GONZÁLEZ, C. G., and J. L. GONZÁLEZ. *A Faith More Precious than Gold: A Study of 1 Peter* (Braille). n.p: John Milton Society for the Blind, 1989.

901   GOPPELT, L. "Der Staat in der Sicht des Neuen Testaments," *Christologie und Ethik. Aufsätze zum Neuen Testament.* Göttingen: Vandenhoeck & Ruprecht, 1968, 190-207.
        Review: Delling, G., *TZ* 94 (1969) 667-668.

902   ———. "Mission ou Révolution? La responsibilité du chrétien dans la société d'après la première épître de Pierre," *Positions Luthériennes* (1969) 202-216.

903   ———. "Prinzipien neutestamentlicher Sozialethik nach dem I. Petrusbrief," *Neues Testament und Geschichte. Historisches Geschehen und Deutung im Neuen Testament. Oscar Cullmann zum 70. Geburtstag.* Ed. H. Baltensweiler and B.

Reicke. Zurich: Theologischer Verlag and Tübingen: Mohr-Siebeck, 1972, 285-296.

904   GREEN, G. L. *Theology and Ethics in 1 Peter*. Ph.D. thesis, Aberdeen University, 1980.

905   GRIFFITHS, C., and S. HATHWAY. *Don't Give In: Discovering the Strength to Keep Going: Explorations in 1 Peter*. Serendipity Bible Studies for Small Groups, Discipleship Series. London: Scripture Union, 1986.

906   GRYGLEWICZ, F. "Pierwotna liturgia chrztu św. jako zrodlo pierwszego listu św. Piotra [Eine ursprüngliche Taufliturgie als Quelle des 1. Briefes des Hl. Petrus]," *Ruch Biblijny i Liturgiczny* 11 (1958) 206-210.

907   GUTHRIE, D. "Petrine Theology," *New Dictionary of Theology*. Ed. S. B. Ferguson and D. F. Wright. Downers Grove: InterVarsity and Leicester: Inter-Varsity, 1988, 507-508.

908   HALLENCREUTZ, C. F. "Ett Folk pa Väg," *Svensk Missionstidskrift* 66 (1978) 13-29.

909   HALL, R. "For to This You Have Been Called: The Cross and Suffering in 1 Peter," *Restoration Quarterly* 19 (1976) 137-147.

910   HAMBLIN, R. L. *Triumphant Strangers: A Contemporary Look at First Peter*. Nashville: Broadman, 1982.
         Review: Omanson, R. L., *RevExp* 80 (1983) 138-139.

911   HEUSSI, K. "Der erste Petrusbrief," *Die römische Petrustradition in kritischer Sicht*. Tübingen: Mohr-Siebeck, 1955.

912   HILL, D. "On Suffering and Baptism in 1 Peter," *NovT* 18 (1976) 181-189.

913   ———. "'To Offer Spiritual Sacrifices . . .' (1 Peter 2:5): Liturgical Formulations and Christian Paraenesis in 1 Peter," *JSNT* 16 (1982) 45-63.

914   HILLYER, N. "'Rock-Stone' Imagery in 1 Peter," *TynBul* 22 (1971) 58-81.

915   HOCKING, D. *First Peter: Your Personal Study Guide*. La Mirada, Cal.: Biola University, 1982.

916   HOLDSWORTH, J. "The Sufferings in 1 Peter and 'Missionary Apocalyptic,'" *Studia Biblica* 1978. JSNTSup 3. Ed. E. A. Livingstone. Sheffield: JSOT Press, 1980, 3:225-232.

917   HOOPS, M. H. "First Peter: A Community at Witness," *Trinity Seminary Review* 7,2 (Fall 1985) 30-39.

918   ———. "First Peter: A Renewed Appreciation (A Review of Selected Issues in Petrine Studies)," *Trinity Seminary Review* 5,2 (Fall 1983), 3-14.

919   HUGHS, H. D. *A Developmental Approach to the Christology of the Petrine Canonical Tradition.* Ph.D. dissertation, Baylor University, 1971, Chapter 4.

920   JANSE, W. "De verhouding tussen 'vlees' en 'geest' in 1 Petrus," *Theologia Reformata* 25 (1982), 244ff; 26 (1983), 13ff.

921   JOHNSTON, G. "The Will of God: V. In I Peter and I John," *ExpTim* 72 (1960-61) 237-240.

922   JONES, R. B. "Christian Behavior Under Fire (The First Epistle of Peter)," *RevExp* 46 (1949) 56-66.

923   JONSEN, A. R. "The Moral Theology of the First Epistle of St. Peter," *ScEccl* 16 (1964) 93-105.

924   KAYALAPARAMPIL, T. "Christian Suffering in 1 Peter," *Biblehashyam* 3 (1977) 7-19.

925   KEARNS, W. P. *Petrine Christology and Its Relation to the Old Testament.* Ph.D. dissertation, Bob Jones University, 1960.

926   KENDALL, D. W. "The Christian's Vocation: The Call to Holiness According to the First Epistle of Peter," *The Asbury Seminarian* 40 (1985) 3-12.

927   KENNARD, D. W. "Petrine Redemption: Its Meaning and Extent," *JETS* 30 (1987) 399-405.

928   KIRK, G. E. "Endurance in Suffering in 1 Peter," *BSac* 138 (1981) 46-56.

929   KIRKPATRICK, W. D. "The Theology of First Peter," *Southwestern Journal of Theology* 25,1 (Fall 1982) 58-81.

930 KLEIN, G. "Der erste Petrusbrief," *Die zwölf Apostel. Ursprung und Gehalt einer Idee.* FRLANT 59. Göttingen: Vandenhoeck & Ruprecht, 1961, 83-84.
Reviews: Boismard, M.-É., *RB* 69 (1962) 617-618; Lohse, E., *ZKG* 73 (1962) 138-139; Schulze-Kadelbach, G., *TLZ* 87 (1962) 927-929.

931 KÖGEL, J. *Die Gedankeneinheit des ersten Briefes Petri. Ein Beitag zur neutestamentlichen Theologie.* BFCT 6,5-7. Gütersloh: Bertelsmann, 1902.

932 KOHLER, M. E. "La communauté des chrétiens selon la première Épître de Pierre," *RTP* 114 (1982) 1-21.

933 KOSALA, K. C. P. *Taufverständnis und Theologie im Ersten Petrusbrief.* Dissertation, Kiel, 1985.

934 KRAFFT, E. "Christologie und Anthropologie im 1. Petrusbrief," *EvT* 10 (1950-51) 120-126.

935 LAMAU, M.-L. "Exhortation aux esclaves et hymne au Christ souffrant dans la « Premère Épître de Pierre »," *MScRel* 43 (1986) 121-143.

936 LAND, D. T. *The Concept of Christian Hope in I Peter.* Ph.D dissertation, Southwestern Baptist Theological Seminary, 1981.

937 LASH, C. J. A. "Fashionable Sports: Hymn Hunting in 1 Peter," *SE* 7. Berlin: Akademie-Verlag, 1982, 293-297.

938 LEANEY, A. R. C. "I Peter and the Passover: An Interpretation," *NTS* 10 (1963-64) 238-251.

939 LEA, T. D. "The Priesthood of All Christians According to the New Testament," *Southwestern Journal of Theology* 30,2 (Spring 1988) 15-21.

940 LEPELLEY, C. "Le Contexte historique de la première lettre de Pierre. Essai d'interprétation," *Études sur la première lettre de Pierre. Congrès de l'ACFEB, Paris 1979.* LD 102. Ed. C. Perrot. Paris: Cerf, 1980, 43-64.

941 LEWIS, J. M. *The Christology of the First Epistle of Peter.* Ph.D. dissertation, Southwestern Baptist Theological Seminary, 1952.

942   LIPPERT, P. "Der erste Petrusbrief," *Leben als Zeugnis. Die werbende Kraft christlicher Lebensführung nach dem Kirchenverständnis neutestamentlicher Briefe.* SBM 4. Stuttgart: Katholisches Bibelwerk, 1968, 61-87.
Reviews: Du Toit, A. P., *TZ* 27 (1971) 57-58; Kugelman, R., *CBQ* 32 (1970) 139-140; Murphy-O'Connor, J., *RB* 77 (1970) 130-132; Roloff, J., *TLZ* 95 (1970) 352-354.

943   ———. "Leben als Zeugnis. Ein Beitrag des ersten Petrusbriefes zur pastoral-theologischen Problamatik der Gegenwart," *Studia Moralia* 3 (1965) 226-268.

944   LOHSE, E. "Paränese und Kerygma im ersten Petrusbrief," *ZNW* 45 (1954) 68-89; *Die Einheit des Neuen Testaments. Exegetische Studien zur Theologie des Neuen Testaments.* Göttingen: Vandenhoeck & Ruprecht, 1973, 307-328.

945   ———. "Paranesis and Kerygma in 1 Peter," trans. J. Steely, *Perspectives on First Peter.* Ed. C. H. Talbert. National Association of Baptist Professers of Religion Special Studies Series 9. Macon, Ga: Mercer University Press, 1986, 37-59.

946   LOSADA, D. "Sufrir por el nombre de Christiano en la Primera Carta de Pedro," *RevistB* 42 (1980) 85-101.

947   MALTE, E. C. "The message of the First Epistle of Peter for our day," *CTM* 20 (1949) 728-774.

948   MANKE, H. *Leiden und Herrlichkeit. Eine Studie zur Christologie des 1. Petrusbriefs.* Dissertation, Münster, 1975.

949   MARTELET, G. "'Das Lamm, erwält vor Grundlegung der Welt {1 Peter 1:17-20},'" *Internationale katholische Zeitschrift 'Communio'* 9 (1980) 36-44.

950   MARTIN, T. W. *Metaphor and Composition in 1 Peter.* Ph.D. dissertation, University of Chicago, 1990.

951   ———. *Metaphor and Composition in 1 Peter.* SBLDS 131. Atlanta, Ga.: Scholars Press, 1992.
Reviews: Bechtler, S. R., *Princeton Seminary Bulletin* 14 (1993) 81-83; Michaels, J. R., *JBL* 112 (1993) 358-360.

952   McCAUGHEY, J. D. "On Re-Reading 1 Peter," *AusBR* 31 (1983) 33-44.

953 ———. "Three 'Persecution Documents' of the New Testament {Mark, Revelation, 1 Peter}," *AusBR* 17 (1969) 27-40.

954 McKELVEY, R. J. "The New Temple in 1 Peter and Miscellaneous Texts," *The Church in the New Testament*. Oxford Theological Monographs. Oxford and London: University Press, 1969, 125-139.

955 MEECHAM, H. G. "The First Epistle of St. Peter," *ExpTim* 48 (1936-37) 22-24.

956 MEUSE, S. "The Family: Old Covenant/New Covenant," *Searching Together* 14,2 (Summer 1985) 7-17.

957 MEYER, F. B. *Tried by Fire: Expositions of the First Epistle of Peter*. London: Morgan and Scott and New York, Chicago, and Toronto: Revell, n.d.

958 MICHAELS, J. R. *1 Peter*. Word Biblical Themes. Dallas, London, Sydney, and Singapore: Word, 1989.

959 ———. "Jewish and Christian Apocalyptic Letters: 1 Peter, Revelation, and 2 Baruch 78-87," SBLSP 26 (1987) 268-275.

960 MILLAUER, H. *Leiden als Gnade. Eine traditionsgeschichtliche Untersuchung zur Leidenstheologie des ersten Petrusbriefes*. Europäische Hochschulschriften 23,56. Bern: Herbert Lang and Frankfurt: Peter Lang, 1976.

961 MILLER, D. G. "Deliverance and Destiny: Salvation in First Peter," *Int* 9 (1955) 413-425.

962 MORRIS, L. "The First Epistle General of Peter," *The Cross in the New Testament*. Exeter: Paternoster and Grand Rapids: Eerdmans, 1965, 316-333.

963 MOULE, C. F. D. "The Nature and Purpose of I Peter," *NTS* 3 (1956-57) 1-11.

964 MUÑOZ LEÓN, D. "Las referencias a Ex 19,6 en la carta 1.ª de San Pedro," in "Un reino de sacerdotes y una nación santa (Ex 19,6)," *EstBib* 37 (1978) 170-182 (section), 149-212 (article).

965 MUNRO, W. *Authority in Paul and Peter: The Identification of a Pastoral Stratum in the Pauline Corpus and 1 Peter*. SNTSMS 45. Cambridge: University Press, 1983.

Reviews: Bruce, F. F., *HeyJ* 27 (1986) 190-191; Court, J. M., *ExpTim* 94 (1983) 345; Holmes, M., *Trinity Journal* 5 (1984) 192-195; Merk, O., *TLZ* 114 (1989) 278-280; Trevijano, R., *Salmanticensis* 32 (1985) 247-250; Ziesler, J. A., *JTS* 36 (1985) 213-214.

966   NEUGEBAUER, F.   "Zur Deutung und Bedeutung des 1. Petrusbriefes," *NTS* 26 (1979-80) 61-86; "Zur Deutung und Bedeutung des 1. Petrusbriefes," *Das Petrusbild in der neueren Forschung*. Ed. C. P. Thiede. Wuppertal: Brockhaus, 1987, 109-144.

967   NEYREY, J. H. "First Peter and Converts," *The Bible Today* 22 (1984) 13-18.

968   OLSON, V. S. *The Atonement in 1 Peter*. Th.D. dissertation, Union Theological Seminary (Virginia), 1979.

969   OLSSON, B. "Mission à la Lukas, Johannes och Petrus," *SEÅ* 51-52 (1986) 180-191.

970   OSBORNE, T. P. *Christian Suffering in the First Epistle of Peter*. S.T.D. dissertation, Université de Louvain, 1981.

971   PAPA, B. "Spirito Santo e battesimo nella Prima Lettera di Pietro," *Nicolaus* 8 (1980), 295ff.

972   PEAK, I. H. *Moral Issues in 1 Peter: Resources for Daily Living: A Study Guide*. Jefferson City, Mo.: Department of Christian Moral Concerns, Missouri Baptist Convention, 1982.

973   PERDELWITZ, R. *Die Mysterienreligion und das Problem des I. Petrusbriefes. Ein literarischer und religionsgeschichtlicher Versuch*. Religiongeschichtliche Versuche und Vorarbeiten 11,3. Giessen: Töpelmann, 1911.

974   PHILIPPS, K. *Kirche in der Gesellschaft nach dem 1. Petrusbrief*. Gütersloh: Mohn, 1971.

975   PHILLIPS, M. A. "Suffering in the General Epistles and Hebrews: 1 Peter," *A Theological Analysis of Suffering as a Christian Lifestyle in the New Testament*. Ph.D. dissertation, Southern Baptist Theological Seminary, 1978, 159-173, 195.

976   PIETRANTONIO, R. "Sacerdocio corporativo y ministereos eclesiales en la 1. Carta de Pedro," *RevistB* 42 (1980) 195-208.

977   PIPER, J. "Rom 12:17 and I Pt 3:9" and "I Peter," *'Love Your Enemies': Jesus' Love Command in the Synoptic Gospels and in the Early Christian Paraenesis: A History of the Tradition and an Interpretation of Its Uses*. SNTSMS 38. Cambridge: University Press, 1979, 14-17, 19-128.

978   PLÜMACHER, E. "1. Petrusbrief," *Identitätsverlust und Identitätsgewinn. Studien zum Verhältnis von kaiserzeitlicher Stadt und frühem Christentum*. Biblisch-theologische Studien 11. Neukirchen-Vluyn: Neukirchener Verlag, 1987, 39-44.

979   PRICE, J. J. H. *Submission-Humility in 1 Peter: An Exegetical Study*. Ph.D. dissertation, Vanderbilt University, 1977.

980   PROSTMEIER, F.-R. *Handlungsmodelle im ersten Petrusbrief.* FB 63. Würzburg: Echter, 1990.
       Review: Elliott, J. H., *JBL* 111 (1992) 553-555.

981   PRYOR, J. W. "First Peter and the New Covenant," *The Reformed Theological Review* 45 (January-April 1986) 1-4, (May-August 1986) 45-51.

982   RAINEY, K. T., SR. *The Death of Christ in Petrine Thought*. Ph.D. dissertation, New Orleans Baptist Theological Seminary, 1967.

983   RASCO, E. "Il « sangue prezioso » di Cristo nella prima lettera di Pietro," *Sangue e antropologia biblica (Roma, 10-15 marzo 1980). Atti della settimana* 1. Ed. F. Vattioni. Roma: Pia unione Preziosissmo Sangue, 1981 2:851-864.

984   REFOULÉ, F. "Bible et éthique sociale: Lire aujourd'hui 1 Pierre," *Supplément* 131 (1979) 457-482.

985   REICHERT, A. *Eine urchristliche Preparatio ad Martyrium. Studien zur Komposition, Traditionsgeschichte und Theologie des 1. Petrusbriefes.* Doctoral thesis, Evangelisch-theologischen Fakultät der Westfällischen Wilhelms-Universität, Münster, 1988.

986   ———. *Eine urchristliche Preparatio ad Martyrium. Studien zur Komposition, Traditionsgeschichte und Theologie des 1. Petrusbriefes*. BBET 22. Frankfurt: Lang, 1989.

987   RENNER, F. "Exkurs 7. Einheit und Structur des ersten Petrusbriefes," *„An die Hebräer"—ein pseudepigraphischer*

Brief. Münsterschwarzacher Studien 14. Münsterschwarzach: Vier-Türme, 1970, 156-60.

988   RIBER, M. "Un modelo de catequesis bautismal. Sugerencias, en torno a la carta primera de Pedro, para una catequesis de adultos," *Cultura Bíblica* 23 (1966) 323-331.

989   RICE, G. E. *A Living Hope.* Boise, Id. and Oshawa, Ontario, Canada: Pacific Press, 1992.

990   RICHARD, E. "The Functional Christology of First Peter," *Perspectives on First Peter.* Ed. C. H. Talbert. National Association of Baptist Professors of Religion Special Studies Series 9. Macon, Ga: Mercer University Press, 1986, 121-139.

991   RICHARDSON, R. L., JR. "From 'Subjection to Authority' to 'Mutual Submission': The Ethic of Subordination in 1 Peter," *Faith and Mission* 4,2 (Spring 1987) 70-80.

992   RITT, H. "Die Verantwortung des Christen in der Gesellschaft. Bibel-theologische Aspecte (1 Petr; Offb)," *Wissen— Glaube—Politik.   Festschrift für Paul Asveld.* Ed. W. Gruber, J. Ladriere, N. Leser, and O. König. Graz, Wien, and Köln: Styria, 1981, 217-225.

993   ROBERTSON, P. E. "Is I Peter a Sermon?" *Theological Educator* 13, (Fall 1982) 35-41.

994   ROBINSON, M. "The First and Second Epistles General of Peter," *Incarnation: Contemporary Writers on the New Testament.* Ed. A. Corn. New York: Viking, 1990, 305-315.

995   ROUSSEAU, J. *A Multidimensional Approach towards the Communication of an Ancient Canonized Text: Towards Determining the Thrust, Perspective and Strategy of 1 Peter.* PhD dissertation, University of Pretoria, 1986.

996   RUSSELL, R. "Eschatology and Ethics in 1 Peter," *EvQ* 47 (1975) 78-84.

997   SCHARFE, E. "Die schriftstellerische Originalität des 1. Petrusbriefes," *TSK* 62 (1889) 633-670.

998   SCHELKLE, K. H. "Das Leiden des Gottesknechtes als Form christlichen Lebens (nach dem 1. Petrusbrief)," *BK* 16 (1961) 14-16; *Wort und Schrift. Beiträge zur Auslegung und Ausle-*

gungsgeschichte des Neuen Testaments. Kommentare und Beiträge zum Alten und Neuen Testament. Düsseldorf: Patmos, 1966, 162-165.

999   SCHEMBRI, G. "Il messaggio pastorale di S. Pietro nella sua Prima Epistola," *Anton* 42 (1967) 376-398.

1000 SCHLATTER, A. *Petrus und Paulus nach dem ersten Petrusbrief.* Stuttgart: Calwer, 1937.

1001 SCHLIER, H. "Die Kirche nach dem 1. Petrusbrief," *Mysterium Salutis* 4,1. Einsiedeln, 1972, 195-200.

1002 ———. "Eine Adhortatio aus Rom. Die Botschaft des ersten Petrusbriefes," *Strukturen christlicher Existenz. Beiträge zur Erneuerung des geistlichen Lebens.* Würzburg: Echter, 1968, 59-80, 369-371; *Das Ende der Zeit, Exegetische Aufsätze und Vorträge.* Freiburg, Basel, and Wien: Herder, 1971, 3:271-296.

1003 SCHLOSSER, J. "Ancien Testament et christologie dans la *Prima Petri,*" *Études sur la première lettre de Pierre. Congrès de l'ACFEB, Paris 1979.* LD 102. Ed. C. Perrot. Paris: Cerf, 1980, 65-96.

1004 SCHMIDT, D. H. "I Peter," *The Peter Writings: Their Redactors and Their Relationships.* Ph.D. dissertation, Northwestern University. Evanston, Illinois, 1972, 19-74, 206-219.

1005 SCHMIDT, P. "Zwei Fragen zum ersten Petrusbrief," *ZWT* 1 (1908) 24-52.

1006 SCHROEDER, D. "Once You Were No People . . . {1 Peter 2:11-3:12}," *The Church as Theological Community: Essays in Honour of David Schroeder.* Ed. H. Huebner. Winnepeg, Man.: Canadian Mennonite Bible College, 1990, 37-65.

1007 SCHRÖGER, F. "Ansätze zu den modernen Menschenrechtsforderungen im 1. Petrusbrief," *Der Dienst für den Menschen in Theologie und Verkündigung. Festschrift für Alois Brems Bischof von Eichstatt zum 75. Geburtstag.* Ed. R. M. Hübner, B. Mayer, and E. Reiter. Regensburg: Pustet, 1981, 179-191.

1008 ———. "Die Verfassung der Gemeinde des ersten Petrusbriefes," *Kirche im Werden. Studien zum Thema Amt und*

Gemeinde im Neuen Testament. Ed. J. Hainz. Müchen, Paderborn, and Wien: Schöningh, 1976, 239-252.

1009 ———. *Gemeinde im 1. Petrusbrief. Untersuchungen zum Selbstverständnis einer christlichen Gemeinde an der Wende vom 1. zum 2. Jahrhundert.* Katholische Theologie 1. Passau: Passavia Universitätsverlag, 1981.

1010 SCHÜCKLER, G. "Wandel im Glauben als missionarisches Zeugnis," *ZMR* 51 (1967) 289-299.

1011 SCHUTZ, H. G. *„Kirche" in spät-neutestamentlichen Zeit. Untersuchungen über das Selbstverständnis des Urchristentums an der Wende vom 1. zum 2. Jahrhundert anhand des 1 Petr., des Hebr. und der Past.* Dissertation, Bonn, 1964.

1012 SCHWEIZER, E. "Zur Christologie des Ersten Petrusbriefs," *Anfänge der Christologie. Festschrift für Ferdinand Hahn zum 65. Geburtstag.* Ed. C. Breytenbach and H. Paulsen. Göttingen: Vandenhoeck & Ruprecht, 1991, 369-382.

1013 SELWYN, E. G. "Eschatology in 1 Peter," *The Background of the New Testament and its Eschatology (In Honour of Charles Harold Dodd).* Ed. W. D. Davies and D. Daube. Cambridge: University Press, 1956, 394-401.

1014 SHIMADA, K. "Is I Peter a Composite Writing?—a stylistic approach to the two-document hypothesis," AJBI 11 (1985) 95-114.

1015 ———. *The Formulary Material in First Peter: A Study According to the Method of "Traditionsgeschichte."* Th.D. dissertation, Union Theological Seminary (New York), 1966 and Ann Arbor: University Microfilms, 1968.

1016 SIEFERT, E. A. "Die Heilsbedeutung des Leidens und Sterbens Christi nach dem ersten Briefe des Petrus," *Jahrbücher für Deutsche Theologie* 20 (1875) 371-440.

1017 SLEEPER, C. F. "Political Responsibility according to I Peter," *NovT* 10 (1968) 270-286.

1018 SMALLEY, S. S. "The Imitation of Christ in I Peter," *Churchman* 75 (1961) 172-178.

1019 SOLTAU, W. "Die Einheitlichkeit des 1. Petrusbriefes," *TSK* 78 (1905) 302-315.

1020 ———. "Nochmals die Einheitlichkeit des ersten Petrusbriefes," *TSK* 79 (1906) 456-460.

1021 SOUČEK, J. B. "Das Gegenüber von Gemeinde und Welt nach dem ersten Petrusbrief," *Communio Viatorum* 3 (1960) 5-13; *Stimmen aus der Kirche der ČSSR. Dokumente und Zeugnisse.* Ed. B. Ruys and J. Smolik. München: Kaiser, 1968, 56-69.

1022 SPICQ, C. "*Agape* and *Agapan* in SS. Peter and Jude," *Agape in the New Testament.* Trans. M. A. McNamara and M. H. Richter. St. Louis: Herder, 1965, 2:342-383.

1023 ———. "'Αγάπη-'Αγαπᾶν dans les épitres de Saint Pierre et de Saint Jude," *Agapè dans le Nouveau Testament. Analyse des textes.* Ebib. Paris: Gabalda, 1958-59, 2:307-363.

1024 ———. "La 1ª Petri et le témoignage évangélique de saint Pierre," *ST* 20 (1966) 37-61.

1025 SPÖRRI, T. *Der Gemeindegedanke im ersten Petrusbrief. Ein Beitrag zur Structur des urchristlichen Kirkenbegriffs.* NTF 2,2. Gütersloh: Bertelsmann, 1925.

1026 STELZENBERGER, J. "Das Innere (Hebr 9, 9; 9, 14; 10, 2; 10, 22; 13, 18. 1 Petr 3, 21. 2 Tim 1, 3)" and "Das gute Gewissen (1 Kor 4, 4. 1 Petr 3, 16. 1 Tim 1, 5; 1, 19; 3, 9. 2 Tim 1, 3)," *Syneidesis im Neuen Testament.* Abhandlungen zur Moraltheologie 1. Paderborn: Schöningh, 1961, 56-68 and 82-90.
      Review: Schnackenburg, R., *BZ* 8 (1964) 122-123.

1027 STÖGER, A. *Bauleute Gottes. Der 1. Petrusbrief als Grundlegung des Laienapostolats.* Lebendiges Wort 3. München: Pfeifer, 1954.

1028 STROUSE, T. M. *The Theology of the Petrine Epistles.* Ph.D. dissertation, Bob Jones University, 1978.

1029 SUPARSCHI, M. "Idei moral-sociale în epistolele sf. Ap. Petru," *Studii Teolgice* 8 (1956) 167-179.

1030 TALBERT, C. H. "Once Again: The Plan of 1 Peter," *Perspectives on First Peter.* Ed. C. H. Talbert. National Association of Baptist Professers of Religion Special Studies Series 9. Macon, Ga.: Mercer University Press, 1986, 141-151.

98 EXPOSITIONS OF THE ENTIRE BOOK

1031 TÀRRECH, A. P. "Le milieu de la Première épître de Pierre," *Revista Catalana de Teología* 5 (1980) 95-129, 331-402.

1032 TAYLOR, R. *Studies in First and Second Peter.* Shreveport, La: Lambert Books, 1979 and Ripley, Tenn: Taylor Publications, 1992.

1033 THILS, G. *De leer van den H. Petrus.* Brugge: Beyaert, 1946.

1034 ———. *L'enseignement de Saint Pierre.* Ebib. Paris: Lecoffre, 1943.

1035 THORNTON, T. C. G. "1 Peter, a Paschal Liturgy?" *JTS* 12 (1961) 14-26.

1036 THURÉN, L. *The Rhetorical Strategy of 1 Peter with Special Regard to Ambiguous Expressions.* Th.D. dissertation, Åbo Akademi, 1990.

1037 ———. *The Rhetorical Strategy of 1 Peter with Special Regard to Ambiguous Expressions.* Åbo: Åbo Akademis Forlag, 1990.

1038 THURSTON, R. W. "Interpreting First Peter," *JETS* 17 (1974) 171-182.

1039 TIEDE, D. L. "An Easter Catechesis: The lessons of 1 Peter," *WW* 4 (1984) 192-201.

1040 TIGERT, J. J. "The Paulinism of First Peter," *Methodist Quarterly Review* 47 (1898) 426-435.

1041 TRILLING, W. "Zum Petrusamt im Neuen Testament. Traditionsgeschichtliche Überlegungen anhand von Matthäus, 1. Petrus und Johannes," *TQ* 151 (1971) 110-133; *Theologische Versuche* 4. Ed. J. Rogge and G. Schille. Berlin: Evangelische Verlagsanstalt, 1972, 27-46.

1042 TUÑI, J. O. "Jesus of Nazareth in the Christology of 1 Peter," *HeyJ* 28 (1987) 292-304.

1043 UNTERGAßMAIR, F. G. "Diaspora und Ökumene aus der Sicht des Neuen Testaments," *Catholica: Vierteljahresschrift für Kontroverstheologie* 38 (1984) 18-30.

1044   VANHOYE, A. "1 Pierre au carrefour des théologies du Nou-
       veau Testament," *Études sur la première lettre de Pierre.
       Congrès de l'ACFEB, Paris 1979.* LD 102. Ed. C. Perrot.
       Paris: Cerf, 1980, 97-128.

1045   VANNI, U. "La promozione del regno come responsabilità
       sacerdotale dei Cristiani secondo l'Apocalisse e la Prima Let-
       tera di Pietro," *Greg* 68 (1987) 9-56.

1046   VAN UNNIK, W. C. "Christianity according to I Peter,"
       ExpTim 68 (1956-57) 79-83; *Sparsa Collecta: The Collected
       Essays of W. C. van Unnik.* NovTSup 29-31. Leiden: Brill,
       1973-83, 2:111-120.

1047   ———. "The Teaching of Good Works in I Peter," *NTS* 1
       (1954-55) 92-110; *Sparsa Collecta: The Collected Essays of
       W. C. van Unnik.* NovTSup 29-31. Leiden: Brill, 1973-83,
       2:83-105.

1048   VIDIGAL, J. R. "A Catechese Baptismal na Primeira Carta de
       Sao Pedro," *RCB* 5 (1981) 76-84.

1049   VILLIERS, J. L. de. "Joy in Suffering in 1 Peter," *Neot* 9:
       Essays on the General Epistles of the New Testament (1975,
       [2]1980) 64-86.

1050   VITTI, A. "Eschatologia in Petri epistula prima," *VD* 11
       (1931) 298-306.

1051   VÖLKL, R. "Die erste Petrusbrief," *Christ und Welt nach
       dem Neuen Testament.* Würzburg: Echter Verlag, 1961, 370-
       380.
       Reviews: Alszeghy, Z., *Greg* 43 (1962) 811-813; Lohse, E., *TLZ* 88
       (1963) 40-42; Schnackenburg, R., *BZ* 8 (1964) 120-122.

1052   VOLKMAR, G. "Über die katholischen Briefe und Henoch,"
       ZWT 4 (1961) 422-436.

1053   VOWINKEL, E. *Die Grundgedanken des Jakobusbriefes
       verglichen mit den ersten Briefen des Petrus und Johannes.*
       BFCT 2,6. Gütersloh: Gütersloher Verlagshaus, (1898),
       1899, 1-74.

1054   WARDEN, P. D. *Alienation and Community in 1 Peter.* Ph.D.
       dissertation, Duke University, 1986.

1055 WATSON, D. L. *The Implications of Christology and Eschatology for a Christian Attitude toward the State in I Peter.*
Ph.D. dissertation, The Hartford Seminary Foundation, 1970.

1056 WEISS, B. *Der petrinische Lehrbegriff. Beiträge zur biblischen Theologie, sowie zur Kritik und exegese des ersten
Briefes Petri und der petrinischen Reden.* Berlin: Schultze,
1855.

1057 WENDLAND, H.-D. "Der 1. Petrus-Brief. Christus, das Ur-
bild des Lebens und Leidens," *Ethik des Neuen Testaments:
Eine Einfürung.* GNT 4. Göttingen: Vandenhoeck & Ruprecht, 1970, ²1975, 101-104.

1058 WENSCHKEWITZ, H. "Der erste Petrusbrief," *Die Spirituali-
sierung der Kultusbegriffe Tempel, Priester und Opfer im
Neuen Testament.* ΑΓΓΕΛΟΣ Archiv für neutestamentliche
Zeitgeschichte und Kulturkunde 4. Leipzig: Pfeiffer, 1932,
160-162.

1059 WINBERY, C. L. "Ethical Issues in I Peter," *Theological
Educator* 13,1 (Fall 1982) 63-71.

1060 WINDISCH, H. "Der entsündigte Christ im 1. Petrusbriefe
(sic)," *Taufe und Sünde im ältesten Christentum bis auf Ori-
genes. Ein Beitrag zur altchristlichen Dogmengeschichte.*
Tübingen: Mohr, 1908, 227-243.

1061 WINTER, B. W. "'Seek the Welfare of the City': Social Ethics According to 1 Peter," *Themelios* 13,3 (April/May 1988)
91-94.

1062 WOLFF, C. "Christ und Welt im 1. Petrusbrief," *TLZ* 100
(1975) 333-342.

1063 WOLFF, H. W. "Jes. 53 im 1. Petrusbrief," *Jesaja 53 im Urchristentum. Die Geschichte der Prophetie 'Siehe, es siegt
mein Knecht' bis Justin.* Bethel: Buchdruckerei der Anstalt
Bethel, 1942 and Berlin: Evangelische Verlaganstalt, ²1950,
³1952, ⁴1984, 88-92.
Review: Ellis, E. E., *Southwestern Journal of Theology* 33 (Fall 1990)
56.

1064 WREDE, W. "Miscellen 3. Bemerkungen zu Harnacks Hy-
pothese über die Addresse des I. Petrusbriefes," *ZNW* 1
(1900) 75-85.

1065 YATES, T. "The Message of the Epistles. The First Epistle of Peter," *ExpTim* 45 (1933-34) 391-393.

SECTION 6

MISCELLANEOUS

Many topics concerning 1 Peter occur with insufficient regularity to warrant collecting their titles in separate sections. The following is a list of works that fall into such categories.

Authorship

1066 BEST, E. "I Peter and the Gospel Tradition," *NTS* 16 (1969-70) 95-113.

1067 BROX, N. "Tendenz und Pseudepigraphie im ersten Petrusbrief," *Kairos* 20 (1978) 110-120.

1068 CARRINGTON, P. "Saint Peter's Epistle," *The Joy of Study: Papers on New Testament and Related Subjects Presented to Honor Frederick Clifton Grant.* Ed. S. E. Johnson. New York: Macmillan, 1951, 57-63.

1069 EBRIGHT, H. K. *The Petrine Epistles: A Critical Study of Authorship.* Cincinnati: Methodist Book Concern, 1917.

1070 GUNDRY, R. H. "Further *Verba* on *Verba Christi* in First Peter," *Bib* 55 (1974) 211-232.

1071 ———. "'Verba Christi' in I Peter: Their Implications Concerning the Authorship of I Peter and the Authenticity of the Gospel Tradition," *NTS* 13 (1966-67) 336-350.

1072 MORTON, A. Q. *The Authorship and Integrity of the New Testament.* London: SPCK, 1965.
   Review: Martin, R. A., *Indian Journal of Theology* 14 (1965) 210-211.

1073 MUßNER, F. "Das Pseudonym 'Petrus' im 1 Petrusbrief," *Petrus und Paulus, Pole der Einheit: Eine Hilfe für die Kirchen.* QD 76. Freiburg, Basel, and Wien: Herder, 1976, 49-57.

1074 RADERMACHER, L. "Der erste Petrusbrief und Silvanus, mit einem Nachwort in eigener Sache," *ZNW* 25 (1926) 287-299.

1075 SCHMIDT, D. H. "The Pseudonimity of I Peter," *The Peter Writings: Their Redactors and Their Relationships.* Ph.D.

dissertation, Northwestern University. Evanston, Illinois, 1972, 7-18.

1076 SELWYN, E. G. "Unsolved New Testament Problems: The Problem of the Authorship of 1 Peter," *ExpTim* 59 (1947-48) 256-258.

1077 SEUFERT, W. "Titus Silvanus (ΣΙΛΑΣ) und der Verfasser des ersten Petrusbriefes," *ZWT* 28 (1885) 350-371.

Address

1078 HEMER, C. J. "The Address of 1 Peter," *ExpTim* 89 (1977-78) 239-243.

Church and Church Order

1079 STREETER, B. H. "The Church in Asia: The First Epistle of St. Peter," *The Primitive Church, Studied with Special Reference to the Origins of the Christian Ministry.* The Hewett Lectures, 1928. London and New York: Macmillan 1929, 115-136.

Compendia and Collected Essays

1080 GAROFALO, S., M. MACCARONE, and J. RUYSSCHAERT, eds. *Studi Petriani.* Roma: Ist. di studi romani, 1968.

1081 PERROT, C., ed. *Études sur la première lettre de Pierre. Congrès de l'ACFEB, Paris 1979.* LD 102. Paris: Cerf, 1980.
Review: Anonymous, *SR* (1982) 90-92.

1082 TALBERT, C. H., ed. *Perspectives on First Peter.* National Association of Baptist Professors of Religion Special Studies Series 9. Macon, Ga.: Mercer University Press, 1986.
Reviews: Chevallier, M. A., *RHPR* 69 (1989) 239; Lea, T. D., *Southwestern Journal of Theology* 29,3 (Summer 1987) 57-58; Michaels, J. R., *Perspectives in Religious Studies* 15 (Fall 1988) 286-288.

1083 THIEDE, C. P., ed. *Das Petrusbild in der neueren Forschung.* Monographien und Studienbücher. Wuppertal: Brockhaus, 1987.
Reviews: Ellis, E. E., Southwestern Journal of Theology 32 (1989) 55; Vogler, W., *TLZ* 112 (1987) 816-817.

1084 VAN UNNIK, W. C. "I Peter," *Sparsa Collecta: The Collected Essays of W. C. van Unnik.* NovTSup 29-31. Leiden: Brill, 1973-83, 2:3-120.

Reviews: Best, E., *JTS* 33 (1982) 549-551; Epp, E. J., *JBL* 102 (1983) 158-159; Holtz, T., *TLZ* 106 (1981) 750.

Concordance

1085 BAIRD, J. A., and J. D. THOMPSON. *A Critical Concordance to I, II Peter.* Computer Bible 32. Wooster, Ohio: Biblical Research Associates, 1989; revised 1989.

Date

1086 BAUER, J. B. "Der erste Petrusbrief und die Verfolgung unter Domitian," *Die Kirche des Anfangs. Festschrift für Heinz Schürmann zum 65. Geburtstag.* ETS 38. Ed. R. Schnackenburg, J. Ernst, and J. Wanke. Leipzig: St. Benno, 1978, 513-527.

1087 HUNZINGER, C. H. "Babylon als Deckname für Rom und die Datierung des 1. Petrusbriefs," *Gotteswort und Gottesland. Hans-Wilhelm Hertzberg zum 70. Geburtstag.* Ed. H. G. Reventlow. Göttingen: Vandenhoeck & Ruprecht, 1965, 67-77.

1088 LEWIS, F. W. "Note on the Date of the First Epistle of Peter," *Expositor* 5,10 (1899) 319-320.

1089 MCNABB, V. "Date and Influence of the First Epistle of St. Peter," *Irish Ecclesiastical Record* 45 (1935) 596-613.

1090 RAMSAY, W. M. "Christian Authorities for the Flavian Period: I. The First Epistle of Peter. II. Later Date Assigned to I Peter," *The Church in the Roman Empire Before A.D. 170.* Mansfield College Lectures. London: G. P. Putnam's Sons, 1893; London: Hodder and Stoughton, [5]1897, [7]1903, [8]1904 (279-290); London and New York: Hodder and Stoughton, [10]n.d., 279-295; reprint of [8]1904 Boston: Longwood, 1978.

1091 ———. "The Church and the Empire in the First Century: III. The First Epistle attributed to St. Peter," *Expositor* 4,8 (1893) 282-296.

1092 SELWYN, E. G. "The Persecutions in I Peter," *Bulletin of the Studiorum Novi Testamenti Societas* 1 (1950) 39-50.

1093   WARDEN, D. "Imperial Persecution and the Dating of 1 Peter and Revelation," *JETS* 34 (1991) 203-212.

Grammar

1094   DAUBE, D. "Appended Note: Participle and Imperative in I Peter," *The First Epistle of St. Peter* by E. G. Selwyn. London: Macmillan, 1946, ^{2}1947; reprint Grand Rapids: Baker, 1981, 467-488.

1095   DIJKMAN, J. H. L. " "Οτι as an Introductory Formula to the Catechetical References in 1 Peter," *A South African Perspective on the New Testament: Essays by South African New Testament Scholars Presented to Bruce Manning Metzger during His Visit to South Africa in 1985.* Ed. J. H. Petzer and P. J. Hartin. Leiden: Brill, 1986, 260-270.

1096   FINK, P. R. "The Use and Significance of *en hoi* in 1 Peter," *Grace Journal* 8,2 (Spring 1967) 33-39.

1097   HAMBLIN, R. L. *An Analysis of First Peter with Special Reference to the Greek Participle.* Ph.D. dissertation, Southwestern Baptist Theological Seminary, 1960.

1098   VILLEY, L. *Hypo dans la 1re épître de Pierre*, cited in É. Cothenet, "Les orientations actuelles de l'exégèse de la première lettre de Pierre," *Études sur la première lettre de Pierre. Congrès de l'ACFEB, Paris 1979.* LD 102. Ed. C. Perrot. Paris: Cerf, 1980, 31-32 and n. 36.

Hermeneutics

1099   ESCOBAR, S. "Our Hermeneutic Task Today {1 Peter 1:3, 10-12, 22-23}," *Conflict and Context: Hermeneutics in the Americas.* Ed. M. L. Branson and C. R. Padilla. Grand Rapids: Eerdmans, 1986, 3-8.

History

1100   RAMSAY, W. M. "Christian Authorities for the Flavian Period: III. Official Action according to I Peter," *The Church in the Roman Empire Before A.D. 170.* Mansfield College Lectures. London: G. P. Putnam's Sons, 1893; London: Hodder and Stoughton, ^{5}1897, ^{7}1903, ^{8}1904 (290-295); London and New York: Hodder and Stoughton, ^{10}n.d., 279-295; reprint of ^{8}1904 Boston: Longwood, 1978.

History of Exegesis

1101   FEDALTO, G. "Il toponomo di 1 Petr 5,13 nella esegesi di Eusebio di Cesarea," *Vetera Christianorum* 20 (1983) 461-466.

1102   LA BONNARDIÈRE, A.-M. "Evodius et Augustin. Lettres 163 et 164," *Saint Augustin et la Bible*. Bible de tous les temps 3. Ed. A.-M. la Bonnardière. Paris: Beauchesne, 1986, 213-227.

1103   ———. "La prédication du Christ aux esprits en prison. 1 P 3,18-19 d'après l'interprétation de Sainte Augustin," *Études sur la première lettre du Pierre. Congrès de l'ACFEB, Paris 1979*. LD 102. Ed. C. Perrot. Paris: 1980, 247-267.

1104   OTRANTO, G. "Il sacerdozio comune dei fedeli nei riflessi della 1 *Petr.* 2,9 (I e II secolo)," *Vetera Christianorum* 7 (1970) 225-246.

History of Religions Research

1105   PERDELWITZ, R. *Die Mysterienreligion und das Problem des I. Petrusbriefes. Ein literarischer und religionsgeschichtlicher Versuch*. Religionsgeschichtliche Versuche und Vorarbeiten 11,3. Giessen: Töpelmann, 1911.

History of Research

1106   COTHENET, É. "La Première de Pierre. Bilan de 35 ans de recherches," *Principat 25,5. Religion (vorkonstaninisches Christentum. Leben und Umwelt Jesu. Neues Testament)*. Ed. W. Hasse. Berlin and New York: de Gruyter, 1988, 3685-3712.

1107   ———. "Les orientations actuelles de l'exégèse de la première lettre de Pierre," *Études sur la première lettre de Pierre. Congrès de l'ACFEB, Paris 1979*. LD 102. Ed. C. Perrot. Paris: Cerf, 1980, 13-42.

1108   ELLIOTT, J. H. "The Rehabilitation of an Exegetical Stepchild: 1 Peter in Recent Research," *JBL* 95 (1976) 243-254; *Perspectives on First Peter*. Ed. C. H. Talbert. National Association of Baptist Professors of Religion Special Studies Series 9. Macon, Ga.: Mercer University Press, 1986, 3-16.

1109   FRY, E. "Commentaries on James, 1 and 2 Peter, and Jude," *BT* 41 (1990) 326-336.

1110   MARTIN, R. P. "The Composition of I Peter in Recent Study," *Vox Evangelica* {1} (1962) 29-42.

1111   PEARSON, B. A. "James, 1-2 Peter, Jude," *The New Testament and Its Modern Interpreters.* Ed. E. J. Epp and G. W. MacRae. Philadelphia: Fortress and Atlanta: Scholars Press, 1989, 371-406.

1112   SCHIERSE, F. J. "Ein Hirtenbrief und viele Bücher. Neue Literatur zum ersten Petrusbrief," *BK* 31 (1976) 86-88.

1113   SYLVA, D. "1 Peter Studies: The State of the Discipline," *BTB* 10 (1980) 155-163.

1114   ——. "A 1 Peter Bibliography," *JETS* 25 (1982) 75-89.

1115   ——. "The Critical Exploration of 1 Peter," *Perspectives on First Peter.* Ed. C. H. Talbert. National Association of Baptist Professers of Religion Special Studies Series 9. Macon, Ga.: Mercer University Press, 1986, 17-36.

1116   WAND, J. W. C. "The Lessons of First Peter: A Survey of Recent Interpretation," *Int* 9 (1955) 387-399.

1117   WEIß, B. *Der erste Petrusbrief und die neuere Kritik.* Biblische Zeit- und Streitfragen 4. Berlin: E. Runga, 1906.

Household Codes

1118   BALCH, D. L. *Let Wives be Submissive: The Domestic Code of 1 Peter.* SBLMS 26. Ed. J. Crenshaw. Chico: Scholars Press, 1981.
Reviews: Kaufman, P. L., *Journal of Psychology and Theology* 10 (1982) 154-155; Martin, R. P., *JSNT* 17 (1983) 103-105; Michaels, J. R., *JBL* 103 (1984) 305-306; Osborne, T. P., *ETL* 58 (1982) 399-400; Osiek, C., *CBQ* 46 (1984) 138-140; Strecker, G., *TLZ* 108 (1983) 746-747; Timbs, D., *AusBR* 30 (1982) 66-67; Walton, W. J., *Bib* 64 (1983) 444-446; Wire, A., *RelSRev* 10 (1984) 209-216.

1119   ——. *"Let Wives Be Submissive . . .": The Origin, Form, and Apologetic Function of the Household Duty Code (Haustafel) in I Peter.* Ph.D dissertation, Yale University, 1974; Ann Arbor: University Microfilms, 1979.

1120 FIORENZA, E. S.   "1 Peter and the Household Code {1 Peter
      2:11-3:12}," *In Memory of Her: A Feminist Theological Re-
      construction of Christian Origins.* New York: Crossroad,
      1983, 260-266.

      Reviews: Anderson, J. C., *CR* (1991) 21-44; Arthur, R. H., *CBQ* 46
      (1984) 567-568; Barton, S. C., *Theology* 88 (1985) 134-137; Bird, P.
      A., *PSTJ* 38 (Winter 1985) 41-43; Braun, W., *Conrad Grebel Review* 3
      (1985) 324-328; Bryan, C., *Saint Luke's Journal of Theology* 28 (1985)
      235-236; Butler, M. Y., *JAAR* 53 (1985) 161-162; Davies, J. G.,
      ExpTim 95 (1984) 375-376; Durka, G., *Religious Education* 79 (1984)
      135-137; Gaventa, B. R., *Lexington Theological Quarterly* 20 (April
      1985) 58-60; Grant, R. M., *JR* 65 (1985) 83-88; Harrison, B. W., *Hori-*
      zons 11 (1984) 150-153, rejoinder by E. S. Fiorenza, 154-157; Hughes,
      F. W., *ATR* 69 (1987) 287-299; King, U., *RelS* 20 (1984) 699-702;
      Koenig, J., *Horizons* 11 (1984) 144-146, rejoinder by E. S. Fiorenza,
      154-157; Kraemer, R. S., *JBL* 104 (1985) 722-725; Kraemer, R. S.,
      RelSRev 11 (1985) 6-9; Kress, R., *TS* 45 (1984) 729-731; Mayer, H. T.,
      CurTM 11 (1984) 311-312; Mercadante, L. A., *Theological Students*
      Fellowship Bulletin 8,3 (Jan-Feb 1985) 28-30; Micks, M. H., *Christi-*
      anity and Crisis 43 (1983) 388-389; Mollenkott, V. R., *Sojourners* 12
      (Oct 1983) 35-36; Murphy-O'Connor, J., *RB* 91 (1984) 287-294;
      O'Connor, J, *Christian Century* 100 (1983) 1114-1117; Orr, E., *Faith*
      and Mission 2,1 (Fall 1984) 98-100; Osiek, C., *BTB* 14 (1984) 166-
      167; Padgett, A., *EvQ* 58 (1986) 121-132; Pellauer, M., *TToday* 40
      (January 1984) 472-; Perkins, P., *Horizons* 11 (1984) 142-144, rejoin-
      der by E. S. Fiorenza, 154-157; Plaskow, J., *Anima* 10 (1984) 98-102,
      rejoinder by E. S. Fiorenza, 109-112; Reuther, R. R., *Horizons* 11
      (1984) 146-150, rejoinder by E. S. Fiorenza 154-157; Sabourin, L., *Re-*
      ligious Studies Bulletin 4 (1984) 102-104; Schneiders, S. M., *Union*
      Seminary Quarterly Review 39 (1984) 236-240; Scroggs, R., *Chicago*
      Theological Seminary Register 75,3 (Fall 1985) 27-30; Setta, S. M.,
      Anima 10 (1984) 95-97, rejoinder by E. S. Fiorenza 109-112; Strug, M.
      C., *WW* 4 (1984) 332-333; Thistlethwaite, S. B., *Anima* 10 (1984) 102-
      105, rejoinder by E. S. Fiorenza 109-112; Tyson, J. B., *Int* 38 (1984)
      106+; West, C., *RelSRev* 11 (1985) 1-4; Wire, A. C., *Anima* 10 (1984)
      105-109, rejoinder by E. S. Fiorenza 109-112.

1121 GOPPELT, L.   "Jesus und die 'Haustafel'-Tradition," *Orien-*
      tierung an Jesus. Zur Theologie der Synoptiker. Festschrift
      für Josef Schmid zum 80. Geburtstag am 26. Januar 1963.
      Ed. P. Hoffman, N. Brox, and W. Pesch. Freiburg, Basel, and
      Wien: Herder, 1973, 93-106.

1122 GÜLZOW, H.   "Die Haustafeln.   Der erste Petrusbrief,"
      Christentum und Sklaverei in den ersten drei Jahrhunderten.
      Bonn: Habelt, 1969, 67-76.

1123 KAMLAH, E.   "ΥΠΟΤΑΣΣΕΣΘΑΙ in den neutestamentlichen
      'Haustafeln'," *Verborum Veritas. Festschrift für Gustav*
      Stählin zum 70. Geburtstag. Ed. O. Böcher and K. Haaker.
      Wuppertal: Brockhaus, 1970, 237-243.

1124 MOTYER, S. "The Relationship between Paul's Gospel of 'All One in Christ Jesus' (Gal 3:28) and the 'Household Codes' {Colossians 3:18-4:1; Ephesians 5:22-6:9; 1 Peter 2:18-3:7}," *Vox Evangelica* 19 (1989) 33-48.

1125 SCHROEDER, D. "Die Erweiterungen der Haustafel in 1.Pet.3,1-7" *Die Haustafeln des Neuen Testaments. Ihre Herkunft und ihr theologischer Sinn.* Doctoral dissertation, Universität Hamburg, 1959.

1126 WEIDINGER, K. "Die Haustafel des I. Petr. (2. 13-3. 7)," *Die Haustafeln. Ein Stück urchristlicher Paränese.* UNT 14. Leipzig: Hinrichs, 1928, 62-66.

Introduction

1127 BEASLEY-MURRAY, G. R. *The General Epistles: James, 1 Peter, Jude, 2 Peter.* Bible Guides 21. London: Lutterworth and New York and Nashville: Abingdon, 1965.

1128 BLEVINS, J. L. "Introduction to 1 Peter," *RevExp* 79 (1982) 401-413.

1129 ELLIOTT, J. H. *1 Peter: Estrangement and Community.* Herald Biblical Booklets. Chicago: Franciscan Herald, 1979.

1130 FARRAR, F. W. "Special Features of the First Epistle of St. Peter," *The Early Days of Christianity.* London: Cassell, Petter, Galpin, 1882 and New York: Funk and Wagnalls, 1883, 67-83.

1131 GLAZE, R. E., JR. "Introduction to 1 Peter," *Theological Educator* 13,1 (Fall 1982) 23-34.

1132 HAYES, D. A. "The First Epistle of Peter," *The New Testament Epistles: Hebrews, James, First Peter, Second Peter, Jude.* Biblical Introduction Series. New York and Cincinnati: Methodist Book Concern, 1921, 121-183.

1133 LOVE, J. P. "Studia Biblica XXIV: The First Epistle of Peter," *Int* 8 (1954) 63-87.

1134 SCHELKLE, K. H. "La prima lettera di Pietro," *Pietro nella Sacra Scrittura.* I maestri di ieri e di oggi 3. Trans. K. Schelkle. Ed. M. G. Rosito. Firenze: Città di Vita, 1975, 101-114.

1135 SENIOR, D. "The First Letter of Peter," *The Bible Today* 22 (1984) 5-12.

1136 STOLT, J. "Isagogiske problemer vedrorende 1. Petersbrev," *DTT* 44 (1981) 166-173.

1137 VÖLTER, D. *Der erste Petrusbrief. Seine Entstehung und Stellung in der Geschichte des Urchristentums.* Strassburg: Heitz-Mündel, 1906.

1138 WILLMINGTON, H. L. "Peter's Two Epistles {adapted from *Wilmington's Visualized Study Bible* (Wheaton: Tyndale, 1984)}," *Fundamentalist Journal* 4,5 (May 1985) 59.

1139 WINBERY, C. L. "Introduction to the First Letter of Peter," *Southwestern Journal of Theology* 25 (1982-83) 3-16.

Lexicon

1140 LYKINS, W. A. *I Peter.* A Word by Word Verse by Verse Lexicon of the Greek New Testament. Portsmouth, Oh.: W. A. Lykins (the author), 1991.

Miscellaneous

1141 ELLIOTT, J. H. "Peter, Silvanus and Mark in I Peter and Acts: Sociological-Exegetical Perspectives on a Petrine Group in Rome," *Wort in der Zeit. Neutestamentliche Studien. Festgabe für Karl Heinrich Rengstorf.* Ed. W. Haubeck and M. Bachmann. Leiden: Brill, 1980, 250-267.

1142 ———. "The Roman Provenance of I Peter and the Gospel of Mark: A Response to David Dungan," *Colloquy on New Testament Studies: A Time for Reappraisal and Fresh Approaches.* Ed. B. Corley. Macon, Ga.: Mercer University Press, 1983, 182-194.

1143 GROSS, C. *Sociology and 1 Peter.* Melbourne, 1984.

1144 LANDWEHR, A. J. "Christian Faith in a Declining Civilization: Pastoral Care in the Light of First Peter," *Quarterly Review* 1,2 (Spring 1981) 59-67.

1145   MARXSEN, W. "Der Mitälteste und Zeuge der Leiden Christi.
       Eine martyrologische Begründung des 'Romprimats' im 1.
       Petrus-Brief?" *Theologia Crucis—Signum Crucis: Fest-
       schrift für Erich Dinkler zum 70. Geburtstag.* Ed. C. Andre-
       sen and G. Klein. Tübingen: Mohr-Siebeck, 1979, 377-393.

1146   QUACQUARELLI, A. "Similtudine, sentenze e proverbi in S.
       Pietro," *San Pietro. Atti della XIX settimana biblica.* Bre-
       scia: Paideia, 1967, 425-442; *Saggi Patristici (retorica ed
       esegesi biblica).* Quaderni di « Vetera Christianorum ». Bari:
       Adriatica, 1971, 307-325.

Mission and Evangelism

1147   O'CONNOR, D. "Holiness of Life as a Way of Christian Wit-
       ness {1 Peter}," *International Review of Mission* 80 (1991)
       17-26.

1148   QUERE, R. W. "The AIDS Crisis: A Call to Mission Based
       on 1 Peter," *CurTM* 14 (1987) 361-369.

Provenance

1149   MANLEY, G. T. "Babylon on the Nile," *EvQ* 16 (1944) 138-
       146.

1150   SEUFERT, W. "Der Abfassungsort des ersten Petrusbriefes,"
       ZWT 28 (1885) 146-156.

1151   SMOTHERS, E. R. "A Letter from Babylon," *Classical Jour-
       nal* 22 (1926-27) 202-209, 418-426.

Style

1152   FINK, P. R. *The Literary Style of Peter and Its Relationship
       to the Exegesis of the Petrine Epistles.* Ph.D. dissertation,
       Dallas Theological Seminary, 1969.

1153   WIFSTRAND, A. "Stylistic Problems in the Epistles of James
       and Peter," *ST* 1 (1948) 170-182.

Teaching

1154 BELCHER, R. P. *Teaching Helps in First Peter.* Columbia, S. C.: Richbarry, 1982.

1155 JONES, P. R. "Teaching First Peter," *RevExp* 79 (1982) 463-472.

Use of the Old Testament, Passages and Concepts

1156 BAUCKHAM, R. "James, 1 and 2 Peter, Jude," *It Is Written: Scripture Citing Scripture.* Ed. D. A. Carson and H. G. M. Williamson. Cambridge, New York, New Rochelle, Melbourne, and Sydney: Cambridge University Press, 1988, 309-313.

1157 DAVEY, G. R. "Old Testament Quotations in the Syriac Version of 1 and 2 Peter," *Parole de l'Orient* 3 (1972), 353-364.

1158 DETERDING, P. E. "Exodus Motifs in First Peter," *Concordia Journal* 7 (1981) 58-65.

1159 GLENNY, W. E. *The Hermeneutics of the Use of the Old Testament in 1 Peter.* Th.D. dissertation, Dallas Theological Seminary, 1987.

1160 GOPPELT, L. *Typos. Die typologische Deutung des Alten Testaments im Neuen.* BFCT 2, Sammlung wissenschaftlicher Monographien 43. Gütersloh: Bertelsmann, 1939; reprint Darmstadt: Wissenschaftliche Buchgesellschaft, 1966.

1161 ——. *TYPOS: The Typological Interpretation of the Old Testament in the New.* Trans. D. H. Madvig. Grand Rapids: Eerdmans, 1982, 152-158.

Reviews: Allen, R. J., *Encounter* 45 (1984) 90-91; Bock, D. L., *BSac* (1983) 274-275; Evans, C. A., *Bib* 64 (1983) 274-275; Hanson, A. T., *JSNT* 22 (1984) 125-126; Hummel, H. D., *Concordia Journal* 9 (1983) 200-201; Karlberg, M. W., *JETS* 26 (1983) 490-493; Sigal, P., *Reformed Journal* 34,11 (N 1984) 24-27; Smith, R. H., *CurTM* 12 (1985) 180-181; Surburg, R. F., *Concordia Theological Quarterly* 49 (1985) 233; Vander Werff, L., *Reformed Review* 39,1 (Autumn 1985) 78; Yanney, R., *Coptic Church Review* 5,2 (Sum 1984) 69-70.

1162 GOTAAS, D. S. *The Old Testament in the Epistle of the Hebrews, the Epistle of James and the Epistle of Peter.* Th.D. dissertation, Northern Baptist Theological Seminary, 1958.

1163 GREEN, G. L. "The Use of the Old Testament for Christian Ethics in 1 Peter," *TynBul* 41 (1990) 276-289.

1164 HILLYER, N. "First Peter and the Feast of Tabernacles," *TynBul* 21 (1970) 39-70.

1165 LEA, T. D. *Peter's Use of the Old Testament*. Ph.D. dissertation, Southwestern Baptist Theological Seminary, 1968.

1166 MCCARTNEY, D. *The Use of the Old Testament in the First Epistle of Peter*. Ph.D. dissertation, Westminster Theological Seminary, 1989.

1167 OSBORNE, T. P. "L'utilisation des citations de l'Ancien Testament dans la première épître de Pierre," *RTL* 12 (1981) 64-77.

1168 OSS, D. A. "The Interpretation of the 'Stone' Passages by Peter and Paul: A Comparative Study," *JETS* 32 (1989) 181-200.

1169 SCHUTTER, W. L. *Hermeneutic and Composition in I Peter*. WUNT 2,30. Tübingen: Mohr-Siebeck, 1989.

1170 VOORWINDE, S. "Old Testament Quotations in Peter's Epistles," *Vox Reformata* 49 (1987) 3-16.

PARALLELS, RELATIONSHIPS, BACKGROUNDS

Here are works that in some way investigate parallels and backgrounds to and relationships with 1 Peter outside the Old Testament. Influences considered in these items may be from the parallels to 1 Peter or vice versa.

1171   ADINOLFI, M.   "La deontologia stoica di Jerocle e il codice domestico della *1 Pt*," *Ellenismo e Bibbia: saggi storici ed esegetici.* Roma: Dehoniane, 1991, 105-122.

1172   ——. "La metanoia della tavola di Cebete alla luce della *1 Pt*," *Anton* 60 (1985) 579-601; *Ellenismo e Bibbia: saggi storici ed esegetici.* Rome: Dehoniane, 1991, 123-143.

1173   ——. *La prima lettera di Pietro nel mondo greco-romano.* Roma: Antonianum, 1988.
Reviews: Osborne, T. P., *RTL* 20 (1989) 222; Rasco, E., *Greg* 69 (1988) 776-777.

1174   ——. "L'Autorità civile nelle diatribe di Epitteto alla luce della *1 Pt*," *Ellenismo e Bibbia: saggi storici ed esegetici.* Roma: Dehoniane, 1991, 93-103.

1175   BARNETT, A. E.   "The First Epistle of Peter," *Paul Becomes a Literary Influence.* Chicago: University Press, 1941, 51-69.

1176   BOISMARD, M.-É.   "Une liturgie baptismale dans la *Prima Petri.* I. —Son influence sur Tit., 1 Jo. et Col.," *RB* 63 (1956) 182-208

1177   ——. "Une liturgie baptismale dans la *Prima Petri.* II. — Son influence sur l'épître de Jacques," *RB* 64 (1957) 161-183.

1178   BOOBYER, G. H.   "The Indebtedness of 2 Peter to 1 Peter," *New Testament Essays: Studies in Memory of Thomas Walter Manson 1893-1958.* Ed. A. J. B. Higgins. Manchester: University Press, 1959, 34-53.

1179   BROX, N.   "Der erste Petrusbrief in der literarischen Tradition des Urchristentums," *Kairos* 20 (1978) 182-192.

1180   CARRINGTON, P.   "I Peter and Parallels," *The Primitive*

Christian Catechism: A Study in the Epistles. Cambridge: University Press, 1940, 22-29.

1181 CLARKE, W. K. L. "The First Epistle of St Peter and the Odes of Solomon," *JTS* 15 (1914) 47-52.

1182 CLEMEN, C. "The First Epistle of St. Peter and the Book of Enoch," *Expositor* 6,6 (1902), 316-320.

1183 DOWNING, F. G. "Pliny's Prosecutions of Christians: Revelation and 1 Peter," *JSNT* 34 (1988) 105-123.

1184 ELLIOTT, J. H. "Ministry and Church Order in the NT: A Traditio-Historical Analysis (1 Pt 5,1-5 and plls.)," *CBQ* 32 (1970) 367-391.

1185 FERRIS, T. E. S. "A Comparison of 1 Peter & Hebrews," *CQR* 111 (1930-31) 123-127.

1186 ———. "The Epistle of James in Relation to 1 Peter," *CQR* 128 (1939) 303-308.

1187 FOSTER, O. D. *The Literary Relations of "The First Epistle of Peter" with their Bearing on Place and Date of Authorship*. Ph.D. dissertation, Yale University, 1911.

1188 ———. "The Literary Relations of 'The First Epistle of Peter' with their Bearing on Date and Place of Authorship," *Transactions of the Connecticut Academy of Arts and Sciences* 17 (1913) 363-538.

1189 GALLOWAY, A. "1 Peter and *The Seafarer*," *English Language Notes* 25 (1988) 1-10.

1190 GOLDSTEIN, H. "Die politischen Paränesen in 1 Petr 2 und Röm 13," *Bibel und Leben* 14 (1973) 88-104.

1191 ———. *Paulinische Gemeinde im Ersten Petrusrief*. Stuttgarter Bibelstudien 80. Stuttgart: Katholisches Bibelwerk, 1975.

1192 HOFRICHTER, P. "Strukturdebatte im Namen des Apostels. Zur Abhängigkeit der Pastoralbriefe untereinander und vom ersten Petrusbrief," *Anfänge und Theologie. XAPIΣTEION Johannes B. Bauer zum Janner 1987*. Ed. N. Brox, A. Felber, and W. Gombocz. Graz, Wien, and Köln: Styria, 1987, 101-116.

1193   KLINZING, G. "1 Pt 2,4 ff," *Die Umdeutung des Kultus in der Qumran-gemeinde und im Neuen Testament.* SUNT 7. Göttingen: Vandenhoek & Ruprecht, 1971, 191-196.

1194   LACONI, M. "Tracce dello stile e dal pensiero di Paolo nella prima lettera di Pietro," *San Pietro. Atti della XIX settimana biblica.* Brescia: Paideia, 1967, 367-394.

1195   MAIER, G. "Jesustradition im 1. Petrusbrief?" *The Jesus Tradition Outside the Gospels.* Gospel Perspectives. Ed. D. Wenham. Sheffield: JSOT Press, 1984, 5:85-128.

1196   McNABB, V. "Date and Influence of the First Epistle of St. Peter," *Irish Ecclesiastical Record* 45 (1935) 596-613.

1197   MIGLIASSO, S. "Il paolinismo di prima Pietro," *RivB* 34 (1986) 519-541.

1198   MITTON, C. L. "The Relationship Between 1 Peter and Ephesians," *JTS* 1 (1950) 67-73.

1199   PALMER, C. L. *The Use of Traditional Materials in Hebrews, James and 1 Peter.* Ph.D. dissertation, Southwestern Baptist Theological Seminary, 1985.

1200   POELMAN, R. "St. Peter and Tradition," *Lumen Vitae* 21 (1966) 50-65.

1201   RIGG, W. H. "Does the First Epistle of St. Peter Throw any Light on the Johannine Problem?" *Expositor* 9,1 (1924) 221-229.

1202   SCHARFE, E. *Die petrinische Strömung der neutestamentlichen Literatur. Untersuchungen über die schriftstellerische Eigentümlichkeit des ersten Petrusbriefes, des Marcusevangeliums und der petrinischen Reden der Apostelgeschichte.* Berlin: Reuther & Reichard, 1893.

1203   SCHATTENMANN, J. "The Little Apocalypse of the Synoptics and the First Epistle of Peter," *TToday* 11 (1954-55) 193-198.

1204   SCHMID, J. "Der Epheserbrief und I Petr.," *Biblische Studien* 22 (1928) 333-362.

1205   SELAND, T. "The 'Common Priesthood' of Philo and 1 Peter: A Philonic Reading of 1 Peter 2.5,9," *JSNT* 57 (1995) 87-119.

1206 SEUFERT, W. "Das Abhängigkeitsverhältnis des 1. Petrusbriefs vom Römerbrief," *ZWT* 17 (1874) 360-388.

1207 ———. "Das Verwandtschaftsverhältnis des ersten Petrusbriefes und Epheserbriefes," *ZWT* 24 (1881) 178-197, 332-380.

1208 TENNEY, M. C. "Some Possible Parallels between 1 Peter and John," *New Dimensions in New Testament Study.* Ed. M. C. Tenney and R. N. Longenecker. Grand Rapids: Zondervan, 1974, 370-377.

1209 VAN ASSELDONK, O. "Le Lettere di S. Pietro negli scritti di S. Francesco," *Collectanea Franciscana* 48 (1978), 67-76.

1210 VAN DODEWAARD, J. "Die sprachliche Übereinstimmung zwischen Markus-Paulus und Markus-Petrus. II. Markus-Petrus," *Bib* 30 (1949) 218-238.

1211 VAN UNNIK, W. C. "A Classical Parallel to I Peter ii 14 and 20," *NTS* 2 (1955-56) 198-202; *Sparsa Collecta: The Collected Essays of W. C. van Unnik.* NovTSup 29-31. Leiden: Brill, 1973-83, 2:106-110.

1212 WILKES, C. G. *The Synoptic Tradition in 1 Peter: An Investigation into Its Forms and Development.* Ph.D. dissertation, Southwestern Baptist Theological Seminary, 1985.

1213 WILSON, C. A. "I Peter {1 Peter 1:22; 3:7; 5:3ff}," *New Light on New Testament Letters.* London: Lakeland, 1971 and Grand Rapids: Baker, 1975, 100-102.

PETER IN THE NEW TESTAMENT

Most books and articles on the life, character, and thought of Peter touch on 1 Peter in some way, though with varying agenda and organization. When they do intersect with 1 Peter, they are included here. Any page numbers listed indicate the pages of the relevant work specifically devoted to an examination of 1 Peter. Books and articles devoted to individual New Testament books and passages outside 1 Peter are not listed here, but works on multiple books and passages outside 1 Peter are included. Excluded is anything about Peter in archaeology or church history outside the New Testament and everything intentionally fictional.

1214   ALAND, K. "Petrus in Rom," *Historische Zeitschrift* 183 (1957) 497-516.

1215   ALCOTT, W. A. *The Life of Peter the Apostle*. Boston: Massachusetts Sabbath School Society, 1836, [2]1839.

1216   ALEXANDER, P., ed. "Peter," *The Lion Encyclopedia of the Bible*. Tring, Batavia: Lion and Sydney: Albatross, 1978, [2]1986, 210.

1217   ALEXANDER, W. L. "Peter," *The Cyclopaedia of Biblical Literature*. Ed. J. Kitto. New York: American Book Exchange, 1880, 2:502-505.

1218   ALLISON, D. C., JR. "Peter and Cephas: One and the Same," *JBL* 111 (1992) 489-495.

1219   ALLMEN, J.-J. von. "Names (Personal): N. T. § 3. Peter," *A Companion to the Bible*. Ed. J.-J. von Allmen. New York: Oxford University Press, 1958, 295-297.

1220   ANONYMOUS. "Peter," *A Concise Cyclopedia of Religious Knowledge*. Ed. E. B. Sanford. Hartford, Conn.: Scranton, 1904, 731-733. {Copyright by Charles L. Webster & Co., 1890.}

1221   ANONYMOUS. "Peter," *A Concise Dictionary of the Bible*. Ed. W. Smith. London: Murray, [3]1872, 714-718.

1222 ANONYMOUS. "Peter," *A Dictionary of the Bible*. Ed. W. Smith. Hartford, Conn.: Scranton, 1900, 725-729.

1223 ANONYMOUS. "Peter," *Cyclopaedia of Biblical, Theological, and Ecclesiastical Literature*. Ed. J. M'Clintock and J. Strong. New York: Harper, 1867-87, 8:4-15; reprint Grand Rapids: Baker, 1981.

1224 ANONYMOUS. "Peter," *Encyclopedia of Religious Knowledge*. Ed. J. N. Brown. Brattleboro', Vt.: Fessenden, 1836, 929-930.

1225 ANONYMOUS. "Peter," *NIV Compact Dictionary of the Bible*. Ed. J. D. Douglas and M. C. Tenney. Grand Rapids: Zondervan, 1989, 448-451.

1226 ANONYMOUS. "Peter," *Peloubet's Bible Dictionary*. Based upon the foundation laid by William Smith. Ed. F. N. Peloubet and A. D. Adams. Philadelphia and Chicago: Winston, 1912, 1925; New York: Holt, Rinehart and Winston, 1913; reprint Grand Rapids: Zondervan, 1971, 503-504.

1227 ANONYMOUS. "Peter, Saint, or Simon Peter," *International Reference Work*. New York, Chicago, and San Francisco: International, 1925, 6:2172.

1228 ANONYMOUS. "Peter, Saint," *The American Cyclopaedia*. New York: Appleton and London: Caxton, 1883 (originally published 1857-63), 13:351-353.

1229 ANONYMOUS. "Peter, Saint," *The Illustrated Columbia Encyclopedia*. New York and London: Columbia University Press, [3]1963, 16:4816-4817.

1230 ANONYMOUS. "Peter, Saint," *The New Columbia Encyclopedia*. New York and London: Columbia University Press, 1975, 2118.

1231 ANONYMOUS. "Peter, Simon," *Concise Dictionary of the Bible*. London: Lutterworth, 1966, 2:244-245.

1232 ANONYMOUS. "Peter (Simon)," *Illustrated Dictionary & Concordance of the Bible*. Ed. (Gen. Ed.) G. Wigoder. New York: Macmillan and London: Collier Macmillan, 1986, 778-779.

1233   ANONYMOUS.   "Peter, Simon," *Nelson's Illustrated Bible Dictionary*. Nashville: Nelson, 1986, 824-827.

1234   ANONYMOUS.   "Peter, St," *Cambridge Biographical Dictionary*. Ed. M. Magnusson. Cambridge, New York, Port Chester, Melbourne, and Sydney: Cambridge University Press, 1990, 1148-1149. (Published in the U. K. as *Chamber's Biographical Dictionary*.)

1235   ANONYMOUS.   "Peter, St," *Chambers's Encyclopaedia*. London: Chambers, 1860, ²1868, ³1878, ⁴1879, 7:445-446.

1236   ANONYMOUS.   "Peter, St," *Chambers's Biographical Dictionary*. Ed. J. O. Thorne. New York: St Martin's and Edinburgh and London: Chambers, 1961 (originally published in 1897), 998.

1237   ANONYMOUS.   "Peter, St., Prince of the Apostles," *The Concise Oxford Dictionary of the Christian Church*. Ed. E. A. Livingstone. Oxford, London, New York: Oxford University Press, 1977, 394.

1238   ANONYMOUS. "Peter, St., Prince of the Apostles," *The Oxford Dictionary of the Christian Church*. Ed. F. L. Cross, 2ⁿᵈ edn. also ed. E. A. Livingstone. Oxford: University Press, 1957, ²1974, 1049-1050 (1ˢᵗ edn.), 1067-1068 (2ⁿᵈ edn.).

1239   ANONYMOUS.   "Peter the Apostle, Saint," *Encyclopaedia Britannica Micropaedia*. Chicago, London, Toronto, Geneva, Sydney, Tokyo, Manila, Seoul, Johannesburg: Encyclopaedia Britannica, ¹⁵1974, 7:909-910.

1240   ANONYMOUS.   "Peter,"   *The Comprehensive Critical and Explanitory Bible Encyclopaedia*. Ed. E. Robinson. Toledo, Ohio: Snow, n.d. {O. A. Browning, 1881}, 739-742.

1241   ANONYMOUS.   "Peter,"   *The Encyclopedia of the Bible*. Originally published as *Elseviers Ecyclopedie van de Bijbel*. Trans. D. R. Welsh; emendations by C. Jones. Englewood Cliffs, N. J.: Prentice-Hall, 1965, 192-193.

1242   ANONYMOUS.   "Peter,"   *The New International Encyclopaedia*. New York: Dodd, Mead, 1902-06, 15:646-647 and 1916-22, 17:414-416.

1243   ANONYMOUS. "Peter," *The New Westminster Dictionary of the Bible*. Ed. H. S. Gehman. Philadelphia: Westminster, 1970, 737-738.

1244   ANONYMOUS. "Peter," *The New World Dictionary-Concordance to the New American Bible*. New York: World, n.d. {copyright 1970 by C. D. Stampley Enterprises Inc.}, 526-528.

1245   ANONYMOUS. "Peter," *Today's Dictionary of the Bible*. Compiled by T. A. Bryant. Minneapolis: Bethany House, 1982, 486-488.

1246   ANONYMOUS. "Peter," *Webster's Biographical Dictionary*. Ed. W. A. Nielson. Springfield, Mass.: Merriam, 1972, 1170.

1247   ANONYMOUS. "Petrus," *Conversations-Lexikon*. Leipzig: Broadhaus, [12]1875-79, 11:665-667.

1248   ANONYMOUS. "Petrus," *Der Große Herder Nachschlagerwerke für Wissen und Leben*. Freiburg: Herder, [4]1931-35, 9:545-548.

1249   ANONYMOUS. "Petrus," *Herders Konversations-Lexikon*. St. Louis: Herder, [3]1902-10, 6:1478 and Beilage I-III.

1250   ANONYMOUS. "Petrus," *Lexikon zur Bibel*. Ed. F. Rienecker. Wuppertal: Brockhaus, 1960, [2]1960, [3]1961, [4]1962, 1057-1059 (for [4]1962 only).

1251   ANONYMOUS. "Petrus," *Meyers kleines Konversations-Lexikon*. Leipzig and Wien: Bibliographisches Institut, 1898-99, 2:887.

1252   ANONYMOUS. "Petrus," *Meyers Lexikon*. Leipzig: Bibliographisches Institut, [7]1924-33, 9:664-665.

1253   AYRE, J. "Peter," *The Imperial Bible-Dictionary*. Ed. P. Fairbairn. London, Glasgow, and Edinburgh: Blackie and Son, 1867, 2:574-580; 1891 ed. by Blackie and Son reprinted as *Fairbairn's Imperial Standard Bible Dictionary*, Grand Rapids: Zondervan, 1957, 5:202-208.

1254   BARKER, W. P. "Peter," *Everyone in the Bible*. Westwood, N.J.: Revell, 1966, 280-281.

1255   BENNET, J. E. *God and Peter.* Grand Rapids: Zondervan, 1939.

1256   BEST, E. "Simon Peter," *The Oxford Companion to the Bible.* New York and Oxford: Oxford University Press, 1993, 695-696.

1257   BOURKE, D. J. "Peter, St., Apostle," *Encyclopedic Dictionary of Religion.* Washington, D. C.: Corpus, 1979, 3:2745-2746.

1258   BOURKE, M. M. "Peter," *The Encyclopedia Americana.* New York, Chicago, and Washington, D. C.: Americana Corporation, 1960 and Danbury, Conn.: Americana Corporation, 1978, 21:656-657.

1259   ———. "Saint Peter," *Encyclopedia Americana.* New York and Chicago: Americana, 1951, 24:163-165.

1260   BRANDES, G. *Petrus.* København: Gyldendal, 1926.

1261   BRANDON, S. G. F. "Peter, St.," *Dictionary of Comparative Religion.* Ed. S. G. F. Brandon. New York: Charles Scribner's Sons, 1970, 493-494.

1262   BROOKS, J. A. "Peter," *Mercer Dictionary of the Bible.* Ed. W. E. Mills (Gen. Ed.). Macon, Ga.: Mercer University Press, 1990, 671-672.

1263   BROWN, R. E., K. P. DONFRIED, and J. REUMANN (eds.). *Peter in the New Testament: A Collaborative Assessment by Protestant and Roman Catholic Scholars.* Minneapolis: Augsburg and New York, Paramus, and Toronto: Paulist, 1973, 149-154.

   Reviews: Beasley-Murray, G. R., *RevExp* 71 (1974) 539-540; Brashler, J., *JES* 13 (1976) 108-109; Brownell, D., *TZ* 33 (1977) 50-51; Dederen, R., *AUSS* 12 (1974) 140-141; Elliott, J. H., *JBL* 95 (1976) 676-678; Granskou, D., *LW* 21 (1974) 98-100; Grassi, J. A., *Horizons* 1 (1974) 106-107; Harrisville, R. A., *Worship* 48 (1974) 30-34; Higgins, A. J. B., *SJT* 31 (1978) 491-492; Jones, J. L., *ATR* 56 (1974) 365-366; MacRae, G. W., *Worship* 48 (1974) 35-39; Mitton, C. L., *ExpTim* 85 (1974) 323-324; Quinn, J. D., *TS* 35 (1974) 554-556; Rhys, J. H., *Saint Luke's Journal of Theology* 17 (1974) 69-70; Schnackenburg, R., *CBQ* 36 (1974) 577-580; Shires, H. M., *Religious Education* 69 (1974) 515; Talbert, C. H., *Religion in Life* 43 (1974) 388-389; Thompson, W. G. and J. H. Elliott, *America* 130 (1974) 53-54; Tyson, J. B., *PSTJ* 27 (1974) 38-39.

1264 ———. *Der Petrus der Bibel. Eine ökumenische Untersuchung.* Trans. E. Füßl. Stuttgart, 1976.

1265 ———. *Saint Pierre dans le Nouveau Testament.* LD 79. Trans. J. Winandy. Paris: Cerf, 1974.
Reviews: Dubois, J. D., *ETR* 52 (1977) 444-445; H. M., *Irénikon* 48 (1975) 586-587; Léon-Dufour, X., *RSR* 64 (1976) 423-425; Rigaux, B., *RHE* 70 (1975) 758-761.

1266 BROWN, R. E. "Peter," *IDBSup.* Nashville: Abingdon, 1976, 654-657.

1267 BROWNRIGG, R. "Andrew and Peter, Brothers from Bethsaida," *The Twelve Apostles.* London: Weidenfeld and Nicholson and New York: Macmillan, 1974, 41-83.

1268 ———. "Peter," *Who's Who in the New Testament* by Ronald Brownrigg. New York: Holt, Rinehart and Winston, 1971, 345-356.

1269 BRUCE, F. F. "Peter and the Eleven," *Men and Movements in the Primitive Church: Studies in Early Non-Pauline Christianity.* The Didsbury Lectures. Exeter: Paternoster, 1979, 15-48.

1270 ———. *Peter, Stephen, James, and John: Studies in Early Non-Pauline Christianity.* Grand Rapids: Eerdmans, 1979.
Reviews: Boys, M. C., *CBQ* 43 (1981) 457-458; Edwards, E. G., *Princeton Seminary Bullitin* 3 (1982) 319-321; Hammer, R., *SJT* 34 (1981) 281; Hultgren, A. J., *Dialog* 19 (1980) 309-310; Kiehl, E. H., *Concordia Journal* 7 (1981) 212; Page, S. H. T., *JETS* 24 (1981) 274-275; Sanders, B., *JRT* 37 (1980-1981) 68-72; Silva, M., *WTJ* 44 (1982) 161-163.

1271 ———. "Peter the Apostle," *Twentieth Century Encyclopedia of Religious Knowledge.* Grand Rapids: Baker, 1955, 869.

1272 БЋКВАИНЬ, С. *Свцамые Пемр ц Иоанн.* Paris: Y.M.C.A., 1926.

1273 BYRUM, E. E. *Peter the Fisherman Preacher.* Anderson, Ind.: Warner, 1931.

1274 CASE, S. J. "Peter," *Dictionary of the Apostolic Church.* Ed. J. Hastings. New York: Charles Scribner's Sons and Edinburgh: T. & T. Clark, 1918, 2:191-201.

1275 CASTELOT, J. J. "Peter, Apostle, St.," *New Catholic Encyclopedia*. New York, St. Louis, San Francisco, Toronto, London, and Sydney: McGraw-Hill, 1967, 11:200-205.

1276 CHASE, F. H. "Peter (Simon)," *A Dictionary of the Bible*. Ed. J. Hastings. New York: Charles Scribner's Sons and Edinburgh: T. & T. Clark, 1898-1904, 3:756-779.

1277 CHEVROT, G. *Simon Pedro*. Madrid: Rialp, 1956.

1278 ———. *Simon Peter*. Chicago, Dublin, and London: Scepter, 1959.

1279 ———. *Simon-Pierre*. Paris: Bloud & Gay.

1280 CIPRIANI, S. "Pedro Apóstol, San," *Gran Enciclopedia Rialp*. Madrid: Rialp, 1971, 18:159-165.

1281 COGGINS, R. "Peter," *Who's Who in the Bible*. Totowa, N.J.: Barnes & Noble, 1981, 217-220.

1282 COOK, F. C. "Peter," *A Dictionary of the Bible*. By (sic) William Smith. Rev. F. N. and M. A. Peloubet. Grand Rapids: Zondervan, 1948, 1967, 502-504. ("Copyright 1884 by Porter and Coates.")

1283 ———. "Peter," *Dictionary of the Bible*. Ed. W. Smith. London: John Murray and London: Walton and Maberly, 1863, 2:797-810.

1284 ———. "Peter," with an editorial addition by E. Abbot, *Dr. William Smith's Dictionary of the Bible*. Rev. and ed. by H. B. Hackett. New York: Hurd and Houghton and Cambridge: Riverside, 1872, 3:2445-2460.

1285 COSTELLOE, M. J. "Peter, St.", *Collier's Encyclopedia*. N.p.: Macmillan, 1974 and New York, Toronto, and Sydney: Collier, 1993, 18:617-618.

1286 COTRELL, R. F. "Peter," *Seventh-Day Adventist Bible Dictionary*. Commentary Reference Series 8. Washington, D. C.: Review and Herald, 1960, 844-846.

1287 CULLMANN, O. *Peter: Disciple—Apostle—Martyr: A Historical and Theological Study*. Trans. F. V. Filson. London: SCM, 1953; ²1962; Philadelphia: Westminster, 1953, (2)1962.

Reviews: Allen, E. L., *JTS* 5 (1954) 59-62; Bailey, J. W., *JBR* 22 (1954) 211-212; Caird, G. B., *ExpTim* 73 (1962) 297; Green-Armytage, A. H. N., *Downside Review* 72 (1954) 201-204; Jennings, K. N., *Indian Journal of Theology* 12 (1962) 158-159; Johnston, G., *CJT* 1 (1955) 53-55; Jones, J. E., *RevExp* 51 (1954) 538-539; Lampe, G. W. H., *CQR* 155 (1954) 176-178; McArthur, H. K., *Religion in Life* 23 (1954) 462-464; McCaughey, J. D., *Reformed Theological Review* 13 (1954) 21-22; McConnell, J. F., *CBQ* 16 (1954) 362-366; McConnell, J. F., *CBQ* 24 (1962) 456-457; Niel, W., *SJT* 7 (1954) 207-210; Sasse, H., *Reformed Theological Review* 21 (1962) 58-60; Wand, J. W. C., *CQR* 163 (1962) 519; Wikgren, A., *JR* 35 (1955) 252-254; Wilder, A. N., *CH* 23 (1954) 278-279.

1288 ——. *Petrus. Jünger-Apostel-Märtyrer. Das historische und das theologische Petrusproblem.* Zürich and Stuttgart: Zwingli 1952, ²1960.

Reviews: Benoit, P., *RB* 69 (1962) 442-443; Burgess, J., *TZ* 17 (1961) 226; Gnilka, J., *ZKG* 73 (1962) 135-137; Michaelis, W., *TLZ* 86 (1961) 921-922; Rasco, E., *Greg* 44 (1963) 881; Weis, E. A., *TS* 23 (1962) 280-282.

1289 ——. *Saint Pierre. Disciple-apôtre-martyr. Histoire et théologie.* Bibliothèque théologique. Neuchâtel and Paris: Delachaux & Niestlé, 1952.

Reviews: Benoit, P., *RB* 60 (1953) 565-579; Goguel, M., *RHPR* 35 (1955) 196-209; Wikgren, A., *JR* 35 (1955) 252-25 {thus the ATLA *Index*; cf. the Wikgren review of the English *Peter: Disciple, Apostle, Martyr* above.}.

1290 DALLMAN, W. *Peter: Life and Letters.* St. Louis: Concordia, 1930.

1291 DE HAAN, M. R. *Simon Peter: Sinner and Saint.* Grand Rapids: Zondervan, 1954.

1292 DELANEY, J. J., and J. E. TOBIN. "Peter, St.," *Dictionary of Catholic Biography.* Garden City, N.Y.: Doubleday, 1961, 916.

1293 DELANEY, J. J. "Peter," *Dictionary of Saints.* Garden City, N.Y.: Doubleday, 1980, 457.

1294 DINKLER, E. "Die Petrus-Rom-Frage. Ein Forschungsbericht," *TRu* 25 (1959) 189-230, 289-335; 27 (1961) 33-64.

1295 DODD, P. S. *A View of the Evidence, Afforded by the Life and Ministry of St. Peter, to the Truth of the Christian Revelation.* London: Rivington, 1837.

1296   ELERT, W. *Die Religiosität des Petrus. Ein religionspsy-chologischer Versuch.* Leipzig: Deichert, 1911.

1297   ELTON, G. E. *Simon Peter: A Study of Discipleship.* London: P. Davies, 1965, ²1967; Garden City, N. Y.: Doubleday, 1966.
       Review: James, A., *Downside Review* 84 (1966) 85-86.

1298   EMMERICH, A. C. *Der heilige Petrus, ein Schuler, Apostel, Martyrer und Stellvertreter Jesu Christi.* Ed. B. Smeddinck. Baltimore: Kreuzer, 1869.

1299   ENGLISH, E. S. *The Life and Letters of Saint Peter.* New York: Our Hope/Gabelein, 1941, 149-232.

1300   ESSIG, M. F. "Peter," *The Railway Through the Word or, The Holy Bible Analyzed.* Nashville: Southwestern, 1908, 402-405.

1301   FARMER, D. H. "Peter," *The Oxford Dictionary of Saints.* Oxford: Clarendon, 1978, 320-322.

1302   FARRAR, F. W. "St. Peter," *The Early Days of Christianity.* London: Cassell, Petter, Galpin 1882 and New York: Funk and Wagnalls, 1883, 60-66.

1303   FASCHER, E. "Petrus {'Jünger und Apostel Jesu Christi'}," PW. Stuttgart: Metzler, 1894-1963, 38:1335-1361; *Socrates und Christus. Beiträge zur Religionsgesichte.* Leipzig, 1959, 175-223.

1304   FAUSSET, A. R. "Peter," *Bible Cyclopaedia.* Hartford, Conn.: Scranton, 1907, 560-562; reprint as *Fausset's Bible Dictionary,* Grand Rapids: Zondervan, 1961.

1305   FELDMEIER, R. "Die Darstellung des Petrus in den synoptischen Evangelien," *Das Evangelium und die Evangelien.* WUNT 28. Tübingen: Mohr-Siebeck, 1983, 267-271.

1306   FILLION, L. "Pierre (Saint)," *Dictionnaire de la Bible.* Paris: Letouzey et Ané, 1895-1912, 7:356-379.

1307   FILSON, F. V. "Peter," *IDB.* New York and Nashville: Abingdon, 1962, 3:749-757.

1308 ———. "Peter," *Pioneers of the Primitive Church*. New York, Cincinnati, and Chicago: Abingdon, 1940, 19-51.

1309 FINDLAY, J. A. *A Portrait of Peter*. New York, Cincinnati, and Chicago: Abingdon, 1935.

1310 FITZMYER, J. A. "Aramaic Kepha' and Peter's Name in the New Testament," *Text and Interpretation: Studies in the New Testament Presented to Matthew Black*. Ed. E. Best and R. McL. Wilson. Cambridge, London, New York, and Melbourne: Cambridge University Press, 1979, 121-132.

1311 ———. "Aramaic Kepha' and Peter's Name in the New Testament," *To Advance the Gospel: New Testament Studies*. New York: Crossroad, 1981, 112-124.

1312 FOAKES-JACKSON, F. J. *Peter: Prince of the Apostles: A Study in the History and Tradition of Christianity*. London: Hodder and Stoughton and New York: Doran, 1927.

1313 FOUARD, C. [H]. *Saint Peter and the First Years of Christianity*. Trans. G. F. X. Griffith from the 2nd edition of *Saint Pierre et les premières années du christianism*. New York, London, Bombay, and Calcutta: Longmans, Green, 1892.

1314 ———. *Saint Pierre et les premières années du christianism*. Paris: Lecoffre, 1886, ^{3}1893.

1315 FRANCIS, P. J., and S. JONES. *The Prince of the Apostles: A Study*. Garrison, N. Y.: Lamp. 1907.

1316 GAECHTER, P. *Petrus und seine Zeit. Neutestamentliche Studien*. Innsbruck, Wien, and München: Tyrolia, 1958.
Reviews: Danker, F. W., *CTM* 30 (1959) 947-948; Fitzmyer, J. A., *TS* 26 (1965) 300-303; Hasler, V., *TZ* 22 (1966) 215-217; R. H. F., *ATR* 42 (1960) 383-384; Vawter, B., *CBQ* 26 (1964) 485-486.

1317 GALLAGHER, M. "Peter," *The Popular and Critical Bible Encyclopaedia and Scriptural Dictionary*. Ed. S. Fallows. Chicago: Howard-Severance, 1901, 2:1318-1319.

1318 GEORGES, N. "Peter, Saint; and Epistles of," *The New Catholic Dictionary*. New York: Universal Knowledge, 1929, 749-750.

1319 GILMORE, G. W. "Peter the Apostle," *The New Schaff-Herzog Encyclopedia of Religious Knowledge*. New York and London: Funk and Wagnalls, 1908-14; reprint Grand Rapids: Baker, 1957-60, 8:479-488.

1320 GOETZ, K. G. *Petrus als Gründer und Oberhaupt der Kirche und Schauer von Gesichten nach den altchristlichen Berichten und Legenden. Eine exegetisch-geschichtliche Untersuchung.* UNT 13. Leipzig: Hinrichs, 1927.

1321 GRANT, M. *Saint Peter.* London: Weidenfeld & Nicholson, 1994.

1322 GRAY, J. M. "Peter, Simon," *The International Standard Bible Encyclopedia.* Chicago: Howard-Severance, 1915, [2]1929, 4:2348-2351.

1323 GRYGLEWICZ, F. "Opis Końca swiata u św. Piotra i w Qumran," *Ruch Biblijny i Liturgiczny* 12 (1959) 278-282.

1324 GUTHRIE, D. "Peter the Apostle," *The New International Dictionary of the Christian Church.* Ed. J. D. Douglas. Grand Rapids: Zondervan, 1974, 770.

1325 HAENCHEN, E. "Petrus-Probleme," *NTS* 7 (1960-61) 187-197.

1326 HALL, J. F. "Peter," *Encyclopedia of Mormonism.* Ed. D. H. Ludlow. New York: Macmillan and Toronto: Maxwell Macmillan, 1992, 3:1077-1079.

1327 HANSON, R. P. C. "Peter, St," *A Dictionary of Christian Theology.* Ed. A. Richardson. Philadelphia: Westminster, 1969, 257.

1328 HARDON, J. A. "Peter," *Modern Catholic Dictionary.* Garden City, N. Y.: Doubleday, 1980, 418-419.

1329 HASELHURST, R. S. T. "Mark, My Son," *Theology* 13 (1926) 34-36.

1330 HIEBERT, D. E. "Peter," *The New International Dictionary of the Bible.* Grand Rapids: Zondervan and Basingstoke: Marshall Pickering, 1987, 771-773. {Originally published as *The Zondervan Pictorial Bible Dictionary.*}

1331 ——. "Peter," *The Zondervan Pictorial Bible Dictionary.* Grand Rapids: Zondervan, 1963, [2]1963, [3]1964, 640-642.

1332   HOBERG, {no forename given}. "Petrus, der hl., der Apos-
        telfürst," *Wetzer und Welte's Kirchenlexikon*. Ed. J. Hergen-
        röther and F. Kaulen. Freiburg, Wein, Straßburg, München,
        and St. Louis: Herder, ²1882-1903, 9:1857-1868.

1333   HOFSTETTER, K. *Das Petrusamt in der Kirche des 1-2.
        Jahrhunderts: Jerusalem-Rom*. Frankfurt, 1960.

1334   HOLWECK, F. G. "Peter, The Prince of the Apostles," *A Bio-
        graphical Dictionary of the Saints*. St Louis and London:
        Herder, 1924; reprint Detroit: Gale, 1969, 797.

1335   HOTCHKIN, S. F. "Peter, St.," *The Church Cyclopaedia: A
        Dictionary of Church Doctrine, History, Organization and
        Ritual, and Containing Original Articles on Special Topics,
        Written Expressly for this Work by Bishops, Presbyters, and
        Laymen*. Ed. A. A. Benton. New York: Mallory, 1883, 588-
        591.

1336   HOULDEN, J. L. "Peter," *A Dictionary of Biblical Interpreta-
        tion*. Ed. R. J. Coggins and J. L. Houlden. London: SCM
        and Philadelphia: Trinity, 1990, 532-534.

1337   HUBER, R. M. "Peter, St., First Bishop of Rome," *An Ency-
        clopedia of Religion*. Ed. V. Ferm. New York: The Philo-
        sophical Library, 1945, 578-579.

1338   IRMSCHER, J., and A. W. CARR. "Peter," *The Oxford Dic-
        tionary of Byzantium*. New York and Oxford: Oxford Uni-
        versity Press, 3:1636-1637.

1339   JANVIER, P. D. *Leben des heiligen Petrus, des Apostelfürsten
        und ersten Papstes*. Einsiedeln and New York: Benziger,
        1879.

1340   JAVIER, J. *Historia s. Petri persice conscripta, simulque
        multi modis contaminata*. Lvgdvni Batavorvm: Elseviriana,
        1639.

1341   JOHNSON, L. T. "Peter, Saint," *Encyclopedia Americana*.
        Danbury, Conn.: Grolier, 1989, 21:800-801.

1342   JONES, B., and M. V. DIXON. "Peter, St," *The St. Martin's
        Press Dictionary of Biography*, the revised edition of *The
        Macmillan Dictionary of Biography* (1981). New York: St.
        Martin's, 1986, 661.

1343 KALT, E. "Petrus," *Biblisches Reallexikon.* Paderborn: Schöningh, Wein: Fürlinger, and Zürich: B. Götschmann, ²1938-39, 2:347-352.

1344 KARRER, O. *Peter and the Church: An Examination of Cullmann's Thesis.* QD 8. Trans. R. Walls. Freiburg and New York: Herder and London and Edinburgh: Nelson, 1963.
Reviews: Butler, C., *Downside Review* 81 (1963) 371-372; Green, E. M. B., *Churchman* 77 (1963) 267-268; McCue, J. F., *TS* 24 (1963) 676-678.

1345 ——. *Um die Einheit der Christen. Die Petrusfrage. Ein Gespräch mit Emil Brunner, Oskar Cullmann, Hans von Campenhausen.* Frankfurt: Knecht, 1953.

1346 KELLY, J. N. D. "Peter, St, Apostle," *The Oxford Dictionary of Popes.* Oxford and New York: Oxford University Press, 1986, 5-6.

1347 KENNARD, D. W. *The Doctrine of God in Petrine Theology.* Th.D. dissertation, Dallas Theological Seminary, 1986.

1348 KIRSCH, J. P. "Peter, Saint, Prince of the Apostles," *The Catholic Encyclopedia.* New York: Enclopedia Press, 1913, 11:744-752.

1349 KNABENBAUER, I. "Petrus," *Lexicon Biblicum.* Cursus Scripturae Sacrae. Ed. M. Hagen. Parisiis: Lethielleux, 1905-11, 3:572-576.

1350 KNOCH, O. *Die „Testamente" des Petrus und Paulus: Die Sicherung der apostolischen Überlieferung in der spätneutes-tamentlichen Zeit.* SBS 62. Stuttgart: Katholisches Bibel-werk, 1973.

1351 KNOPF, {no forename given}. "Petrus, Apostel," *RGG.* Tübingen: Mohr-Siebeck, 1909-13, 4:1408-1412.

1352 KOBAYASHI, T. *The Role of Peter According to the Theo-logical Understanding of Paul, Mark, and Luke-Acts.* Ph.D. dissertation, Drew University, 1962.

1353 KOGER, A. D., JR. *The Question of a Distinctive Petrine Theology in the New Testament.* Ph.D. dissertation, Baylor University, 1988.

1354   KOHLER, K.   "Simon Cephas (Better Known as Peter)," *The Jewish Encyclopedia*. New York: Ktav and London: Funk and Wagnalls, 1901-06, [2]1925, 11:366-368.

1355   KOWALSKI, S.   *Zstąpienie do piekieł Chrystusa Pana wedle nauki św. Piotra Apostoła (Rozbiór krytyczny Dz. II,27, 31 i 1 Piotr. III, 19,20; IV, 6)*. Poznań, 1938.

1356   LAFFERTY, O. J.   "Peter, St.," *The Catholic Encyclopedia for School and Home*. New York, San Francisco, Dallas, Toronto, London, and Sydney: McGraw-Hill, 1965, 8:352-354.

1357   LAKE, K.   "Peter, St," *Encyclopaedia Britannica*. Cambridge: University Press and New York: Encyclopaedia Britannica, [11]1911, 21:285-288; London and New York: Encyclopaedia Britannica, [13]1926, 21:285-288.

1358   LAMARCHE, P.   "Pedro (san)," *Vocabulario de Teología Biblica*. Ed. X. Léon-Dufour. Trans A. E. Lator Ros from *Vocabulaire de théologie biblique* (Ed. X. Léon-Dufour, Paris: Cerf, [5]1970). Barcelona: Herder, 1965, [9]1977, [12]1982, 670-672.

1359   ——.   "Peter," trans. J. J. Kilgallen, *Dictionary of Biblical Theology*. Ed. X. Léon-Dufour. Trans. under the direction of P. J. Cahill from *Vocabulaire de théologie biblique* (Ed. X. Léon-Dufour, Paris: Cerf, 1962, [2]1968). New York: Seabury, 1967, [2]1973, 427-428.

1360   ——.   "Saint Pierre," *Vocabulaire de théologie biblique*. Ed. X. Léon-Dufour. Paris: Cerf, 1962, 830-831; [2]1968; [6]1988 {"Pierre (Saint)"} 996-998.

1361   LANG, J. P.   "Peter, Apostle, St.," *Dictionary of the Liturgy*. New York: Catholic Book, 1989, 505.

1362   LÉON-DUFOUR, X.   "Peter (Saint)," *Dictionary of the New Testament*. Trans. T. Prendergast. San Francisco: Harper & Row, 1980, 320.

1363   LOWE, J.   *Saint Peter*. London and New York: Oxford University Press and Oxford: Clarendon, 1956.

1364   LYONETTE, S.   "De ministerio romano S. Petri ante adventum S. Pauli," *VD* 33 (1955) 143-154.

1365   MacDuff, J. R. *The Footsteps of St. Peter: Being the Life and Times of the Apostle.* New York: Carter, 1877; reprint Minneapolis: Klock, 1982, 562-580. {Cf. also the section on commentaries.}

1366   MacGregor, G. "Peter," *Dictionary of Philosophy and Religion.* New York: Paragon, 1989, 479.

1367   MacInnis, J. M. *Peter the Fisherman Philosopher: A Study in Higher Fundamentalism.* New York and London: Harper, 1927 and 1930.

1368   Mackintosh, C. H. *Simon Peter: His Life and Its Lessons.* New York: Loizeaux, 1945.

1369   Malloch, J. M. "Peter, Saint," *A Practical Church Dictionary.* Ed. K. Smallzried. New York: Morehouse-Barlow, 1964, 363-364.

1370   Martin, R. P. "Peter," *ISBE.* Grand Rapids: Eerdmans, ³1979-88, 3:802-807.

1371   Marucchi, O. *Pietro e Paolo a Roma.* Torino and Roma: Marietti, ⁴1934.

1372   McCue, J. F. "Peter The Apostle," *The Encyclopedia of Religion.* New York: Macmillan and London: Collier Macmillan, 1987, 11:258-260.

1373   McKenzie, J. L. "Peter," *Dictionary of the Bible.* Milwaukee: Bruce, 1965, 663-666.

1374   Meinertz, M. "Petrus," *Lexikon für Theologie und Kirche.* Freiburg: Herder, ²1929-38, 8:131-135.

1375   Miller, M. S., and J. L. Miller. "Peter," *Harper's Bible Dictionary.* New York: Harper, 1952, 541-542; New York, Evanston, and London: Harper & Row, ⁷1961, 541-542.

1376   Moret, J. *Simon Bar Jona, un homme de foi.* Paris: Apostolat des Éditions, 1967.

1377   Moule, C. F. D. "Some Reflections on the 'Stone' *Testimonia* in Relation to the Name Peter," *NTS* 2 (1955-56) 56-58.

1378   Myrant, R. W. *Petrine Theology.* Th.D. dissertation, Dallas Theological Seminary, 1956.

1379   NEVINS, A. J. "Peter, St.," *The Maryknoll Catholic Diction-
        ary*. New York: Grosset & Dunlap, 1965, 443.

1380   NOURSE, E. E. "Peter, Simon, The Apostle," *A New Standard
        Bible Dictionary*. New York and London: Funk & Wagnalls,
        ²1925, ³1936, 696-699.

1381   ——. "Saint Peter," *The Encyclopedia Americana*. New
        York: Scientific American, 1903-06, 13:n.p.

1382   O'BRIEN, I. *Peter and Paul, Apostles: An Account of the
        Early Years of the Church*. Paterson, N. J.: St. Anthony
        Guild, 1950.

1383   O'CONNOR, D. W., JR. *Peter in Rome: An Investigation into
        the Literary, Liturgical and Archaeological Evidence for the
        Residence, Martyrdom and Burial of Peter in Rome*. Ph.D.
        dissertation, Columbia University, 1959.

1384   O'CONNOR, D. W. *Peter in Rome: The Literary, Liturgical
        and Archaeological Evidence*. New York and London: Co-
        lumbia University Press, 1969, 14-18, 64.
        Reviews: Allen, F., *Journal of the Canadian Church Historical Society*
        12 (Mr 1970) 17; Barnes, T. D., *JTS* 21 (1970) 175-179; Buehler, W.
        W., *Christianity Today* 13 (Je 6 1969) 23-24; Shepherd, M. H., Jr.,
        JAAR 37 (1969) 180-181.

1385   ——. "Peter the Apostle," *Abingdon Dictionary of Living
        Religions*. Ed. K. Crim. Nashville: Abingdon, 1981, 566-
        567.

1386   ——. "Peter the Apostle, Saint," *Encyclopaedia Britannica
        Macropaedia*. Chicago, London, Toronto, Geneva, Sydney,
        Tokyo, Manila, Seoul, and Johannesburg: Encyclopaedia
        Britannica, ¹⁵1974, 14:153-157.

1387   ——. "Peter the Apostle, Saint," *Encyclopaedia Britannica
        Macropaedia*. Chicago, London, Toronto, Geneva, Sydney,
        Tokyo, Manila, Seoul, and Johannesburg: Encyclopaedia
        Britannica, ¹⁵1987, 9:330-333.

1388   OSBORNE, G. R. "Peter, The Apostle," *Baker Encyclopedia
        of the Bible*. Ed. W. A. Elwell. Grand Rapids: Baker, 1988,
        2:1659-1667.

1389 ———. "Peter the Apostle," *Who's Who in Christian History.* Ed. J. D. Douglas and P. W. Comfort. Wheaton: Tyndale House, 1992, 549-555.

1390 PACIOREK, A. "Obraz Piotra w pierwotnej gminie [Das Petrusbild der Urgemeinde]," *Studia Theologica Varsaviensia* 14 (1976) 85-98.

1391 PANIMOLLE, S. A. "L'autorité de Pierre en *Ga* 1-2 et *Ac* 15," *Paul de Tarse, Apôtre de notre temps.* Ed. L. De Lorenzi. Rome: Abbaye de S. Paul, 1979, 269-289.

1392 PATRICK, W. "Peter," *A Dictionary of Christ and the Gospels.* Ed. J. Hastings. New York: Charles Scribner's Sons and Edinburgh: T. & T. Clark, 1908, 2:349-351.

1393 PENNA, A. *San Pietro.* [Brescia]: Morcelliana, 1954.

1394 PENNINGTON, M. B. *Daily We Follow Him: Learning Discipleship from Peter.* Originally published as *In Peter's Footsteps.* Garden City, N. Y.: Image Books, 1987.

1395 ———. *In Peter's Footsteps: Learning to Be a Disciple.* Garden City, N.Y.: Doubleday, 1985.

1396 PERKINS, D. W. "Simon Rock: An Appraisal of Peter in the New Testament Witness," *Theological Educator* 13,1 (Fall 1982) 42-54.

1397 PERKINS, P. "Peter," *Harper's Bible Dictionary.* Ed. P. J. Achtemeier (Gen. Ed.). San Francisco: Harper & Row, 1985, 776-778.

1398 PESCH, R. "Peter in the Mirror of Paul's Letters," *Paul de Tarse, Apôtre de notre temps.* Ed. L. De Lorenzi. Roma: Abbaye de S. Paul, 1979, 291-309.

1399 ———. *Simon-Petrus. Geschichte und geschichtliche Bedeutung des ersten Jüngers Jesu Christi.* Päpste und Pappstum 15. Stuttgart: Hiersemann, 1980.
   Reviews: Benko, S., *American Historical Review* 86 (1981) 579-580; Betz, O., *TLZ* 109 (1984) 38-39; Hall, S. G., *JEH* 33 (1982) 586-589.

1400 RICHARDS, L. O. "The Apostle Peter," *The Bible Reader's Companion.* Wheaton: Victor Books, 1991, 711.

1401 ROBERTSON, A. T. *Epochs in the Life of Simon Peter.* New York and London: Charles Scribner's Sons, 1933; reprint in the A. T. Robertson Library, Grand Rapids: Baker, 1974.

1402 ROBINSON, C. S. *Simon Peter: His Early Life and Times.* New York: American Tract Society, 1889.

1403 ——. *Simon Peter: His Later Life and Labours.* New York, London, and Edinburgh: Nelson, 1894.

1404 ROSITO, M. G., ed. *Pietro nella Sacra Scrittura.* I maestri di ieri e di oggi 3. Firenze: Città di Vita, 1975.

1405 SALDARINI, A. J. "Peter, Saint," *Academic American Encyclopedia.* Princeton: Aretê, 1981 and Danbury, Conn.: Grolier, 1986, 15:199-200.

1406 SALVONI, F. "Il servizio di Pietro," *Ricerche bibliche e religiose* 17 (1982) 130-136.

1407 SCHELKLE, K. H. "Petrus in den Briefen des Neuen Testaments," *BK* 23 (1968) 46-50.

1408 SCHMID, J. "Petrus der 'Fels' und die Petrusgestalt der Urgemeinde," *Begegnung der Christen. Studien evangelischer und katholischer Theologen.* Ed. M. Roesle and O. Cullmann. Stuttgart: Evangelisches Verlagswerk and Frankfurt: Knecht, 1959, ^{2}1960, 347-359.

1409 SCHMIEDEL, P. W. "Simon Peter," *Encyclopaedia Biblica.* Ed. T. K. Cheyne and J. S. Black. London: Black, 1899-1903, 4:4559-4567.

1410 SCHNACKENBURG, R. "Das Petrusamt. Die Stellung des Petrus zu den anderen Aposteln," *Wort und Wahrheit* 26 (1971) 206-216.

1411 SCHNEIDER, R. "Der Glaube des Petrus," *Das Unzerstörbare. Religiöse Schriften.* Gesamelte Werke. Frankfurt: Insel, 1978, 9:89-96.

1412 SCHULZ-KADELBACH, G. "Die Stellung des Petrus in der Urchristenheit," *TLZ* 81 (1956) 1-14.

1413 SCOTT, E. F. "Peter," *An Encyclopedia of Religion.* Ed. V. Ferm. New York: The Philosophical Library, 1945, 577.

1414 ——. "Peter, The Apostle," *A Dictionary of Religion and Ethics*. Ed. S. Matthews and G. B. Smith. New York: Macmillan, 1921, 334.

1415 SENIOR, D. P., and F. W. NORRIS. "Peter," *Encyclopedia of Early Christianity*. Ed. E. Ferguson. New York and London: Garland, 1990, 719-723.

1416 SEYLER, G. "Ueber die Gedankenordnung in den Reden und Briefen des Apostels Petrus," *TSK* (1832) 44-70.

1417 SHEEN, F. J., and M. C. TENNEY. "Peter, Saint," *The World Book Encyclopedia*. Chicago, Frankfurt, London, Paris, Rome, Sydney, Tokyo, and Toronto: World Book-Childcraft, 1978, 15:284-285.

1418 SHERWOOD, J. C. "Saint Peter: Simon," *Great Lives From History: Ancient and Medieval Series*. Ed. F. N. Magill. Pasadena and Englewood Cliffs, N. J.: Salem, 1988, 5:1580-1583.

1419 SIEFFERT, F. "Peter, The Apostle," *A Religious Encyclopedia or Dictionary of Biblical, Historical, Doctrinal, and Practical Theology* (based on the Real-Encyclopädie of Herzog, Plitt and Hauck). Ed. P. Schaff. New York and London: Funk and Wagnalls, ³1891, 3:1813-1817.

1420 SMITH, D. "Peter," *Dictionary of the Bible*. Ed. J. Hastings. New York: Charles Scribner's Sons, 1909, 713-714; new edition ed. F. C. Grant and H. H. Rowley, article revised by H. M. Shires, New York: Charles Scribner's Sons, 1963, 752-754.

1421 ——. *The Life of St. Peter*. New York: Mason and Lane for The Sunday School Union of the Methodist Episcopal Church, 1840.

1422 SMITH, T. V. *Petrine Controversies in Early Christianity: Attitudes towards Peter in Christian Writings of the First Two Centuries*. Doctoral thesis, University of London, 1981.

1423 ——. *Petrine Controversies in Early Christianity: Attitudes towards Peter in Christian Writings of the First Two Centuries*. WUNT 2,15. Tübingen: Mohr-Siebeck, 1985.
   Reviews: Achtemeier, P. J., *JBL* 107 (1988) 337-339; Ellis, E. E., *Southwestern Journal of Theology* 30 (1988) 68; Grappe, C., *RHPR* 66 (1986) 237-238; Harrington, D. J., *CBQ* 49 (1987) 352-353; Horst, P.

W. van der, *NedTTs* 41 (1987) 320-321; Lieu, J. M., *ExpTim* 97 (1986) 180; Norelli, E., *Christianesimo nella Storia* 9 (1988) 177-181; Orbe, A., *Greg* 68 (1987) 432-433.

1424   SMYTH-VAUDRY, T. *Peter's Name or A Divine Credential in a Name*. Techny, Ill.: Society of the Divine Word, 1909.

1425   STEINMUELLER, J. E., and K. SULLIVAN. "Peter, Saint," *Catholic Biblical Encyclopedia: New Testament*. New York: Wagner, 1950, 503-504.

1426   STRATHMANN, H. "Die Stellung des Petrus in der Urkirche," *ZST* 20 (1943) 223-282.

1427   STRATON, H. H. *Peter, the Man Jesus Made*. Grand Rapids: Zondervan, 1938.

1428   TAYLOR, W. M. *Peter the Apostle*. New York: Harper, 1876, 332-348.

1429   THIEDE, C. P. *Simon Peter: From Galilee to Rome*. Exeter: Paternoster, 1986; Grand Rapids: Zondervan, 1988, 169-194 (Section III, "Peter's Last Years in his letters and in Church History").
Reviews: Bauckham, R., *Scottish Bulletin of Evangelical Theology* 6 (1988) 41-43; Brown, R. E., *Bib* 68 (1987) 583-584; Bruce, F. F., *ExpTim* 98 (1987) 281-282; Ellis, E. E., *Southwestern Journal of Theology* 32 (1990) 55-56; Frend, W. H. C., *JEH* 41 (1990) 137-138; Jensen, P., *Reformed Theological Review* 46 (1987) 92; Marshall. I. H., *Themelios* 12 (1987) 103; Osborne, T. P., *RTL* 19 (1988) 88-89.

1430   THOMAS, W. H. G. *The Apostle Peter: Outline Studies in His Life, Character, and Writings*. London: The Religious Tract Society, 1906 and New York, Chicago, and Toronto: Revell, 1904; reprint Grand Rapids: Eerdmans, 1946.

1431   TURNER, C. H. "St. Peter in the New Testament," *Theology* 13 (1926) 66-78.

1432   UNDERHILL, F. L. *Saint Peter*. London: Centenary, 1937 and New York and Toronto: Longmans, Green, 1938.

1433   UNGER, M. F. "Peter," *Unger's Bible Dictionary*. Chicago: Moody, 1957, 847-850.

1434   VAN DODEWAARD, J. A. E. "Peter." Trans. L. A. Bushinski. *Encyclopedic Dictionary of the Bible*. Ed. L. F. Hartman. Trans. and adapted from A. van den Born's *Bijbels Woorden-*

boek, ²1954-57. New York, Toronto, and London: McGraw-Hill, 1963, 1814-1818.

1435   VAN ELDEREN, B. "Peter, Simon," *Zondervan Pictorial Encyclopedia of the Bible.* Grand Rapids: Zondervan, 1975, 4:733-739.

1436   VAN STEMPVOORT, P. A. "Proloog: Petrus," *Petrus en zijn graf te Rom.* Bibliotheek van boeken bij de bijbel. Baarn: Bosch & Keuning, 1960, 7-14.
       Review: Sevenster, P., *NedTTs* 15 (1960-1961) 306-307.

1437   WALLS, A. F. "Peter," *Baker's Dictionary of Theology.* Ed. E. F. Harrison. Grand Rapids: Baker, 1960, 405-406.

1438   ———. "Peter the Apostle," *Evangelical Dictionary of Theology.* Ed. W. A. Elwell. Grand Rapids: Baker, 1984, 848-849.

1439   ———. "Peter," *The Illustrated Bible Dictionary.* Ed. J. D. Douglas. Leicester: Inter-Varsity, Wheaton: Tyndale, and Sydney and Auckland: Hodder and Stoughton, 1980, 3:1199-1202.

1440   ———. "Peter," *The New Bible Dictionary.* Leicester: Inter-Varsity and Wheaton: Tyndale, 1962, ²1982, 916-918.

1441   WALSH, W. T. *Saint Peter The Apostle.* New York: Macmillan, 1948.

1442   WARFIELD, B. B. "Peter," *Davis Dictionary of the Bible,* 1898, ⁴1924; reprint Grand Rapids: Baker, 1972, 624-627.

1443   WARREN, C. C. *Peter's Difficulty about the Conversion of the Gentiles.* Th.D. dissertation, Southern Baptist Theological Seminary, 1928.

1444   WEED, G. L. *A Life of St. Peter for the Young.* Philadelphia: Jacobs, 1901.

1445   WEGNEGAST, K. "Petros," *Der Kleine Pauly Lexikon der Antike.* München: Druckenmüller, 1964-75, 4:674-676.

1446   WENHAM, J. "Did Peter go to Rome in AD 42?" *TynBul* 23 (1972) 94-102.

1447   WEST, D. *Scenes in the Life of St. Peter, Sometime a Fisherman of Galilee, Afterwards an Apostle of Christ: A Course of Lectures*. London: Heylin, 1854.

1448   WILHELM-HOOIJBERG, A. E. "The Martyrdom of Peter was before the Fire in Rome," *Studia Biblica* 1978. JSNTSup 3. Ed. E. A. Livingstone. Sheffield: JSOT Press, 1980, 3:431-433.

1449   WOLSTON, W. T. P. *Simon Peter: His Life and Letters*. London: Nesbit, 1892; reprint Denver: Wilson Foundation, 1962, 251-329.

1450   YVER, C. [A. (de Bergivin) Huzard]. *Saint Pierre*. Les grands coeurs. Ed: E. Flammarion. Paris: Grevin, 1927.

1451   ZAMPINI, G. M. *San Pietro, a cui nostro Signor lasciò le chiave. Epistole*. Manuali Hoepli. Milano: Hoepli, 1922.

SECTION 9

SERMONS AND PREACHING

1452 ANONYMOUS. {"1 Peter,"} *The Great Texts of the Bible*. Ed. J. Hastings. New York: Charles Scribner's Sons and Edinburgh: T. & T. Clark, 1912, 19:31-150.

1453 ANONYMOUS. "The First Epistle of Peter," *The Speaker's Bible*. Ed. J. Hastings. Aberdeen: Speaker's Bible Office, 1923, 36:1-305; reprint Grand Rapids: Baker, 1961.

1454 BECKMANN, J. "Die Kirche und die Friede in der Welt {includes *Predigt* on 1 Peter 4:12-19}," *Bis an das Ende der Erde. Ökumenische Beiträge zum 70. Geburtstag von Martin Niemöller*. Ed. H. Krüger. München: Kaiser, 1962, 182-192.

1455 BRISCOE, D. S. *When the Going Gets Tough {sermon-like studies from 1 Peter}*. Ventura, Cal.: Regal Books, 1982.

1456 BURDSALL, J. "The Spirit's Prophetic Testimony Concerning the Sufferings and the Glory of Christ: A Sermon (1 Peter I.11)," *Methodist Magazine* 6 (1823) 121-127, 161-174. {Reprinted from the *Wesleyan Methodist Magazine*.}

1457 BURTNESS, J. H. "Sharing the Suffering of God in the Life of the World: From Text to Sermon on I Peter 2:21," *Int* 23 (1969) 277-288.

1458 CARTER, J. E. "You Don't Have to Live Like a Refugee {1 Peter 2:9-12}," *The Christian Ministry* 16,5 (September 1985) 27-29.

1459 CHAPPELL, C. G. *Sermons on Simon Peter*. New York: Abingdon, 1959.

1460 DETZLER, W. [A.] *Living Words in 1 Peter*. Welwyn, Hertfordshire: Evangelical Press, 1982.

1461 DIETZFELBINGER, H. "Dienet einander. Predigt über die Jahreslosung 1968 {1 Peter 4:10}," *Wort Und Wagnis. Festgabe zum 80. Geburtstag von Erich Stange am 23. Marz*

1968. Ed. W. Arnold. Kasel: Erichenkreuzverlag, 1968, 9-12.

1462 EDGEWORTH, R. *Sermons Very Fruitfull, Godly, and Learned: Preaching in the Reformation.* Ed. J. Wilson. Cambridge and Rochester, N.Y.: Brewer, 1993.

1463 GADDY, W. "Preaching from 1 Peter," *RevExp* 79 (1982) 473-485.

1464 GEORGI, D. "Predigt {1 Peter 3:18-22}," *EvT* 31 (1971) 187-192.

1465 GILLESPIE, T. W. "House of Living Stones {1 Peter 1:22-2:10}," *Princeton Seminary Bulletin* 4 (1983) 168-172.

1466 HERROD, R. *Faith under Fire: Inspiration and Instruction for the Modern Christian from the First Epistle of Peter.* Kenner, La.: R. Herrod (Author), 1982.

1467 JI, W. Y. "Homiletical Helps on *LW* One-Year Series—Epistles: Fourth Sunday of Easter: 1 Peter 2:21-25, April 24, 1983," *Concordia Journal* 9 (1983) 65-66.

1468 KLEIN, G. "Ein Stück aus dem Tollhaus. Predigt über 1 Petrus 2,1-10," *Vom Amt des Laien in Kirche und Theologie. Festschrift für Gerhard Krause zum 70. Geburtstag.* Theologisch Bibliothek Töpelman 39. Ed. H. Schröer and G. Müller. Berlin and New York: Walter De Gruyter, 1982, 85-91.

1469 KNIPPEL, C. T. "Homiletical Helps on *LW* One-Year Series—Epistles: Second Sunday of Easter, 1 Peter 1:3-9, April 10, 1983," *Concordia Journal* 9 (1983) 62-64.

1470 KOCH, M. "Predigt über 1 Petrus 4,7-11," *Botschafter von der Versöhnung. Festschrift für Walter Arnold zum 50. Geburtstag am 11.7.1979.* Ed. H. Kraft and H. Mayr. Stuttgart, 1979, 95-101.

1471 LUTHER, M. *Epistel Sanct Petri gepredigt und ausgelegt.* Wittenberg, 1523; *D. Martin Luthers Werke. Kritische Gesamtausgabe.* Weimar: Böhlaus, 1883 ff, 12:259-399; "Sermons on the First Epistle of St. Peter." Trans. M. H. Bertram. *Luther's Works.* St. Louis: Concordia, 1955-86, 30:1-145. {Apart from the 1523 original, these are representative editions only.}

1472   MacDONALD, G. "The Sending Church {1 Peter 2:9-10}," *Confessing Christ as Lord: The Urbana 81 Compendium.* Ed. J. W. Alexander. Downers Grove: InterVarsity, 1982, 95-105.

1473   MATTHEWS, C. D. "On Being Humble: 1 Peter 5:1-11," *Preaching in Today's World.* Ed. J. C. Barry. Nashville: Broadman, 1984, 26-31.

1474   MAY, G. "Die Zeit ist da, dass das Gericht anfange am Hause Gottes. Eine biblische Meditation über 1 Petr 4,17," *Geschichtswirklichkeit und Glaubens: Festschrift für Bp. Friedrich Müller.* Ed. F. C. Fry. Stuttgart: Evangelisches Verlagswerk, 1967, 41-49.

1475   McCOMB, J. H. *Reborn to a Living Hope: Peter's Message to God's Pilgrim Band.* Ed. R. E. McComb. 1983.

1476   McGEE, J. V. *1 Peter.* Pasedena, Cal.: Thru the Bible Books, 1978.

1477   NOLASCO ARRIAGA Y RINCON, J. P. *Panegirico del apostolo San Pedro.* Puebla?: Farríll, 1858.

1478   ORU, N. "The Challenge," *Point* [10],1 (1981) 163-171.

1479   PLUMPTRE, E. H. *The Spirits in Prison: A Sermon on the State of the Dead, Preached in St Paul's Cathedral, on Sunday April 30th, 1871.* London: Strahan, 1871.

1480   REES, P. S. *Triumphant in Trouble: Studies in I Peter.* Westwood, N.J.: Revell, 1962.

1481   ROLSTON, H. *The Apostle Peter Speaks to Us Today.* Atlanta: John Knox, 1977.

1482   SCHREIBER, P. L. "Homiletical Helps on *LW* One-Year Series—Epistles: Sixth Sunday after Pentecost: 1 Peter 2:4-10, July 3, 1983," *Concordia Journal* 9 (1983) 107-108.

1483   SMART, E. R. D. "What's Your Number?" *ExpTim* 88 (1976-77) 269.

1484   TATUM, S. L. "Preaching From I Peter," *Southwestern Journal of Theology* 25,1 (Fall 1982) 46-57.

1485 TOZER, A. W. *I Call It Hearsay: Twelve Sermons in Peter's First Epistle: Selections from His Pulpit Ministry.* Ed. G. B. Smith. Harrisburg, Penn.: Christian Publications, 1974.

1486 TURNER, J. M. "The People of God {1 Peter 2^{1-10}}," *ExpTim* 91 (1979-80) 244-245.

1487 WANGERIN, M. E. "Homiletical Helps on *LW* One-Year Series—Epistles: Twelfth Sunday after Pentecost: 1 Pet 5:5b-11, August 14, 1983," *Concordia Journal* 9 (1983) 152-153.

1488 YOUNG, J. H. "The Sufferings and Glory of Christ: A Sermon," *Methodist Review* 19 (1837) 318-332.

1489 YTTA Y PARRA, B. F. de. *El santo de los santos, n. s^{mo} padre, y señor san Pedro.* Mexico: Hogal, 1736.

SECTION 10
THE TEXT OF 1 PETER

The following are works that in some way examine the text of 1 Peter. It should be noted, however, that they are mostly works *about* the text of 1 Peter rather than simple presentations *of* the text of 1 Peter. Mere versions of the text are excluded.

1490 ALAND, K. "Bemerkungen zu den gegenwärtigen Möglichkeiten textkritischer Arbeit aus Anlass einer Untersuchung zum Cäsarea-Text der Katholischen Briefe," *NTS* 17 (1970-71) 1-9.

1491 BEARE, F. W. "Some Remarks on the Text of I Peter in the Bodmer Papyrus ($\mathfrak{P}^{72}$)," *Studia Evangelica*. Ed. F. L. Cross. Berlin: Akademie-Verlag, 1964, 3:263-265.

1492 ———. "The Text of I Peter in Papyrus 72," *JBL* 80 (1961) 253-260.

1493 CARDER, M. M. "A Caesarean Text in the Catholic Epistles?" *NTS* 16 (1969-70) 252-270.

1494 ———. *An Enquiry into the Textual Transmission of the Catholic Epistles*. Th.D. dissertation, Victoria University (Toronto), 1969.

1495 DARIS, S. *Un Nuovo Frammento della Prima Lettera di Pietro (1 Petr. 2, 20-3, 12)*. Papyrologica Castroctaviana 2. Barcelona: Papyrologica Castroctaviana, 1967.

1496 DAVEY, G. R. *Philological Notes in the Two Epistles of St. Peter: An Examination of the Greek and Syriac Texts of the Two Petrine Epistles, of their Interpretation and their Theology*. Ph.D. dissertation, Melbourne, 1970.

1497 DUPLACY, J., and C.-B. AMPHOUX. "A propos de l'histoire du texte de la première épître de Pierre," *Études sur la première lettre de Pierre*. *Congrès de l'ACFEB, Paris 1979*. LD 102. Ed. C. Perrot. Paris: Cerf, 1980, 155-173.

1498 DUPLACY, J. "'Le Texte Occidentale' des Épîtres Catholiques," *NTS* 16 (1969-70) 397-399.

1499 GARCÍA DEL MORAL, A. "Crítica Textual de 1 Ptr. 4,14," *EstBib* 20 (1961) 45-77.

1500 HARRIS, J. R. "A Further Note on the Use of Enoch in 1 Peter," *Expositor* 6,4 (1901) 346-349.

1501 ———. "An Emendation to 1 Peter i.13," *ExpTim* 41 (1929-30) 43.

1502 ———. "An Emendation to 1 Peter II. 8," *Expositor* (1909-A) 155-163.

1503 ———. "On a Recent Emendation in the Text of St. Peter," *Expositor* 6,5 (1902) 317-320.

1504 ———. "The History of a Conjectural Emendation," *Expositor* 6,6 (1902) 378-390.

1505 KING, M. A. "Notes on the Bodmer Manuscript of Jude and 1 and 2 Peter," *BSac* 121 (1964) 54-57.

1506 MARTINI, C. M., ed. *Petri Epistulae ex Papyro Bodmeriana.* 2 vols. Milan, 1968.

1507 MASSAUX, E. "Le texte de la 1ᵃ Petri du papyrus Bodmer VIII ($\mathfrak{P}^{72}$)," *ETL* 39 (1963) 616-671.

1508 METZGER, B. M. *A Textual Commentary on the Greek New Testament: A Companion Volume to the United Bible Societies' Greek New Testament (third edition).* London and New York: United Bible Societies, 1971, ²1975.

Reviews: Ellicott, J. K., *Theology* 76 (1973) 610-611; Enslin, M. S., *Princeton Seminary Bulletin* 66 (1973) 129-131; Fitzmyer, J. A., *TS* 34 (1973) 522-523; Hoehner, H. W., *BSac* 131 (1974) 276; Hurtado, L. W., *JBL* 92 (1973) 621-622; Kilpatrick, G. D., *TLZ* 104 (1979) 260-270; Kümmel, W. G., *TRu* 38 (1973) 163-164; Parvis, M. M., *ExpTim* 84 (1973) 378-379; Sabourin, L., *Religious Studies Bulletin* 1,3 (May 1981) 81-82; Schnackenburg, R., *BZ* 17 (1973) 106-107; Stagg, F., *RevExp* 70 (1973) 399-400; Watson, N. M., *Reformed Theological Review* 32 (1973) 98-99.

1509 MORRIS, W. D. "1 Peter iii. 19," *ExpTim* 38 (1926-27) 470.

1510 QUINN, J. D. "Notes on the Text of the $\mathfrak{P}^{72}$ 1 Pt 2,3; 5,14; and 5,9," *CBQ* 27 (1965) 241-249.

1511   RICHARDS, W. L. "Textual Criticism on the Greek Text of the Catholic Epistles: A Bibliography," *AUSS* 12 (1974) 103-111.

1512   ——. "The New Testament Greek Manuscripts of the Catholic Epistles," *AUSS* 14 (1976) 301-311.

1513   ——. "The Present Status of Text Critical Studies in the Catholic Epistles," *AUSS* 13 (1975) 261-272.

1514   RODGERS, P. R. "The Longer Reading of 1 Peter 4:14," *CBQ* 43 (1981) 93-95.

1515   SALMON, P. "Le texte Latin des épîtres de S. Pierre, S. Jean et S. Jude dans le MS. 6 de Montpellier," *JTS* 2 (1951) 170-177.

1516   THIELE, W. *Die lateinischen Texte des 1. Petrusbiefes.* Vetus Latina. Aus der Geschichte der lateinischen Bibel 5. Freiburg: Herder, 1965.
       Review: Gribomont, J., *RHE* 61 (1966) 536-539.

1517   VANHOYE, A. "Des textes de la Ire Lettre de Pierre et L'Apocalypse," *Prêtres anciens, prêtre nouveau selon le Nouveau Testament.* Parole de Dieu. Paris: Seuil, 1980, 267-340.

1518   ——. *Old Testament Priests and the New Priest According to the New Testament.* Studies in Scripture. Petersham, Mass.: St. Bede's, 1986, 243-267.

1519   WEISS, B. *Die katholischen Briefe: Textkritische Untersuchungen und Textherstellung.* Leipzig: Hinrichs, 1892.

1520   WILLIS, W. H. "An Unrecognized Fragment of First Peter in Coptic," *Classical, Mediaeval and Renaissance Studies in Honor of Berthold Louis Ullman.* Storia e letteratura. Ed. C. Henderson, Jr. Roma: Storia e letteratura, 1964, 1:265-271.

1521   WILSON, J. P. "In the Text of 1 Peter ii. 17 is πάντας τιμήσατε a Primitive Error for πάντα ποιήσατε?" *ExpTim* 54 (1942-43) 193-194.

UNCLASSIFIED TITLES

Despite a lengthy and thorough search for literature on 1 Peter, some works could neither be examined in hardcopy nor classified from their titles alone. All such works that on the face of it are or might be about Peter or 1 Peter are listed below. Many of the bibliographic details have been accessible for checking via electronic media. Other works have been excluded because neither their titles nor ancillary investigation gave any evidence that they fulfilled the criteria for a place in the bibliography.

1522   AULETTA, G. *Pietro e Paolo. Il timone e la prora.* Napoli-Bologna: Dehoniane, 1968.

1523   BAGATTI, A. "La famiglia di S. Pietro," *Familiare '82.* Brindisi: Amici della « A. de Leo, » 27-32.

1524   BALOCCO, A. A. "Avviando alla lettura de S. Pietro," *Rivista Lasalliana* 33 (1966) 180-213.

1525   BARNES, W. W. *The Place of Peter in the Early Church (up to A.D. 451).* Th.D. dissertation, Southern Baptist Theological Seminary, 1913.

1526   BAUER, F. C. "Der erste petrinische Brief, mit besonderer Beziehung auf das Werk: Der petrinische Lehrbegriff . . . von Bernh. Weiss," *Theologische Jahrbücher* 15 (1856) 193-240.

1527   COCAGNAC, A. M. *Pierre, pêcheur du Christ.* Paris: Cerf, 1968.

1528   COTHENET, É. "Béni soit Dieu (1 Pt)," *Assemblées du Seigneur* 23 (1971) 26-33.

1529   FAULAND, F. *Sankt Peaderer und aun<d>ere Geschichtn.* Graz and Wien: Styria, 1974.

1530   FULLER, E. *Peter the Apostle.* Garden City, N. Y.: Double-day, 1961.

1531   GALE, H. M. *The Validity of the Petrine Tradition in the*

Light of Modern Research. Ph.D. dissertation, Boston University, 1939.

1532 GALOT, J. "La vittoria di Cristo sulle morte," *Civiltà Cattolica* 138 (1987) 118-131.

1533 GEWALT, D. *Petrus. Studien zur Geschichte und Tradition des frühen Christentums*. Doctoral dissertation, Heidelberg, 1966.

1534 GONTARD, L. *Essai critique et historique sur la première épitre de Saint Pierre*. Lyons, 1905.

1535 HARNACK, A. von. "Die Verklärungsgeschichte Jesu, der Bericht des Paulus (I. Kor. 15, 3 ff.) und die beiden Christusvisionen des Petrus," *Sitzungsberichte der Preußichen Akademie der Wissenschaften zu Berlin*. Berlin, 1922, 62-80.

1536 HO-SANG, D. *The New Age and the Interpretation of 1 Peter*. Unpublished Ph.D. thesis, Oxford University, 1989.

1537 *Il messaggio spirituale di Pietro e Paolo*. Roma: Teresianum, 1967.

1538 JOHNSON, E. E. *Peter's Growing Conception of Christ*. Ph.D. dissertation, Southern Baptist Theological Seminary, 1932.

1539 KEMNER, H. *Simon Petrus. Die Geschichte einer Wandlung vom Ich zum Er*. Wuppertal: Sonne und Schild, 1967.

1540 KOPAČ, J. *Na nepremagljivi skali*. Celoveo, Družba sv.: Mahorja, 1954.

1541 KÜGLER, U.-R. *Die Paränese an die Sklaven als Modell urchristlicher Sozialethik*. Dissertation, Erlangen-Nürnberg, 1976.

1542 *La liturgie, expression de la foi*. Ed. A. M. Triacca and A. Pistoia. Conférences Sainte-Serge, XXVe Semaine d'études liturgiques, 27-30 Juin 1978. Paris and Rome: Edizioni Liturgique, 1979, 97-113.

1543 LAUB, F. "Sozialgeschichtlicher Hintergrund und ekklesiologische Relevanz der neutestamentlich-früchristlichen Haus- und Gemeinde-Tafelparänese—ein Beitrag zur Sociologie des Früchristentums," *MTZ* 37 (1986) 249-271.

1544 LEE, A. "Life of the Apostle Peter," *A Series of Practical Discourses*. London: Low, 1853.

1545 LEIGHTON {no forename given}. *Das christliche Leben nach dem ersten Petrusbrief in Bibelstunden dargestellt.* Witten: Bundes-Verlag, 1928.

1546 LE PAS, A. J. *Urteilssprüche des heiligen Petrus*. Trans. V. Gross from the 3rd French edition. Aachen: Jacobi, 1884.

1547 LINNARTZ, F. J. *Petrus, Prinz der Aposteln.* Gravenhage: Uitgeverij Pax, 1946.

1548 LIPSCOMB, A. A. *Lessons from the Life of Saint Peter: Six Essays.* Macon, Ga.: Burke, 1882.

1549 MACARTHUR, J. *Christians in a Hostile World.* Chicago: Moody, 1990.

1550 ———. *Living for Christ in a Cynical World.* Panorama City, Cal.: Grace to You and Chicago: Moody, 1991.

1551 MASTRACCO, G. *Recenti studi e notizie di indole biografica e cronologica sul principe degli apostoli san Pietro papa e martire e de l'apostolo delle genti san Paulo.* Sulmona: Labor, 1972.

1552 MICHL, J. "Petrus als Seelssorger," *BK* 3 (1948) 15-24.

1553 NARDELLI, M. *Pietro e Paolo apostoli a Roma.* Brescia: Franciscanum, 1967.

1554 NOUEL, P. C. "Le christ notre rançon. Le témoignage de Pierre," *Cahiers Évangiles* 25 (1957) 45-50.

1555 PARTH, W. W. *Petrus, anekdotisch. Himmlischer Humor mit höllischen Aspeckten.* München: Kindler, 1969.

1556 PENNA, A. "Il « Senatoconsulto » del 35 B. C. e la prima lettera di S. Pietro," *San Pietro. Atti della XIX settimana biblica.* Brescia: Paideia, 1967, 337-366.

1557 PESCH, W. "Zu Texten des Neuen Testaments über das Priestertum der Getauften," *Verborum Veritas. Festschrift für G. Stählin zum 70. Geburtstag.* Ed. O. Böcher and K. Haaker. Wuppertal: Brockhaus, 1970, 303-315.

150 UNCLASSIFIED TITLES

1558 "Pierre, pêcheur du lac, pêcheur d'hommes," *Le monde de la Bible* 27 (Janv.-Févr. 1983).

1559 POELMAN, R. "Saint Pierre et la tradition," *Lumen Vitae* (Bruxelles) 20 (1965) 632-648.

1560 RATZINGER, J. "'Auferbaut aus lebendigen Steinen,'" *Kirche aus lebendigen Steinen.* Ed. W. Seidel. Mainz: Grünewald, 1975, 30-48.

1561 RHODES, D. E. *Myself with You: The Development of a Curriculum for Use in the Local Church to Enrich Marriage and Family Relationships.* D.Min. dissertation, Eastern Baptist Theological Seminary, 1982.

1562 SAARISALO, A. *Pietari, suuri kalastaja.* Porvoo: Söderstrom, 1967.

1563 SCHELKLE, K. H. "Spätapostolische Schriften als frühkatholisches Zeugnis," *Neutestamentliche Aufsätze. Festschrift für Prof. Josef Schmid zum 70. Geburtstag.* Ed. J. Binzler, O. Kuss, and F. Mussner. Regensburg: Pustet, 1963, 225-232.

1564 SPEYR, A. *Kreuz und Hölle.* Einsiedeln, 1966.

1565 SPICQ, C. "Saint Pierre, apôtre de l'espérance," *La révélation de l'espérance dans le Nouveau Testament.* Avignon: Aubanel and Paris: Dominicaine, 1932, 99-157.

1566 STEGMANN, A. *Silvanus als Missionar und „Hagiograph": Eine exegetische Studie.* Rottenburg: Bader, 1917.

1567 STROCCHI, G. *Al föl 'd sa' Pir.* Ravenna: Girasole, 1974.

1568 SZAFRAŃSKI, W. *Podziemia Watykanu.* Warszawa: Książka i Wiedza, 1965.

1569 THOMPSON, J. *The Church in Exile: God's Counter Culture in a Non-Christian World.* Abilene, Tex.: ACU, 1990.

1570 TURMEL, J. *La descente du Christ aux enfers.* Paris: Bloud, 1908.

1571 VIELHAUER, P. *Oikodome. Das Bild vom Bau in der christlichen Literatur vom Neuen Testament bis Clemens Alexandrinus.* Karlsruhe-Durlach: n. p., 1940.

1572   WENDLAND, H. D.   "Zur sozialethischen Bedeutung des neutestamentlichen Haustafeln," *Die Botschaft an die soziale Welt. Festschrift A. Köberle*. Beiträge zur christlichen Sozialethik der Gegenwart. Hamburg: Furche, 1959, 104-114.

1573   ZAMPINI, S. *Pietro e le sue Epistole*. Milan: Hoepli, 1922.

INDEX OF AUTHORS

INDEX OF EDITORS

INDEX OF FESTSCHRIFT HONOREES

INDEX OF REVIEWERS

INDEX OF TRANSLATORS

NEW TESTAMENT
TOOLS AND STUDIES

edited by

Bruce M. Metzger, Ph.D., D.D., L.H.D., D. Theol., D. Litt.

and

Bart D. Ehrman, Ph.D.

VOL. XX *The New Testament in Greek*, IV. *The Gospel According to St. John*, edited by the American and British Committees of the International Greek New Testament Project. Volume One: *The Papyri*, edited by W. J. Elliott and D. C. Parker. 1995. ISBN 90 04 09940 9

VOL. XXI *Comparative Edition of the Syriac Gospels: Aligning the Sinaiticus, Curetonianus, Peshîttâ and Harklean Versions*, by George A. Kiraz; 4 volumes. Vol. 1: Matthew; Vol. 2: Mark; Vol. 3: Luke; Vol. 4: John. 1996. ISBN 90 04 10419 4 (set)

VOL. XXII *Codex Bezae*. Studies from the Lunel Colloquium, June 1994, edited by D. C. Parker and C.-B. Amphoux. 1996.
ISBN 90 04 10393 7

VOL. XXIII *Bibliography of Literature on First Peter*, by Anthony Casurella. 1996. ISBN 90 04 10488 7